Cakes and Bails

Cakes and Bails

Henry Blofeld's
CRICKET YEAR

SIMON & SCHUSTER
A VIACOM COMPANY

First published in Great Britain by Simon & Schuster, 1998
A Viacom Company

1 3 5 7 9 10 8 6 4 2

Simon & Schuster UK Ltd
Africa House
64-78 Kingsway
London WC2B 6AH

Simon & Schuster Australia
Sydney

A CIP catalogue record for this book is available from the British Library.

ISBN 0-684-85151-2

Typeset by SX Composing DTP, Rayleigh, Essex
Printed and bound in Great Britain by The Bath Press, Bath

For Bitten, Rumple and Bubbles
who weathered the birth pangs with
humour and no little fortitude.

Contents

CHAPTER ONE

A Fine Glass of South African

I was staying with Johnny Wheeler, a *grand cru* wine merchant, on Mersea Island for the Southend cricket week at the end of June in 1997 as the result of a slight miscalculation, because I had thought that Southend and Mersea were reasonably adjacent and I did not look at a map until everything had been arranged. Even allowing for navigational problems, the journey took about an hour and a half. We arrived back at his house one evening after an excellent dinner at a local hostelry and were embarking upon that final glass which seems so eminently sensible at the time, but the next morning can be pinpointed as the major contributor to much blotchiness and throbbing at the temples, when Johnny announced that he had come up with a good idea.

'I think you should come with us on the Atherton trip to Rheims,' was his promising start. 'We've got something like a hundred punters coming over for three days as part of his benefit. You may have to sing for your supper one evening, but bring Bitten (my wife) and it'll be good fun. There'll be some decent champagne, too.'

I couldn't see anything wrong with that and the long and short of it was that on Monday, 29 September at some ungodly hour before breakfast, Bitten and I foregathered at Waterloo station to catch the train to France. Graham Gooch was the first to clock in, followed by Mike Atherton and Derek Pringle and an assortment of paying customers, all of whom were in sparkling form. One of the earlier arrivals was the ubiquitous Ivo Tennant, the smilingly bonhomous cricket writer from *The Times* who loves to dabble in this type of excursion, when he is almost always sponsored up to the hilt. Ivo has turned freeloading into something of an art form and is liable to cadge a lift across a continent if he feels a free lunch coming on. He is a very hard worker and I remember him making his first notes that morning at Waterloo prior to giving some deserving benefactor a mention in the following day's paper.

After much banging of doors and blowing of whistles, the train eased its way out of Waterloo and glided down to Ashford while we all strained our necks to see if we could spot Hercule Poirot, or was it Miss Marple, in our carriage, for it all had a faint feel of the Orient Express about it. At Ashford, we picked up the second half of the party who had travelled by bus from Chelmsford, the other early morning staging post. Nasser Hussain was there with John Stephenson and Mark Ilott and, of course, the ever cheerful Johnny Wheeler whose splendid family wine business had organised the adventure. We had hardly left Ashford station before we descended into the bowels of the earth and it was only about twenty minutes later that we came up for air in the French countryside. As we sped through the Tunnel, I could not help thinking back to the times, almost fifty years ago, when we had to go through the whole business of catching the Channel boat to France. To be seasick was almost obligatory, especially when sailing from Southampton to St Malo and spending the night in just about the most uncomfortable cabin it would be possible to imagine as the wretched thing rolled and floundered its way across to France. It was still pretty exciting and when, on the boat, we were allowed to pay for things with the few French francs we were permitted to take with us, it was thrilling beyond belief. Now, it was all over in less than half an hour. Remarkable.

Two buses from Colchester had been sent ahead to meet us at the station in Lille and take us to Rheims, where they would ferry us about the place for the next three days before decanting us back at Lille. The Hotel de la Paix was our destination and once there, the action was not slow in starting. The first glass of champagne was in our hands before we had even been given a room and was followed by a delicious buffet lunch. The only problem was: would Ivo have time to file his first story before we took the bus to La Maison Veuve Cliquot that evening? Spurred on by the thought of a possible taxi fare, he just made it. We were shown the cellars which stretched for miles underground and we walked past an awesome number of bottles and had worked up a considerable thirst before being allowed to taste the product. The next day, Bollinger made us most welcome and on our last night, it was Laurent Perrier who pushed out the boat. I had always wondered why the England side had found it necessary to have an official supplier of champagne, but from the way Michael Atherton gripped his glass and Graham Gooch, not to mention Nasser Hussain, savoured the bubbles, I began to have serious doubts that one was enough.

Atherton had, not long before, made his decision to continue as England's captain and to take the side to the West Indies the following January. I discuss his decision-making process later in the book. As we now know, and many will have suspected at the time, it was one tour too many. Atherton is very much his own man and he likes to keep his own company. There is a natural reserve, almost a shyness, about him. Even on an occasion like this, I couldn't help feeling that while the paying customers were a necessity, he was not really comfortable unless he was with his colleagues. He is a quiet man who lives his life as he captained England: thoughtfully, undemonstrably, carefully, with an unwillingness to take a risk, with a strong determination to do it his way which can assume the guise of obstinacy, and with a healthy suspicion of much that is going on around him. He has a charming, almost boyish smile tinged with shyness and he is good company with a glass of champagne in his hand. There is also that knowing, slightly quizzical look which seems to say, 'I can see where you are coming from,' or 'I wasn't born yesterday, you know,' or just occasionally, 'You haven't a clue what you're talking about.' Maybe he reserved the latter for the press. It takes time to get to know him. It is easy to see that he was not born an extrovert and it is grossly unfair that he should have been consistently blamed for something that was not his fault. If Atherton is ever asked for a character reference, all he needs to do is to send off a video recording of his 98 not out in the Trent Bridge Test Match against the South Africans. In Rheims, the Atherton I met was still captain of England. The Atherton who took on Donald at Trent Bridge was less reserved and more resolved.

Before we left Rheims, we played an unofficial Test Match. The six Test cricketers in the party were challenged to a game of boules by the local side on a boules park distantly overlooked by the magnificent Rheims cathedral, which miraculously escaped annihilation during two world wars. First, we were all allowed a go and for an hour or two we flung these heavy balls hither and thither, but mostly thither judging from the scoresheets. The in-house competition was won by my side and, not surprisingly, it was generally agreed afterwards that my captaincy had made the difference. Then, the grounds were cleared and the clash of the Titans began. The local side included the French national champion and it was fascinating to watch the technique of the experts who exerted an amazing control over their weighty balls, which are mostly thrown out of the back of the hand to create backspin. Like all the best managed events, it all came down to the final ball and a throw by Mike Atherton, who earlier had shown no great aptitude, was tinged with genius, and England carried off the spoils.

There was one dreadful moment when Ivo Tennant accused a much respected champagne house, barely a stone's throw away from the church guarding the mortal remains of Dom Perignon, one of the truly great men of the world, of producing champagne in which he had detected too many bubbles and which he feared was not the real thing. *Crémant* was the word he used, and it was greeted with a shocked silence which the cartoonist, H.M. Bateman, would surely have immortalised. Really, Ivo.

Three days later, I was in Pakistan driving through the streets of Rawalpindi in the same taxi as Geoffrey Boycott, also known to some as the Greatest Living Yorkshireman although I am not sure how that noble county takes the news. He was much fussed by the transport system or, indeed, the lack of one, and was deeply concerned that the Highway Code was, by and large, completely ignored. If given the chance, he was confident he would be able to sort it out. In fact, there are very few things our Geoffrey does not think he can sort out.

The Third Test Match between Pakistan and South Africa was played in Faisalabad and a wonderful game of cricket it was too, but first we had to get there. This involved a car journey from Lahore of some four hours along a road which would have won a serious prize for awfulness. The GLY set off in the front seat of a taxi with Ramiz Raja, the former Pakistan captain, crouched behind him in the space that the GLY's reclining seat allowed him. Geoffrey was apparently at the top of his form and his pithy comments hurried along the journey. The standard of driving, the state of the roads and the behaviour of the pedestrians all caught his attention and he will undoubtedly have passed on one or two useful tips to the driver.

My friend the Commander – you will hear much more of him later – and I had set off rather earlier but as we drove the last fifty miles we found ourselves increasingly caught up in a political rally or protest. Many thousands of people were bearing down on Faisalabad dressed predominantly in green and the road, which was narrow and full of potholes of magnificent proportions, was unable to cope. We made slow and exceedingly hazardous progress. By the time the GLY arrived on the scene, it had grown worse, which did nothing for the Great Man's humour and by the time they had reached the outskirts of Faisalabad, the traffic had ground to a halt and the entire population appeared to be sitting on their horns. Lorries and buses lurched this way and that like prehistoric mastodons engaged in mortal combat. From his seat beside the driver, Geoffrey had apparently been able to spot a way through but it depended on other drivers being accommodating. After a bit of shouting and gesticulating which had about as much effect as a keep left sign, he decided to take a hand. He got out onto the road to try and enlist the cooperation of the drivers nearest to him but he had not bargained for the language barrier and, like many of his batting partners, they were unable to interpret his gestures. I don't suppose they took a blind bit of notice. History doesn't relate if he was wearing his panama hat but I hope that he was because it would have lent a certain style to the occasion. In the end, he had to make a somewhat undignified withdrawal as there was every chance that he might himself have been run over. He was not amused. I have not heard how his plans for introducing zebra crossings into Pakistan are coming along.

Then, after a rather unsatisfactory one-day competition between the West Indies, South Africa, Sri Lanka and Pakistan played under floodlights and in heavy dew in Lahore, it was back to England by way of Dubai to pick up the obligatory tin of duty-free beluga caviar. It was not only the caviar which made it a memorable journey. The last people to enter the aeroplane that morning in Karachi were four Arabs in their dish-dashes and three of them had a huge falcon on each wrist whilst the fourth, clearly a learner, had only one. The birds, in magnificent plumage, sitting in business class, never put a foot wrong. The reason for this was that they were blindfold when, presumably, they are too frightened to move. They were supremely handsome birds with the most fearsome looking beaks. It was a pity there were no hijackers.

The falcons left the aeroplane in Dubai and when I returned to my pew with my tin of sturgeon's roe, I was treated to another very different but wonderfully exciting diversion. The RAF's Red Arrows were that afternoon rehearsing for a display they were giving the following day at Dubai airport. For almost an hour I watched spellbound as they went through their full repertoire. It was breathtaking stuff as they plunged headlong for the ground at breakneck speed before pulling out of the dive at the very last moment. There was then the formation flying when their wing tips were almost touching as they went through an amazing display of aerobatics. Then they came flat out across the desert about five feet off the ground. It made me frightened to watch them.

After a typically hectic Christmas, it was off to Jamaica for the start of the series against the West Indies, but first I spent four fabulous days on the north coast of the island. It was another

of those agonising 'so nearly, but not quite' series which cul-
minated in England being beaten and poor old Mike
Atherton falling on his sword. For me, it was then time to go
back to England and an exciting evening encounter with a
surgeon's knife and a late start to the cricket season which was
soon to be given the ominous look of so many others in recent
years. Uncluttered with the problems of captaincy, Atherton
began with a fine century at Edgbaston in a Test Match
England might just have won if the last day had not been
washed out by rain. At Lord's the batsmen put together an
impressive reconstruction of the dramatic collapse on the last
day in Antigua. On that occasion the last six wickets fell for
twenty-six runs; now the last seven went down for only eleven
runs, so I suppose you could say that they had improved upon
it. This was followed by another impressive disintegration at
Old Trafford before the new captain, Alec Stewart, and Mike
Atherton batted England to within sight of safety, but it still
needed 188 minutes of stout defence from Robert Croft and
untold gallantry at the end by Angus Fraser for England to
get away with a draw. The scores were level and England had
one wicket left at the finish of a marvellous day's cricket.

Somewhere amongst all this, there was time for an unrivalled bottle of Meursault and a superb dinner at Wilton's, a
hasty fitting of a new suit in Savile Row and, of course,
England's demise in the World Cup in a penalty shoot-out. In
addition to Michael Owen, Tim Henman and Justin Rose
both left their imprints on the summer. Essex overwhelmed
Leicestershire in the last Benson & Hedges Cup final and
Bitten and I were at Lord's again the following Saturday as
guests of Sir Paul Getty, to watch the Princess Diana
Memorial Match. This was most suitably blessed by as good a
hundred as one could wish to see from India's Sachin
Tendulkar who is surely the best batsman of his generation.
Sir Paul's box in the New Mound Stand took cricket watch-

ing to a new dimension and we were lucky enough to have John Major as a fellow guest along with David and Thorunn Gower and those two hubs of West Indian cricket, Derrick Murray and Clive Lloyd. It was a marvellous occasion with an almost-full house and some highly entertaining cricket. The cynics seemed to doubt its value afterwards, presumably because no one swore at anyone very much, there was no dissent to enjoy and it had all been preceded by a spectacular parachute drop which my more stuffy friends feel should be best left to RAF Brize Norton and similar venues. I thought it was amazing how they all landed within feet of each other on the hallowed turf.

Then it was time for Langar. For every Test Match or one-day international at Trent Bridge, the Test Match Special team stay in bulk at Langar Hall, a lovely country house hotel about ten miles from Trent Bridge. It is unique, not because of its comfort or its food, both of which are very classy, but because of its owner, Imogen Skirving, who is one of the great characters. The house belonged to her family and it was where she was brought up. As time went by and the family went their various ways, Imogen stayed on and turned the house into an hotel. She herself trained at the school for benevolent and mildly absent-minded despots. She runs the hotel too beautifully and, in spite of her delightfully inconsequential air, she is firmly in control of everything, and anyone who doubts this does so at their peril. Langar has the wonderful atmosphere of the best sort of well lived in, large-ish country house where it all seems a little bit haphazard but nothing is left to chance. The hotel is a joy although I have one serious complaint. I am always given the charming bedroom which is called Churchyard for the simple reason that the windows open out onto the graveyard of the church, feet rather than yards away from Langar which, I suppose, may once have been a magnificent vicarage. The telephone in Churchyard sits on a little round table by the window which has been its home for years and Imogen will not find a longer lead to enable me to put it on my bedside table. I expect she chuckles happily at the thought of my alarm call coming through at 6 a.m. While I am about it, I also wish the church clock would not chime away in the dead of night with that insufferable mocking resonance. But the excellence of the dining room more than makes up for these deficiencies and her splendid claret has well known anaesthetic qualities. It is presided over with genial efficiency by Michael.

The dining room was full of good cheer and claret when I arrived the evening before the Test Match began, at about ten o'clock, which is more than I can say about myself when I was called at five in the morning with a cup of coffee. I had to make the journey to Nottingham to appear on GMTV at twenty past six. The avuncular night porter got into a muddle with his instructions, which were pinned to the notice board, and thought he had to arrange a taxi for me at 5.30. When it did not turn up on time, he apparently ordered another although GMTV had promised me that they had themselves arranged a taxi for me the night before, and I now reconfirmed this with them in London. At 5.35, I pushed my way out of the front door and stood, in hope, on the gravel. Moments later the night porter rushed out and accused me of being an errant taxi driver; he must presumably have thought that I had come to pick up myself. I was surprised, as he had had a good look at me when delivering the coffee not half an hour before. An extraordinary conversation ensued. I eventually said, with just about all the indignation I could muster, 'Do I look like a taxi driver?' Which I thought might floor him but not a bit of it, for it was on the tip of his tongue to answer in the affirmative. More than a little puzzled, unappreciated and unloved, he shrunk back into the hotel and soon afterwards no less than three taxis in line-ahead formation came up the drive, all keen to take me to Nottingham. It's not easy to travel in three taxis at the same time and so I returned two to sender and kept the one which GMTV had ordered, which may have been a mistake. The driver had no idea where he was taking me and I had no idea where I was going, which created something of an impasse until I came up with the brainwave that he should ring his base and ask them. He did just that and discovered that our destination was the Carlton Studios in Nottingham, but there was a small snag there in that he did not know where the Carlton Studios were. I said that surely anyone who lived in Nottingham must know that and he told me that he had come from Burton-on-Trent. My blood pressure was well on the way towards scoring the equivalent of a hundred before breakfast. After making a prolonged acquaintance with the Ring Road, we arrived with seconds to spare. I felt I had been up for a day and a half and it was still only a quarter past six.

The first time I had caught a glimpse of the new Radcliffe Road Stand had been at 5.58 that morning when we scuttled down the Radcliffe Road itself, past the back of the stand in pursuit of the elusive Carlton Studios. Even from behind, it was stamped with the right pedigree and when I arrived in earnest sometime after ten o'clock this was confirmed. It was a marvellous addition to my favourite Test Match ground of all. It had been built in keeping with the rest of the Trent Bridge architecture and it has taken over the entire Radcliffe Road end of the ground, replacing those old ramshackle two-tier stands that looked as if they might disintegrate in the next gale. Within the body of the new stand are all the accoutrements of a modern cricket academy, including bedrooms where the participants can stay and which at Test Match time become hospitality suites. There is an indoor cricket school, a gymnasium with sauna baths and all the other equipment which, as far as I am concerned, has been designed only to bring on premature heart attacks. I can only say that it is as good as, if not better than, the brilliant stand which has been built at the City end of the Adelaide Oval.

My great affection for Trent Bridge goes back to 1959 when I was lucky enough to play for Cambridge against Nottinghamshire when the former England opening batsman, Reg Simpson, who was captain of Nottinghamshire, persuaded Keith Miller, the famous Australian all-rounder, to turn out against us, presumably in order to swell the weekend gate which I am delighted to say it did. Keith made 62 in the first innings, opened the bowling and I received a quick leg-break in the first over, and then hit 102 in the second innings. When he was in the sixties, he had a tremendous heave at a ball from Alan Hurd, our off-spinner, and the skied catch came to me at deep midwicket in front of the old ladies' stand. I waited under it for an age and of course dropped it, to the great delight of the crowd. A couple of years ago, I found the complete scorecard for this match and with the help of Colin Ingleby-Mackenzie, who took it down to Wormsley where Keith was staying with Paul Getty, the great man signed it. Back it came with the inscription, 'Well dropped, Henry. Keith Miller', which said as much for his memory as it did for his sense of humour.

Soon afterwards in that hot summer of 1959 I had another great piece of luck, which was to play against Keith's great friend, Denis Compton, who was in the MCC side to play Cambridge just before the University match. He scored a marvellous 71 and gave us more than just a glimpse of his genius. Neville Cardus mentioned the innings in one of his books. I kept that scorecard too and persuaded Denis to sign it one afternoon at Lord's the year before he died. Both scorecards evoke wonderful memories and explain why Trent Bridge and Lord's, in that order, are my two most favourite cricket grounds.

Back at Trent Bridge in 1998, Test Match Special has moved over from our rather cramped eyrie in the top of the pavilion, and although we now have much more space and comfort, we are more remote from the cricket and all the other occupants of the pavilion, so, in some ways I feel it was a rather sad departure. Having said that, our new home is the best commentary box in the country and has the best facilities with the exception of the lifts, which work on whim and with an almost complete disregard of any instructions you might have issued. Lifts at cricket grounds are a vexed issue. The lift which goes up four floors to the Oval Press Box and the players' dressing rooms is the most reluctant lift in the world and moves at a pace a snail would sneer at, and yet with great skill still manages to stop with a bit of a jerk. The new lift in the Lord's pavilion, when it works which is not often, has a splendid habit of welcoming you in when the doors open but this is followed by an inordinately long period of total inactivity, so much so that the passengers, certain that it has again broken down, leave the lift preparing to climb the stairs on foot, when the lift doors suddenly shut and it goes up to the top floor completely empty. Temperamental beasts, lifts.

From the new box, we now have an entirely different view of Trent Bridge, looking across the ground past the old, rambling Victorian pavilion. In the distance, over its left shoulder there stands a hill covered with trees and cornfields in about equal proportion. I felt it my duty to describe the setting to our listeners and in talking about the hill, I pointed out the dark red tower which rose up almost on the summit itself and described it as a church tower poking enticingly out of the trees. I speculated on the joy and peace of walking up the hill on a Sunday morning and going to church in such a lovely setting. When I had finished, David Richardson, the former South African wicket keeper who was with us as a comments man, saw some smoke near the church and said that he imagined they were having a barbecue as it was such a lovely day, and what a great setting for a barbecue. The next day, I received a postcard pointing out that my idyllic church on the hill was the Wilford Crematorium. Oh dear.

The Fourth Test Match lived up to the ground it was played on and was a wonderful game of cricket, especially if you happened to be an Englishman. Alec Stewart who, like the legendary C.B. Fry of whom it was originally said, is himself a ministry of all the talents, decided to put South Africa in to bat, always a brave thing to do in a Test Match. We all said that he had been seduced by a pitch which looked deceptively green and that he should have remembered that this was Trent Bridge. Captains who put the opposition in at Trent Bridge and, come to think of it, the Adelaide Oval, age prematurely and almost certainly die young. It was a surprising move for Stewart to make for in his years as Surrey's captain, his highly talented side had never won anything very much and his captain had not been especially imaginative or inspiring, while his instincts had seemed to be defensive. There is a paradox here, for anyone who bats as Alex Stewart does has no business to be defensively minded about anything. His nature, as reflected in his batting, is surely to attack. Perhaps his early captaincy had been paternally orchestrated by his father Mickey who, in his years running the England side, had not been known as a calculated risk taker, let alone for his recklessness. Cricketers usually play the game in step with their characters and I refuse to believe that anyone who can bat as Stewart does can be a man who likes to play life off the back foot. Putting the South Africans in now was an attacking enough move although the pitch looked greener than its behaviour suggested.

It was a decision which didn't go right for him at once, but then it didn't go altogether wrong either. The South Africans finished the first day at 302 for 7. They had been saved by a brilliant hundred from Hansie Cronje, his first for forty-five Test innings and his first against England, while Angus Fraser, who was back to his rhythmical best in the second half of the day, took four wickets and made sure that England hung on. His second, that of Jonty Rhodes who was lbw to one which cut back and looked suspiciously high, was the first of a number of questionable decisions, most of which went England's way.

There was one unforgettable piece of cricket on this first day when Stewart first threw the ball to his leg spinner, Ian Salisbury. When Salisbury had been selected for this match, Bob Woolmer, South Africa's coach, had expressed exaggerated unconcern in a way which made me think that he was a trifle alarmed at the thought of what he might do. From the evidence of county cricket so far in 1998, Salisbury appeared to be a born-again leg-spinner. He had spent the winter in Australia and had put himself in the hands of the former Australian leg-spinner, Terry Jenner, who has looked after Shane Warne. Salisbury had worked hard and had greatly improved his control. In the past, one had reckoned on one ball an over which could be hit for four. That was no longer happening and in achieving this extra control, he had not in any way sacrificed his spin, for he still gave both the leg-break and the googly a good tweak.

When he first gripped the ball at Trent Bridge, he was understandably nervous and one reason for this may have been the presence at the batting crease of Cronje, who is such a fine player of spin bowling. His first over to Jacques Kallis was a more than respectable maiden and there was a loud appeal for lbw when Kallis tried to sweep. He bowled his second over to Cronje, who had obviously thought about Salisbury and had decided that the one thing he was not going to allow him to do was to settle down. In this second over, picking his ball, he danced down the pitch and straight drove Salisbury back over

15

his head with a stroke which must have come as a devastating blow for the bowler. There was a certainty, almost a finality, about that one which signalled Cronje's intent and shook Salisbury's composure. After this first stroke, he began to strain for the crease and his control wavered. In his next over, he pitched a leg-break a fraction short and again Cronje pounced. Although he had all-too-little room in which to work, he swivelled, uncoiled a pull and the ball disappeared over mid-wicket for six – and that brought Salisbury's house crashing down. The old bad habits now reappeared and along came the long hops and full tosses. His line went too, and almost all of the forty-one runs which came in his first seven overs were scored on the leg side. Cronje had done what he set out to do; he had broken Salisbury's confidence; he had knocked him out of the attack as an effective bowler. When Stewart brought him back later, it was abundantly clear what Cronje had done, for in two overs he gave away sixteen runs and he had to be taken off. It had been a brilliant, calculated assault carried out with clinical efficiency. His bat had been the butcher's knife and Salisbury the carcass.

The picking of Andrew Flintoff had come as a breath of fresh air. So often, in the past, when the selectors have picked a young man, they have left him out of the final side and the pressure has built on him, but now they were prepared to throw the huge young Lancastrian in at the deep end and he came through his trial with credit. On this opening day, his first bowl in Test cricket was successful when he brought one back off the seam which found the inside edge of Kallis's bat. He fielded with fair-haired innocence and enthusiasm and later in the match and all too briefly, he showed us how hard he could hit the ball.

On the second morning, the admirable Fraser, whom I had nicknamed the schoolmaster in the West Indies, soon prompted an edged cut from Cronje and South Africa had to be content with 374. Mike Atherton had not had the same opening partner in successive Tests in this series, but at least he now had Mark Butcher back with him after injury and these two had put on 177 for the first wicket at Edgbaston when Allan Donald and Shaun Pollock had not bowled well. They now put on 145 for the first wicket with batting of an even higher quality than they had managed at Edgbaston and, in doing so, had finally solved the vexed problem of who should be Atherton's long-term partner. Atherton had gone from strength to strength as the series had progressed and his form came as no surprise, while Butcher's playing of Donald and Pollock was much more assured than anything I had seen from him before and he showed that he is an excellent player of fast bowling. They were unruffled as the two South African fast bowlers did everything they knew to break up the innings. Not the least of the benefits of this stand was the effect it will have had on others in the dressing room waiting to bat. Donald, whose controlled pace and stamina is extraordinary, took both their wickets in the end, although Butcher was probably unlucky to be given out lbw when Donald was bowling from round the wicket. Stewart and Hussain were also out before the end of the second day when England were 202 for 4 and the match was already building up to its climax.

The third day revolved around an innings of monumental patience, which was born of monumental insecurity, from Mark Ramprakash. At the time it seemed counter-productive but in the final analysis it was an important contribution to England's victory. His 67 not out took him 277 minutes and seemed to be controlled by an all too obvious fear of failure. I know of no one who wears his heart so openly on his sleeve when he is batting. It would be difficult to imagine an innings which was so far removed from the 154 he made in the Barbados Test, but this was not becoming an especially happy series for him, and after a fluent 49 in the First Test, his batting had become increasingly introverted. He likes to explore the dark side of any equation first. It was not until England were nine wickets down that he made an effort to change gear and it worked well enough for him to have been cross with himself for not going for his strokes earlier. As it was, he stayed to the end and made sure that England's deficit was no bigger than thirty-eight.

As I have suggested, the day was spiced up briefly by 'Freddie' Flintoff who, in sharp contrast to Ramprakash, came energetically out of the pavilion relishing the prospect of his first joust at this level. Even though he had to weather a few awkward overs before lunch, he let it worry him less than most. Then, after tucking in to a decent meal, he lent his massive frame into a cover drive against Kallis and the ball raced away to the cover boundary, seeming to say as it went, 'What's all the fuss about?'. In the next over he straight drove Donald to the pavilion rails with the unfussiest of strokes which Donald clearly thought was *lèse-majesté* in the extreme. A humble square cut followed, off Kallis although it is seldom that one sees such power in humility and then he spoiled it all by having a go at a wide one which swung wider still without much footwork, and got an edge. It was an innings which had the same effect as half a glass of vintage champagne. It left one longing for more at the same time as feeling devastated that one had drunk what little there was with such unseemly haste. Experience will teach Flintoff which ball to hit and which ball to leave alone but, please God, don't let anyone try and change him. In those few minutes he showed us that he's going to give us plenty to enjoy in the years ahead. And he's only twenty.

England could hardly believe their luck when South Africa lost three wickets for 21 at the start of their second innings and Kallis could hardly believed his when he was given out caught behind off Dominic Cork and the replays hardly supported the decision. Some sort of order was restored before the close by Cullinan and Cronje, who put on 71, taking South Africa to 92 for 3. There were so many possibilities. On the fourth day, another wonderful effort by the schoolmaster brought him his second five-wicket haul in the match and England had a major piece of luck when Cronje grew frustrated and was caught behind slashing at Cork without any footwork. After Cork had worked his way through the middle order, Fraser finished things off with his usual undemonstrative efficiency. South Africa had had to grit their teeth over one other dismissal, which was probably the worst of the lot. Rhodes had tried to flick Cork down the leg side and there was a huge and ongoing appeal for a catch behind. Umpire Kitchen waited a long time, which can imply doubt, and then up went the finger and even Jonty Rhodes found it hard for a moment or two to remember his devoutly held religious beliefs. Television was quick to confirm that the bat had been nowhere near it, prompting Kitchen to say after the match that he was not sure that he was up to in any more. I felt as sorry for Kitchen, who is the nicest and fairest of men, as I did for Rhodes. These things happen under pressure and will continue to happen until the authorities bite the bullet as they surely must and take full advantage of all electronic evidence over any potential dismissal to which it may be relevant. I know it is going to waste even more time and slow down the over-rates further but it would prevent the absurd situation of a batsman walking off having been given out when the entire ground has already seen from the replay on the big screen that he is not out, well before the victim has reached the pavilion. Much more account must be taken of the available replays even if we all have to wait while the umpire at the bowler's end asks the third umpire if he can see any good reason why he should not give the batsman out. We cannot go on having twenty-first century cricketers – as near as dammit – being ruled over by prehistoric methods. If the cameras have the evidence, it must be used and the Laws must be altered to allow for this with all possible haste. If the evidence is not there, the umpire in the middle will make the decision and if he gets it wrong, it is understandable. But when the world can see that you are out and the umpire says you are in, it is a farce. However, I confidently expect cricket's liberal supply of old farts to throw up their hands in horror at such a suggestion even now.

The inescapable fact at Trent Bridge was that England needed 247 runs to win this Fourth Test Match and to level the series. Only once in Test Matches in England have they scored that many to win in the fourth innings and that was at the Oval in 1902 when Hirst and Rhodes famously scored the last 15 in singles. Atherton and Butcher began the last act, and pretty well they did too. They saw away the immediate threat of the new ball adding 40 for the first wicket before Pollock, from round the wicket, made one straighten on Butcher.

When Hussain comes to the wicket, it is impossible to know what to expect. On his good days he is magnificent, but if the moon is in the wrong quarter, or whatever, he is on his way back after some dreadful stroke looking like A.A. Milne's Eeyore on the worst of days. This was a good day and there was a confident ring to his bat as he helped Atherton combat the pace of the South Africans. The cricket was gripping, the tension was dramatic and not a single millimetre was given by either side. The crowd were spellbound, cheering every England run to the echo and otherwise watching in almost dead silence, but even this did not hint at what was to come.

Atherton had made 27 and Donald was bowling from the pavilion end as if his own reputation and that of his country was in his right hand. The ball had been repeatedly passing

Atherton's face and shoulders at a searing 90 m.p.h., but Atherton's poise and equanimity were remarkable. He was brave Horatius defending the bridge and Donald made Lars Porsena of Clusium look like an imposter. Then, Donald went round the wicket and another furious bouncer tore past Atherton's chest, and this time Donald and the rest of the South Africans were certain the ball had flicked his glove on the way through to Mark Boucher, who went low to his right and held on to a pretty good one. Donald celebrated, Atherton stood stock still and the world with him, umpire Steve Dunne deliberated before giving Atherton the benefit of the doubt. The South Africans could not believe it, Donald seemed to snarl at Atherton, who held his ground and met Donald's stare with one of his own which was firm but not entirely without humour. Donald was the first to look away. There followed one of the fiercest battles between bat and ball it has been my privilege to see. Donald, maintaining control over himself and the ball, was now a primeval force and Atherton, with his jaw stuck out as never before, displayed the raw guts which occasionally prompts human beings to deeds which win them the Victoria Cross. For a handful of overs now, Ernest Hemingway would have fallen in love with cricket if he had been at Trent Bridge. There was not much difference between a bullfight and what was going on between Atherton and Donald. At the end of it, Atherton's cape was too clever for Donald's bull. It was cricket at its unforgettable best, cricket to rival Michael Holding's over at Geoffrey Boycott in the 1980 Barbados Test; cricket to rival Ted Dexter's 70 against Wes Hall and Charlie Griffith in their pomp at Lord's in 1963; cricket to rival any great moment in the game's history; cricket to take to the grave with you.

England survived that night with one wicket down although Hussain should have been caught behind off Donald. England had to score 139 more the next day, but the match ended when Donald failed to take Atherton's wicket. Not surprisingly, the zip had gone out of it the next day for all but the most ridiculously nervous. Atherton never wavered and set his stall to finish the job. Hussain passed 50 and was then brilliantly caught by Kallis at slip and Alec Stewart came in and finished it off with a blaze of strokes you would expect to see in an exhibition match. Atherton failed by two to reach a hundred. In years to come, he may regret those two runs but I wonder if, when he looks back, he will reckon that he ever played a better innings for his country. England won by eight wickets and the next day the entire country was talking cricket, the Fifth Test at Headingley had become a near sell-out; the television audience during England's second innings must have been huge. Cricket was back on the map again, but for how long?

We did not have to wait too long to be able to answer that question because England went on to win an absorbing but distorted Fifth Test Match at Headingley, by the slender margin of twenty-three runs after half an hour's play on the final morning. The joy and the relief was fantastic as England brought to an end a twelve-year period in which they had not won a single five-match Test series against a major Test playing country. They had won in heroic and unlikely circumstances; as we have seen, the Third Test was saved thanks to the batting of Croft and Fraser; the Fourth Test was then won by eight wickets and now, we came to Headingley for the final match.

Mark Butcher's brilliant hundred on the first day saved England's first innings, which folded all too quickly for 230. An epidemic of dropped catches by the safest fielders in the side, on the second afternoon, prevented England from gaining a first innings lead which would probably have been decisive on a typically uncertain Headingley pitch. Even so, the admirable schoolmaster came up with another haul of five wickets and South Africa's lead was kept to 22. Then came Nasser Hussain's 94 which took him just over seven hours and was the sort of innings books are written about, only to be followed by the sort of collapse of which English cricket supporters have such an excellent collection. Six wickets fell on the fourth morning for thirty-four runs and South Africa were left to score 219 to win.

Ten for one at lunch became 12 for 4 shortly afterwards and 27 for 5 soon after that, at which point Jonty Rhodes whose batting, like his walk to the wicket, was full of the spring and enthusiasm of a man who couldn't wait to get started, was joined by Brian McMillan, a man who is given to fewer excesses of emotion. While Rhodes danced his step at one end and continued to dance as he turned growing English frustration into irritation and on to anger, McMillan provided the roast beef and Yorkshire pud sort of innings that Headingley crowds have been reared on and rather warm to. These two put on 117 before McMillan played one hook too many. Rhodes forgot himself and drove to short mid-wicket and Mark Boucher plonked his pads approximately in front and was the fourth lbw victim of the innings. There was even a controversy about the extra half an hour, which either side could have claimed. The South Africans wanted it, the English did not and the umpires, curiously, decided the South Africans had put in their application too late. Paul Adams had run out to the pitch to deliver the message after the bails had come off.

The last day dawned overcast, England's bowlers were rested and may have sniffed a little swing in the air. Fraser bowled two maidens, unemotionally and efficiently, trudging off to fine leg in between times, while Gough, all arms and legs and ebullience, gave away nine precious runs in three overs. Then the schoolmaster ran in again and found the edge of Donald's forward stroke and in the next over the bounding

Gough hit Makhaya Ntini's pad and Javed Akhtar, who is from Pakistan, raised his finger, something which he had been doing with fair frequency since the match began. Mike Procter, the former South African all-rounder, was beside himself with rage and claimed that the ball would not have hit another set of stumps down the leg side. In calmer, more measured tones, Richie Benaud seemed to think it was fair enough. The celebrations began. Butcher was man of the match, Atherton was England's man of the series and Donald South Africa's and they had all been brilliant.

I couldn't help but feel that it all left a sense of injustice. Faulty umpiring had played too big a part in both of England's victories and I don't blame the South Africans for feeling aggrieved. In this last innings alone, Gerry Liebenberg hit the ball when he was given out lbw; Hansie Cronje walked off grinning broadly and thinking dark thoughts about the caught-behind decision which went against him; Daryl Cullinan's lbw may have been going down the leg side and Ntini could also have been unlucky. In their defence, England will say that Nasser Hussain was not caught behind on the first day, nor Andrew Flintoff at short leg, and that the ball bounced before Mark Ramprakash was caught behind, and then Atherton hit the cover off the ball when he was lbw to the first ball on the third morning. In South Africa's first innings, Gary Kirsten's lbw was too high, Cronje may have been too far forward for his and on it went with the all-seeing eye of television making monkeys of the umpires and a fool of the game, too.

Of course, it was a result which could only have left a nasty taste in most mouths. Two wrongs never make a right and it is a rotten philosophy to suggest that they do. Both sides were affected and neither will have felt it was a level playing field, but more especially so the losers. The sooner all electronic evidence is made available to the umpires the better. It will wash away this particular nasty taste, but I fear it cannot help but produce another which may be just as nasty. The tacit acceptance by the players of the umpires' word has always been a basic tenet of the game of cricket. Now, alas, it is something of the past, gone for ever to be replaced by trial by television. This may be inevitable, but cannot fail to turn it into a different game. Meanwhile, England have won a major series after twelve years of trying but at what a cost, even if the fault was not theirs.

The Fourth Test had been lent a little shaft of excitement by Matthew Fleming's monthly column in the *Daily Telegraph* which had appeared on the Saturday. Fleming is the chairman of the Professional Cricketers' Association, a body which has, as you will discover later in the book, come firmly down on the side of change when discussing the future of England's domestic cricket. They would like to see the Championship take on a league format with promotion and relegation. Fleming had just been across to France to stock up with as much duty-free as he could lay his hands on and upon his return had met up with Jim Swanton's equally informed and entertaining column, 'Personally Speaking', which appears in the same newspaper. Jim is one of the staunchest opponents of change to the championship, and had forcibly expressed his views in this column. He had also taken the PCA to task, writing, 'In the scramble for players (in a likely transfer market) (*my brackets*) salaries would continue to rise, probably sharply; hence the support of the PCA.' Fleming was understandably needled by this, to say the least, and now proceeded to play the bull to Jim's matador. In mild and measured tones, he flicked Swanton away off his pads to the fine leg boundary in an effortless way Ranjitsinghi would have admired, for having the temerity to suggest that the decision of the PCA had been purely financially motivated.

He went on to say that, like Jim and cricket lovers

generally, the PCA want a 'vibrant, healthy game and a successful national team. Our final destination is therefore the same, our chosen routes however differ widely'. There is more about this particular battle in the pages to come but I could think of no better way to start it off than with an eloquent skirmish between these two pillars of Kent cricket. As this debate gathers momentum I can see blood being spilled, because passions are already beginning to run dangerously high.

CHAPTER TWO

New Plans, Same Old Farts

England's cricket is in a mess. It has been for years. You do not have to be an Einstein or a Geoffrey Boycott to know that. The most extraordinary aspect of this is that, while it is obvious to anyone who follows the game, the people whose responsibility it is to try and get English cricket back on course have been unwilling or unable to believe it and hope that, by looking the other way and doing nothing, the problem will go away. Their continued reluctance to confront the matter, except by energetically promoting and voting for the status quo, is astonishing. Pompous platitudes continue to reverberate around Lord's and the other committee rooms of the country and much sucking of teeth and worried frowns from the gurus in charge has heralded a state of deafening indecision. The corridors of power have become increasingly full of minions chosen to run the game and yet England's performances on the field continue to cause despair.

Who could cricket turn to? It needed someone who had the combined qualities of Winston Churchill, Field Marshal

Montgomery and the Secretary-General of the United Nations. Not an easy one and the specification would have had the headhunters themselves in turmoil. Yet there was someone. For long years, after shrewdly marrying into the founder's family, Ian MacLaurin, who went on to acquire a K before gracefully stepping up into ermine, had steered Tesco, the superstore giant, back into competition and then to the top of the league. When taking over Tesco, MacLaurin had insisted on compulsory retirement for all staff at sixty. He may have felt, perhaps, that the enthusiasm of some members, especially of the founding family, not to be a burden on the company's pension fund until they needed a trolley of their own, not to push, but to be pushed in, had been counter-productive. Although in the pink in every possible way, MacLaurin was, at fifty-nine about to be felled by his own axe. His record was more than unblemished, it was one of long and unqualified success.

It was high time a realist took charge of English cricket. MacLaurin was no stranger to the game, having served on the Middlesex committee and having been a good enough player to have turned out for the Kent Second Eleven. He was competitive in every sense, he understood the marketplace and he would keep the gnomes who had been running the game on their toes. He was the one man who stood a reasonable chance of bringing the game into the second half of the twentieth century and eventually into the twenty-first.

After some skilful outmanoeuvring by Brian Downing, the treasurer of the old Test and County Cricket Board, MacLaurin was elected as the first chairman of the new England and Wales Cricket Board (the ECB) late in 1996. Downing had surreptitiously won the approval of the majority of the county chairmen before those at Lord's who disapproved of the whole idea of MacLaurin, knew what was going on. Alan Smith, the chief executive of the TCCB, seemed to be badly wrongfooted and MacLaurin was voted in. The knight in shining armour had arrived.

In December 1996 England toured Zimbabwe, shamefully for the first time, and the by now ennobled MacLaurin visited the country immediately after England had most ingloriously failed to win the First Test Match in Bulawayo. And even more ingloriously after they had failed to win it – the scores were level at the end and England had four wickets in hand – the coach, David Lloyd's, mildly hysterical catchphrase was 'we murdered 'em'. In fact, we did no such thing. The Zimbabweans played good and, much of the time, the better cricket. But Lloyd was unstoppable in his condemnation of Zimbabwe cricket. He was outspoken in his dislike of a charming country and he was appalled at the more than adequate accommodation, to say nothing of the eminently eatable food. He was also downright rude to one or two of the local officials after this First Test.

When MacLaurin arrived with his more or less permanent ADC, Tim Lamb, the Chief Executive of the ECB, he may have wished that he had had a red and not just a yellow card in his pocket. Lloyd will not have forgotten the meetings he had with MacLaurin in Harare. And, for the record, England not only failed to 'murder 'em' in the Second Test as well, they lost all three one-day internationals to boot. The party left Zimbabwe with the sad reputation of being the rudest visitors ever to have peered at the Victoria Falls. A good many of them appeared to be boorish. At parties some formed squares, talking only to themselves; some were uncommunicatively surly; many were scruffy beyond belief and their lack of dress sense was as sensational as the inability of some to find their razors.

MacLaurin will have left Zimbabwe appalled at what he had seen and no doubt staggered that those who had been in charge should have allowed things to disintegrate to this extent. He always knew he was going to have problems but probably didn't realise the scale. It had been a most pertinent introduction for him at the sharp end. By then, he had already begun to immerse himself in the production of a blueprint for the future of English cricket though he still had about six months more to serve as chairman of Tesco. The blueprint was scheduled to be unveiled towards the end of the English season in 1997.

In the intervening period he was to discover that pushing a trolley down the purpose-built gangways in a Tesco super-market was an altogether different ball game from trying to steer one through the labyrinth of highways and byways, to say nothing of the dungeons, of Lord's Cricket Ground. He will have found the enemy within a great deal more of a stumbling block than anyone else. The man on a mission for change was soon banging his head against a solid phalanx of stuffy, stubborn, humourless reactionaries who were apparently myopically defending their own efforts to run the game of cricket over a great many years. They had been presiding over a system which had seen England become progressively more uncompetitive on the international stage and did not have the guts to admit that they might have done it differently.

I am not going into the blueprint which was eventually produced because it was extremely complicated and parts of it, to me at any rate, were quite incomprehensible. And I am sure I am not alone. There were lots of good things to help streamline the progress of talented youngsters through the lower reaches of the system, which were gratefully received. It was the centrepiece, which dealt with the future of the County Championship, which was so arcane. The blueprint proposed that the eighteen first-class counties should be divided into three conferences of six sides each. After that, the only thing which was abundantly clear was that we would all be scurrying for our logarithm tables on a daily basis if we were to have any idea of what was going on. After the first half-a-dozen overs of a match the bowlers themselves would not have been sure they were bowling against the correct opposition.

It was obvious the three-conference plan was not MacLaurin's first choice. What we may never be told is whether or not it was a form of double-bluff. Was MacLaurin so sure the counties would throw up their hands in horror at the conference idea that they would therefore welcome the two-tier system as the lesser of two evils? Since taking office, he and Lamb had gone round all the counties talking to the chairmen and their chief executives. He would have felt out first opinions about his, at that stage, proposed two-tier system. With a two-tier system there would have been a concentration of excellence in the first division with the best sides in the country playing each other all the time. There would have been the promotion and relegation battles for the top three sides in the second division and the bottom three in the first. This would have been bound to keep interest going much later in the season for many more clubs than happens now. It would have avoided, therefore, a great many of those pointless end-of-season games when neither side gives a fig, everyone goes through the motions, the players are demob happy and the crowds bored to death and extremely small.

I watched one such in September 1997, at The Oval, between Surrey and Lancashire. Surrey were too awful for words. Their side was stuffed with Test cricketers and yet no one could bring himself to bother It was an insult to ask people to pay money at the gate to look at such a charade; it was a dreadful imposition to inflict on readers of the following day's newspapers and, for a side as individually talented as Surrey's, it was worthy of a stewards' inquiry.

A new system would invigorate the old corpse of county championship cricket and would bring with it a new sense of purpose for everyone concerned. National interest would be rejuvenated and a competition which has become as boring and inevitable as the weekly shopping expedition to the local supermarket – unless, of course, you are Lord MacLaurin – might one day claim television time. It would give a shot in the arm to what has more and more been regarded, in recent years, as a tired old anachronism which no longer produces cricketers good enough for England to beat other countries on a regular basis.

Of course there is a downside, expressed to me with force and eloquence one evening by the new chairman of Sussex, the redoubtable Robin Marlar whose opinions have never made him eligible for even associate membership of the Most Noble Company of Fencesitters. With a two-tier system, the future for a county destined to finish in the bottom four of the second division is bound to be bleak. The chances were that this might have been Sussex's fate for a year or two after all the recent dramas which ended with most of their best players decamping in the winter of 1996/97. It was only the spirited rescue operation mounted by Tony Pigott, who is now the Chief Executive, and Marlar, who has taken over as Chairman, that has seen the club turn the corner. Marlar said when he agreed to take over that it would only be for one year but, as I thought , he has got a taste for it and one year has become two. Understandably, he wants to see some of the initiatives he has taken come closer to fruition.

He says fiercely, 'I've got a county club to run'. Sussex is one of the poorer clubs, and if those faithful few who have been turning up come hell or high water for years to sit in the deckchairs at Hove, and are the life blood of the county, should decide to stay at home he would have real problems on his hands. No one will realise quicker than they that unless Sussex can lift themselves into the promotion zone at the top of the table, the good players they produce will soon be 'bought' by one of the richer counties in the first division.

These players will want to find a better stage on the road to Test cricket. Under the present system the optimists can always find something to be hopeful about and in 1997, in spite of finishing last in the County Championship, Sussex managed to reach the semi-final of the NatWest Trophy and their victory at Derby in the quarter-final was one of the most heroic of the season. Derbyshire made 327 for 8 in their sixty overs and Sussex, thanks to an extraordinary innings of 158 by Rajesh Rao, won by five wickets with four balls to spare. This could still happen in a one-day competition in the two-tier system but, with the best players gravitating towards the first division, it would be more unlikely. Another reason the deckchairs may then empty is that the spectators will not any longer have the prospect of seeing the country's best players in action when they play Sussex because the former will now be in a higher division. It is a chilling prospect for Marlar and the other chairmen in a similar situation. On the other hand it might be just the spur they need to find ways of making their counties competitive and I know no one fuller of ingenious ideas than the Sussex chairman. In 1998, Sussex showed that a place in the first division might be theirs by right.

Yet has not the point been reached where almost anything is better than nothing? I believe the counties should have voted for the two-tier system for a trial period of three years, at the end of which there would be an extensive postmortem. There may be advantages to come from it which have not been seen, and disadvantages too. The ECB, which controls the purse strings, should for this trial period make good any serious and unavoidable losses the less fortunate counties may suffer because of the new format, to ensure there is no chance of any of them going to the wall. I realise this is hardly a selling point but at least it would guarantee that all the counties would be in a position to return to the status quo or to whatever system would then be agreed upon if the two-tier system was scrapped. It is interesting that a poll of county cricketers by their trade union, the Cricketers Association, has shown that the players themselves have voted strongly in favour of a two-tier or league plan.

When it came to the vote, the six counties which stage Test Matches, Middlesex, Surrey, Nottinghamshire, Yorkshire, Lancashire and Warwickshire were all in favour of the two-tier system and were supported by Worcestershire. The rest voted against. This brings us to the next point which is whether or not the people who decide these things for their counties are anachronisms themselves. In 1998, it is strange that the feudal age should remain in place and county cricketers should be told what is best for them without the right of reply; indeed, with their expressed opinions being ignored. Do as you are told is the message. So much for the brave new world.

It is hardly surprising that cricket in England has become such a laughing-stock. Much is spoken about the big new sponsorship deals and the wads of money coming into the game from television contracts. New, lucrative deals are being unveiled all the time and the game has a much sounder financial base than it did. Satellite television is giving people the opportunity to watch international cricket overseas which they have never had before. Yet the old fuddy-duddies who run English cricket shake their collective head and say that they are not prepared to try anything to improve the standard of domestic cricket and therefore of England's Test side. They can think of nothing which might streamline, make more appetising or improve the main domestic competition which breeds our cricketers and which has been playing to almost empty grounds for years. When the players have spoken out for change they have effectively been told to mind their own business. Is that the way to run anything?

Late in July 1997 I was lucky enough to go to the Colchester Festival, which is one of the best dates on the cricketing calendar. Too many festival weeks have gone to the wall in recent years because, as the number of matches the counties play each year have decreased, there are not enough to go round. It is also expensive for clubs to stage matches away from their main centres and it is only those such as Colchester, Bath, Basingstoke, Cheltenham, Southend and Maidstone, which are able to pay their way, who have survived. Castle Park at Colchester is a delight not only because of the lovely ground and wonderful atmosphere but also because of the sponsorship and hospitality of local wine merchants, who always provide an excellent excuse to visit the country's oldest town, and the proximity of Gerald Milsom's restaurant in Constable country at Dedham, where the browsing and sluicing is unrivalled.

I watched Essex play Leicestershire which gave me the chance to enjoy to the full all the added extras, for it was a wholly unmemorable game except for one curious statistic. Peter Such, the Essex off-spinner, bowled no less than eighty-six overs in Leicestershire's only innings which is a record for a county match. This contest was played a few days before the MacLaurin blueprint, which was called Raising the Standard, was to be unveiled. As I walked round Castle Park behind the many marquees which help give the ground its character for this occasion, I spotted perhaps the most influential figure in English cricket, Doug Insole, who has also been the controlling influence with Essex cricket for a great many years. He played nine Test matches for England as a rather boring middle-order batsman in the 1950s. His companion that day at Castle Park was Alan Smith, recently retired as the chief executive of the old Test and County Cricket Board where he had become the Master of the Most Noble Company of Fencesitters. I have pointed out earlier in the chapter that he was a less than whole-hearted supporter of Lord MacLaurin's appointment as chairman of the ECB.

Insole's feelings on this issue, in case one had any doubts, were made apparent when Essex went against the two-tier system. It would not have needed any great guesswork to have hit upon the subject of their conversation that weekend. Insole has always been a believer in the cyclical nature of things and that England's cricket will in time come right again and that there is, therefore, no need to resort to a great upheaval of the present system. I suggest, too, that if figures like Insole and Smith had been eager to embrace the mood for change it would in effect have been questioning the validity of their own stewardship over so many years. I am sure this will not have been lost on them and their like. As far as MacLaurin was concerned, Insole and Smith were the vanguard of the influential enemy within and if their opposition to his plans for the future was implacable, the way forward was blocked. Insole is in his seventies, Smith will not see sixty again and it is surely not right that people of this generation should be able to control the destiny of the game of cricket in the fast-changing world of today. They have been left far behind.

Of course, cricket, like rugby union, has its old farts and most of them have done long and noble service on behalf of the game they have loved. Their fault has been to go on for too long and to attempt to tackle the problems of the modern world with views which were once highly relevant but are now out of date and inappropriate. Could anyone be less suited to usher in the new world of professionalism in rugger, the most dramatic change that game has ever seen, than a body of men who have given their lives to making sure that the amateur ethic survives. Cricket's old farts found it difficult enough to come to terms with one-day cricket, which began in earnest in 1963, and now many of the same old farts are in the unfortunate but possibly understandable position of wanting to block changes which are being proposed to try to secure the future of England's cricket. They have an unshakeable belief that they know best.

There is an inevitable dichotomy. The present system of county cricket has developed into a cosy club which has produced a splendid way of life that has continued for a long time but, as the Millennium approaches, it has become drastically out of date. The stage has been reached where it is actively working against the development of the England side which must be the top priority. The continued prosperity and success of the game in England can stem only from a strong national side and a firm central government which works to that end. The urge to preserve eighteen individual entities as they are is worthy and understandable but, if it is at the expense of the England side and therefore the health and prosperity of the game, it is nonsense.

1997 was the year of New Labour. The year of change, of Tony Blair and of the People. The latter were told what was good for them and, in their eagerness to welcome the new order, they liked it. Out with the old and in with the new. To hell with tradition. We must have change. Trust cricket to muck it all up. I doubt Tony Blair will spend much time at Lord's, or at the Oval, either, for if he went to Kennington he might find himself in the uncomfortable position of being taught the virtues of keeping bat and pad close together by one of Surrey's newest committee members, John Major. Leicestershire are the county likely to get the most out of New Labour. The club's emblem is a fox and it may soon become an offence to dismiss a Leicestershire batsman. Or maybe they will have to change their emblem. Tony Blair's government has already had an impact on the future of English cricket. The Heritage Secretary, Chris Smith, has decided that the planned academy for the production of sporting excellence will not be giving any support to cricket. Cricket's more than reasonable answer, forcibly expressed to the Minister by Lord

MacLaurin, is that it would therefore be extremely unfair to keep home Test matches on the list of protected events which must be shown on terrestrial television. If the government is refusing to give cricket any financial support, it must allow those who run the game to sell their principal product to the highest bidder, which would be satellite television. MacLaurin met Smith to make his point and the Minister, after listening carefully to the advice of the committee he had appointed to look into the matter, announced to the House of Commons in midsummer 1998 that he had decided to take Test Matches off the list of events preserved for terrestrial television. He made it clear that he had been impressed by the determination of the game's authorities not to let it all go to satellite television and therefore to keep a balance. MacLaurin himself must take a great deal of the credit for this decision.

Although the counties have, in their infinite wisdom, subjected us to three more pointless years with the mixture as before, there is one faint glow of hope. If England's recent mediocrity at international level continues, the cry for something to be done will become even louder. Because all the suggested changes which have been made so far have been returned to sender, there must be just a chance that in the end the administrators will, in complete panic, shut their eyes, hold their noses and jump. They might conceivably agree to bring in the one change which would not only considerably improve the quality of our domestic cricket but would also have an immediate effect.

The magic recipe is simplicity itself. Take the covers off the pitches and leave them off. England's cricket started on a downward path in 1982 when, with an impressive lack of foresight, those in charge of the game decided that first-class cricket in England would from henceforward be played on pitches which would be completely covered against the weather at all times. The result, sixteen years later, is that batting and bowling techniques have suffered irreparable damage. We now have a generation of batsman who cry 'foul' if ever the ball does anything unexpected. When they find themselves on a bad pitch they do not have the technique to cope. On rain-affected pitches batsmen were constantly having to adapt and improvise, and against the spinners they had to know how to use their feet in order both to survive and to score runs. Nowadays, in the commentary box, when one sees a batsman come down the pitch to a spinner, one talks about it rather as if one has just spotted a bird that was thought to be extinct. If we went back to uncovered pitches, the late cut and the leg glance, strokes that are seldom seen today, would re-emerge.

Another blessing would be that the weight of bats would come down. Heavy bats would be a handicap on a difficult pitch for they make it almost impossible for batsmen to indulge in last minute and highly entertaining improvisations because they would be impossible to control. Wristy deflections on both sides of the pitch or hastily improvised defensive strokes have to be part of the repertoire in such conditions. With a bat which weighs scarcely more than two pounds they are more than possible. When a batsman is carrying a tree trunk with the thick grips which are all the vogue today, and it all weighs nearly three pounds, these delicate touches are too dangerous to attempt. On the bland, covered pitches of contemporary cricket the ability to adapt like this is not needed, although the weight of bats has decreased in the last two or three years.

On covered pitches bad batsmen are able to survive for much too long and there is no more boring sight in cricket. In the old days, tail-end batsmen had a go and it was most exciting to watch. Either wickets fell or the ball disappeared to all parts of the ground. In the prevailing conditions, they know they have a chance of staying for a while with, say, the last 'proper' batsman and so they try to put their heads down and behave like a top-of-the-order player. I believe uncovered pitches would help make county cricket a more entertaining game.

The change in the bowling would be no less remarkable. Spin would return with a vengeance. One of the saddest effects of covering pitches has been that it has turned finger spinners – off-spinners and orthodox slow left-armers – into largely defensive bowlers. Long gone are the days when, on a drying pitch, they were rewarded with figures of, say, 7 for 28. On uncovered pitches they toil away for hours on end when their final tally may be 3 for 85 from thirty-seven overs. They bowl largely in order to prevent runs being scored rather than going all out to take wickets, for in the present conditions the odds are stacked against them.

Modern captaincy also works against spin bowlers. In the way the game is now played, containment is the order of the day. This is a virtue or a vice handed down from limited-over cricket which, for the bowling side, is an essentially defensive game. Captains think long and hard before entrusting the ball to the spinners for fear of what might happen if they bowl badly. To no one was this more applicable than to the last England captain, Michael Atherton who brought on his spinners only when he had run through just about every other available option. Except in exceptional circumstances he would then allow them only four or five overs which is hopeless, for on covered pitches a finger spinner has to wage a campaign against a batsman and he cannot do this in such short spells. In any event, if a spinner should get hit for a couple of fours, most contemporary captains rush for shelter behind the nearest seamer who, among other things, slows the game down because he bowls his overs much more slowly.

Present-day finger spinners have therefore become defensive, containing, mean-spirited bowlers who are frightened to give the ball air. Off-spinners, epitomised by John Emburey, push the ball through more and more on the line of the middle or middle and leg stumps with their full quota of five men on the legside rather than tossing it up outside the off stump with a packed offside field, inviting the batsman to drive, hoping first to deceive him in the air. The slow left-armer is nowadays equally reluctant to throw the ball up and invite the batsman on to the front foot. He also pings it in at middle and leg just as Phil Edmonds did for years, and it is all so boring. But it is more than anything, a product of covered pitches. I can understand the need to play one-day matches on covered pitches but, in England, the longer game should always be on uncovered pitches. Cricket would become fun again and, for that, spectators and sponsors would surely be prepared to put up with the odd 'no play today' sign. It would also mean an improvement of standards all round the world. Players who toured England would make it their business to adapt their game to the needs of uncovered pitches.

Another important advantage would be that uncovered pitches would increase the need for spinners which would automatically result in fewer of those dreary old seam bowlers who plod away relentlessly up and down the country from April to September at fourteen overs an hour and bore us all to tears. Teams would be better balanced, the cricket would be more entertaining and one or two of the participants might even look as if they are enjoying it. Standards could not help but improve and England might one day win another Test Match at Lord's. It sounds elementary, so why on earth do the administrators not get on with it.

You have guessed it. There is a snag. The marketing gurus who increasingly run the game, in spite of deafening protestations to the contrary, will not have a bar of it. Now marketing men do not always know too much about cricket and I am not sure even they would say it is an essential requirement for the job. The sponsors, for whom they are trying to produce a good deal, may also have a fairly sketchy knowledge of the finer points. But inevitably sponsors, who have paid a fortune for a Test series or whatever, dread the idea of a clear blue sky and spectators queuing at gates which remain firmly locked because a deluge during the night has left the pitch and surrounds waterlogged. Worse still, the television cameras will be standing idly by and the viewing public will be asked to make do with endless replays of old Test matches. These often come from the black and white era and are usually far more entertaining than the live output. I can never see too much of Fred Trueman bowling out the West Indies at Edgbaston in 1963 or, better still, Jim Laker taking all those wickets against Australia at Old Trafford in 1956. But, as far as the sponsors are concerned, it means that hours go by without their name being mentioned or their logo shown. It is the type of situation which makes marketing men take to drink or go into the church. No, they do not want a return to the bad old days of uncovered pitches and they have, I can assure you, insinuated their influence into every committee which has the chance of doing something positive about the future of English cricket.

This brings us straight to a good old chicken-and-egg question. Which comes first: the successful England side big business is falling over itself to sponsor, or the money from big business which will enable the game to flourish and the England side to improve? Historically, cricket has been strapped for money and for years the marketing guys went out, cap in hand, to potential sponsors and came away grateful for anything they could get. What would have been sillier than to have the game jeopardise their chances of raising a bob or two? But that's all old hat. Cricket has moved light-years from those days and there is much more money coming in, mainly from sponsorship and television that means an awful lot of advertising time. So, let's get tougher with the sponsors and tell them what we are going to do and why we are going to do it and, if they don't like it, that's their bad luck. I bet hardly any of them would want to pick up their bats and go home and, if they did, there would be plenty of others lining up to take their places.

I am getting fed up with continually seeing England walloped all round the world and having to be content with the occasional victory over New Zealand. When that happened in New Zealand early in 1997, we were all led to believe by those in the know that this was the start of an England resurgence. At the moment of writing which is more than a year later England has not resurged very far. In spite of the reassuring victory over South Africa, which came not a moment too soon, much still remains to be done if this is to become the norm rather than an isolated instance. Why does no one do anything except for those who continually try to block the people who *do* try and do something? Suggestions are made, blueprints are produced, ideas go round but the blockers always win and at the end of the day, a few cosmetic changes apart, it is steady as she goes; more sucking of teeth and shaking of heads but little else. Will the time ever arrive when the punters lose interest and stay at home? And, having stayed at home, will the stage eventually be reached when they refuse to turn on their television sets any more? This may be the point we have to get to before anyone in a position of real power will accept that something drastic has to be done if England are ever to be in the wonderful position of having won more Test matches than Australia who, after their 1997 tour of England, were 114-92 ahead? But they will all be dead by then, anyway. Will there ever come a time when the sponsors begin to feel that by supporting a side that continually loses, they are not getting value for money and pull the plug? Is all of this a spurious argument because airtime and newspaper column inches are everything and the product is irrelevant, however chilling that thought may be?

And now for the solution. All first-class cricket in England from now on should be played on uncovered pitches with only the creases being sheltered from the rain. Leave the bowlers run-ups open to the elements and, when they get a bit too squelchy (which will not take too long, one hopes), captains will have to turn to their spinners. I have detected a feeling within cricket that the game belongs to the players. What nonsense. It belongs to the spectators whom it sets out to entertain and who pay the players their salaries. If the public is happier watching cricket at eighteen overs an hour on uncovered pitches, that should be the end of the argument. It would be lovely to think that the country might rise up and march on Hyde Park demanding uncovered pitches and faster over rates. Where would the old farts hide then?

Nor will it be a question of asking England's cricketers to play in one set of conditions for domestic cricket and in another for Test cricket. The ECB should tell the rest of the cricket world that, whether they like it or not, they will play Test matches in England on uncovered pitches. The International Cricket Council will squeal loudly as well and they too must be told where to get off. If the other countries do not like it, there is no need for them to come. You see how many will be able to afford to throw up lucrative tours of England. They may make a lot of noise but they will come just the same. Of course, playing Test cricket on uncovered pitches will give back to England the advantage they always had over visiting sides. All other countries prepare pitches to suit their own sides. Why should the English be so squeamish? We should have the guts to wag our finger much more strongly at the rest of the cricket-playing world and, if need be, to tell them to go and jump.

Who will ever forget the excitement at The Oval in 1968

after heavy rain looked as if it had washed out most of the last day of the final Test when England were poised to beat Australia. The rain stopped, the ground staff were confronted by a waterlogged ground and there were not enough of them to cope in the time available. Realising this, hundreds of spectators helped mop up the pitch and the outfield. Play became possible around teatime and England had Derek Underwood in the side who was a magician in these conditions. He proceeded to mop up the Australians every bit as efficiently as the spectators had mopped up earlier. Who will forget that splendid photograph of Underwood finishing it off when he had John Inverarity, surrounded by almost the entire England side, palpably lbw to his arm ball with umpire Charlie Elliott confirming the obvious in that way of his which seemed to be saying to the batsman, 'this hurts me more than it hurts you'. It was all too glorious for words and the Australians will have whinged for months about the ground not being fit and the spectators being allowed to help with the drying up operations. So what? Those few minutes not only enabled England to draw the series, they made everyone feel much better and did wonders for the game in England and it was all made possible by the fact that the pitch was uncovered.

Why do the people who run the game in England drag their feet so much? English cricket needs people who are going to stand up for it, and take it on the chin if needs be. Which brings me back to the admirable Lord MacLaurin. He was brought in to do a job by some of the people who eventually blocked him. But, being the man he is, he has stayed to fight on and he brings to the game a precious commodity which it is desperately short of: common sense. He has taken the view that he has at least started people thinking and has made a small start in the right direction. As I write, he is almost coming towards the end of his first two-year term of office, and it is essential that he is given a second term for he is the only man with the sense and the vision to shake up the game in England so that it enters the twenty-first century organised and equipped for the battles ahead. I have to admit, though, to a nasty, sneaking feeling that the counties who seized on him so eagerly in 1996 will turn their backs on him in 1999. If they do, the old farts will have won the day. Perish the thought.

On the day I left London late in January for Jamaica and the aborted First Test Match between the West Indies and England, the best possible news broke for English cricket. It was announced that MacLaurin was to become chairman of Vodafone, the company that took over in the autumn of 1997 as the main sponsor of the England side for the next five years. This means that when the chairman of the ECB has to talk over policy with the chairman of Vodafone, he will be talking to himself. And I am sure he will get the answers he wants. I believe, too, that this arrangement strengthens the power of MacLaurin as he struggles to take English domestic cricket forward. But I can hear the old farts in so many of the county clubs shaking their heads and sucking their teeth and 'not being sure about it'.

It is, to say the least, mildly ironic that, having taken over as the main sponsor of England's cricket late in 1997, Vodafone were blocked from taking commercial advantage of their role in the West Indies by Cable & Wireless, the main sponsors of West Indies cricket who are in the same line of country. This was a stupid and short-sighted decision by Cable & Wireless, not least because during the five years of Vodafone's contract the West Indies will make two, if not three, visits to England where I imagine Vodafone will be ready for them. The irony was underlined on my flight to Kingston. Sitting in the font row of the first-class compartment of the British Airways jumbo was the amiable and now ample figure of Sir Michael Marshall, the former Conservative member for Arundel, where they used to weigh his majority, who has for years been a Cable & Wireless consultant. A few rows further back on the other side of the same compartment sat Terry Barwick, the director of corporate affairs of Vodafone who was on a familiarisation trip. They probably did not know each other and certainly did not share a drink. When Chris Gent, the chief executive of Vodafone and a great cricket lover, received a letter from the American chairman of Cable & Wireless telling him that Vodafone would not be able to play more than a walk-on part in the West Indies, he was apparently reminded, most irritatingly, of the necessity of abiding by the umpire's decision. I would have enjoyed Gent's reply.

By then the old farts had done it again. One of the important features of MacLaurin's long-term plan for English cricket was the need to contract the best players to the ECB rather than their county clubs. This was in order to give the board a greater measure of control over its principal employees. It would mean, for example, that if the selectors felt it was important a player should be rested from his county side between Test matches, they could take the decision themselves rather than have to go on bended knee to the county concerned and run the risk of being told to mind their own business. Of course, that was effectively what MacLaurin was now told and the plan was thrown out. The greater good of English cricket again took second place to parochialism.

Who are these people who were apparently happy to see MacLaurin installed at the ECB with a reforming brief before going on to tie both hands behind his back and reduce him to impotency? By and large, county administrators do not rank high in the list of progressive thinkers. Their motto might be 'To have and to hold'. However they might want to disguise it, they must be frightened that a board with sweeping powers would take away their authority to run their own county clubs. Undoubtedly they live in the past. They are not certain that a winning England side would see their own smaller economies boosted; they are terrified they will lose control of their own destinies. Their argument is likely to run along the lines that all counties have their own individual problems and that strong central control would ignore them. More specifically, at the moment they are alarmed that a two-tier county system would at some stage, if not straight away, see them in the second or lower division and that local interest will fall away, if not disappear. And what then? It is depressing that they are unable to approach it with more of an open mind. The paradox is that they are already under a central financial control in that the considerable handout they receive each year from the profits of the ECB makes more than just the difference between solvency and bankruptcy.

Old cricketers usually think they know what is best for modern players and in the way of the world this is understandable, even though they will mostly have played their own cricket in vastly different circumstances. Some who still help control their counties will have retired before the arrival of the one-day game which has made such a difference; others will have played no more than a handful of limited-over matches when the old Gillette Cup began in 1963. Yet they are sure they know what is best for present-day cricketers, although they would find themselves complete strangers in a modern dressing room. They will deplore the lack of technique today; they chortle with disgust at the ease with which they consider today's players appear to give in to injury; they will laugh at the emphasis on physical fitness and the combined sessions of physical jerks which go on before the start of each day's play; they will scoff at what they perceive to be the lack of professional skills in today's lot and they will be amused at the frequent use of the word 'pressure' as if it was an excuse for technical shortcomings. They may be influential among fellow committee members of the same generation who are all likely to feel that what was good enough for them in their era is surely good enough now. They are out of touch with the game as it is, as we approach the third millennium. Yet many of them are still powerful figures and the chief executive of a county club will think long and hard before he fundamentally disagrees with his chairman or whoever the person is who effectively runs the club. Lord MacLaurin will have to break down some strongly entrenched attitudes but he has already begun with seven counties and most of the players with him. That is a useful start as long as he does not weaken. But England is not the only country with cricketing problems as I was to discover when I went to Pakistan in October 1997.

CHAPTER THREE

Eastern Scenes

Some people have doubts about visiting Pakistan and Ian Botham has made it clear he considers it to be the ideal place for his mother-in-law to be dispatched for an all-expenses-paid holiday. On the other hand, I can think of few countries that have made me as welcome and few international airports where my arrival is as painless as it is in Karachi. I clocked in towards the end of the first week in October after my fleeting visit to Rheims with Michael Atherton and company. I landed in the middle of the night as if the victim of some immutable law of nature, and the moment I stepped out of the aeroplane I was confronted by a man holding a notice board with my name on it. This did not surprise me because the influence of my friend the Commander knows no boundaries. The chap with the board took my briefcase and told me to follow him. We arrived eventually, after much passage work, at the end of a long queue leading to the immigration counter. We never paused but strode on to the head of the queue where we waited long enough for one of the immigration officers to finish with his current passenger. More surprisingly, no voices were raised in anger accusing me of queue barging. At the counter the speech was in Urdu, there were looks and smiles, my visa was checked and stamped and, as a hurried after-thought, so too was my passport.

From there we moved on to the baggage claim area where hundreds of green-dungareed porters touted for business as the carousel noisily jerked its way round spilling bags at each hairpin as it went. My guide selected a porter and asked me for my baggage tag, which took a while to find and was even-tually located in the last pocket I tried. It always is. My bag made a surprisingly early appearance and it was on to the Customs who were full of smiles and shook me warmly by the hand. They were not in the least concerned about the contents of anything, solid or liquid. It was amazingly friendly. An official standing by the entrance checked the tag on my case with the one on my ticket and then we were outside where a sea of expectant faces surged towards me, restrained by a line of crush barriers, their faces peering through the dim electric light.

I saw, at once, the cheerful, moustachioed features of Amir Baig, the Commander's driver. He is an old friend and easy to spot because he is not much more than knee-high to a grasshopper and his smiling face was at about waist height and so he did not have too much competition. Amir Baig speaks no English and my Urdu is every bit as good but we smiled at each other like mad and he scuttled round to the head of the exit path where the barriers end and we almost shook each other's hands off. The four of us then set off in line-ahead formation, Amir Baig at the front looking like a rabbit who has scented victory and increasing his lead all the time; I came next, followed by the stout chap who had met me at the door of the aeroplane, who was now going through his limited repertoire of English phrases for the third time; and the porter, who gamely had my heavy suitcase on his shoulder, was bringing up the rear without ever suggesting he would finish in any other position. It took Amir Baig a moment or two to spot the exact location of the car ,which he did amid a flurry of 'I told you so' smiles. The luggage was loaded and, after much enthusiastic pressing of flesh and the unbelting of the odd banknote or two, we set off.

Now, a journey with Amir Baig is never less than memorable and he drives rather as if the massed bands of something or other rather important are playing Colonel Bogey. From the moment he guns his engine Amir Baig more than makes up for his lack of inches. The Commander's car is much like any other in Karachi and yet the traffic has to be extremely heavy for the road not to open up in front of Amir Baig as if we had police outriders on each side. He set a cracking pace, which was not surprising considering it was the middle of the night but he paid not the slightest attention to any speed-limit requirements. More imaginatively, he did not pay the slightest attention, either, to the many traffic lights between the airport and the Commander's house, most of which seemed to be red. With a feudal disregard for such impediments he accelerated triumphantly, if a trifle alarmingly, through the lot of them. He must have taken minutes off the record for the journey. He also showed a healthy contempt for the driving of most of his fellow countrymen as he kept his thumb firmly pressed down on the horn, and if a chap was particularly stupid, rather enjoyed drawing up alongside and letting him have an impressively succulent piece of invective. Sadly, it was in Urdu, so I missed the full flavour of it. When we arrived at our destination, a short but meaningful hoot interrupted the nightwatchman's dreams, the huge wooden door was opened and he drove into the courtyard. Amir Baig leapt out and opened my door, shook me by the hand once again, smiled beamingly and gave a slight shrug of the shoulders as a conjuror might after doing an especially successful trick.

I had arrived at the magnificent house of my great friend Arshad Gilani, a former Commander in the Pakistan Navy who, to this day, walks with a touch of the nautical roll. As you will have gathered, he is the Mr. Fixit to end all Mr. Fixits. He and I met some years before, at one of the many cricket tournaments in Sharjah, and had become the firmest of friends as had our families. In the early 1990s I had been working for TransWorld International (TWI), Mark McCormack's television arm, in the West Indies when South Africa made a short tour soon after the abolition of apartheid and their readmittance to international cricket. We were flying one day on that interminable journey from Kingston to Port of Spain and I was sitting next to Bill Sinrich, the bearded American from Connecticut who lives in London and, among other things, masterminds TWI's cricket coverage. Twelve months hence, the Pakistanis were scheduled to tour the West Indies and TWI, who had bought the rights to televise cricket in the West Indies, were hoping to cover the series but only if they could raise enough money to make it worthwhile. The fragmented economies of the West Indies are unable to make a significant contribution and, if coverage of the series was to be viable, the major proportion of the money would have to come from Pakistan. Bill asked me if I knew anyone in Pakistan who might be able to raise more than a million US dollars so that Pakistan television would be in a position to buy the product at the right price. I said I thought the Commander might be his man and on our return to England I arranged a lunch and it all came to pass. The Commander worked himself to the bone raising the money from a number of different companies in Pakistan and TWI covered a series which the West Indies won, 2–0. The television coverage was a personal triumph for the Commander who was with us for most of the tour and himself provided one or two of the main features. He is the most generous of men and one day in St. Vincent he hired a yacht which took us to Bequia and then on to Mustique in the Grenadines, and it would be impossible to imagine a more beautiful part of the world. Later on, there was another day during the Third Test when he organised a boat trip around Antigua which was just as memorable. But sadly the strain took its toll of the Commander who became extremely unwell for quite a considerable time afterwards. By the time I arrived in Karachi in October 1997 he had been back in harness for three years at least and had now become TWI's man in Pakistan, Bangladesh, Sri Lanka and the United Arab Emirates, where he was crucial to their success.

The Commander is a buoyantly cheerful extrovert and I do not think I have met more than two or three others in my life whom it is such fun to be with. Visits to Pakistan would not be half so amusing without him and every time he comes to London he brings the best out in the old city. Well-known head waiters come at the double when they see him pushing through the swing doors, the wine waiters put their best foot forward and once more life seems jolly. When the Commander summons you for a drink, you discover how catholic his tastes are. You are as likely to find Ian Chappell and Geoffrey Boycott as you are the senior diplomatic staff of the Pakistani Embassy, a television mogul or two, tycoons from a variety of different worlds and many more. All are received with the same bouncing, good-natured hospitality. The pace of life never slackens and you never know what glorious piece of gossip the next telephone call will produce. Life with the Commander is not dull.

I had arrived in Pakistan that morning to make my comeback on television for TWI, who were covering the Test series between Pakistan and South Africa and then a quadrangular one-day tournament in Lahore. It was a comeback because I had jumped ship and joined the Mascarenhas bandwagon after he had won the rights for the 1995/96 World Cup in India and Pakistan. For two years I had steered Mark Mascarenhas in the direction of many of the influential figures in a world cricket, people who had much to do with the buying and selling of television rights and I had been a loyal supporter until, one day, he took me out to lunch at the Halcyon Hotel in London's Bayswater Road and told me he had decided to take a different view from me of an agreement, not to say a contract, which had been agreed by us on a handshake. I shall remember to get it in writing next time.

Mascarenhas is a large, bearded Indian with a cheerful, bluff, hail-fellow-well-met exterior whom it is impossible to ignore. This can be deceptive and in many ways he is the Geoffrey Boycott of television tycoons. He knows exactly what he wants and does not care whose toes he treads on to get it. It is a moot point whether he or Geoffrey changes his hotel room more times in a calendar year and who makes the more noise about it. Head waiters blanch visibly when they see either approaching but once in a restaurant they could hardly be more different. Mascarenhas is expansively generous when it comes to giving hospitality, while Boycott dines more modestly, on the edges. When it comes to making sure a television production is done as cheaply as possible, Mascarenhas's qualities are impressively Scrooge-like; but maybe that explains why he is as rich as he is. He is ruthless and once said to me, 'I don't waste time hating people, I just thank God I am smarter than they are.'

Mascarenhas hails from Bangalore and made a lot of money quickly from a cleverly thought-out television deal for skiing in parts of Europe. He is persuasive but when it comes to cricket, like many movers and shakers, he does not know anything like as much about the game as he professes. Making money is his game and he is very good at that.

For a while, after I left them for Mascarenhas, TWI took a dim view of me and it was thanks largely to the Commander's persistent lobbying on my behalf that I had been asked back. I would have liked to have made a success of television commentary but I am afraid I was never very good at it. Television commentary had increasingly become a formula whereby former Test cricketers comment on the picture which is being beamed into people's homes. Ritchie Benaud, Ian Chappell, Geoffrey Boycott and Michael Holding do this brilliantly. With the help of replays they analyse each ball bowled, each stroke played and any relevant pieces of fielding. It is dry, it is to the point. I was brought up in radio, where the commentator is the listeners' eyes. He has to describe the whole picture and he can talk about anything he likes and has the luxury of being able to indulge in repartee with whoever is alongside him, no matter what the subject. The television commentator has to be subjugated to the picture. It is bad television to talk about something the viewer cannot see. His scope is more limited, therefore, and there is no need for him to talk all the time. It is irritating for viewers to be told continually that so-and-so is coming in to bowl when they can see it for themselves. They want the picture to be explained and put into perspective and, quite rightly, there is no place for the double decker bus going down the Wellington or Harleyford Road. What added extras there are, must come from within and not from without. Established radio commentators do not easily turn into television commentators. I think it is fair to say that Tony Cozier is the only exception. He is brilliant on both radio and television and moves effortlessly from one box to the other, twice an hour, for the five days of most Test matches he covers. I have always found it difficult to commentate from the monitor and it is almost as if I feel that, if I am not looking at the actuality of it, something might be going on behind my back. I do not trust the monitor, which is as silly as it sounds. I also talk too much. So you can see that I have never found television comfortable and will happily settle for making a fool of myself on radio. I do wish, though, that they would be prepared to have a bit more of a laugh on television; but that does not seem to be part of the plan, at any rate since Brian Johnston was sacked by BBC Television in 1970.

Anyway I was back with TWI and was determined to get it right if I could. I think I may have done for about the first day and a half but as my confidence increased, so did my bad habits and I was left yet again doffing my cap to the likes of Geoffrey Boycott, Sunny Gavaskar and the rest who do it so well.

It was about four o'clock in the morning before I put my head on the pillow in the Commander's spare bedroom which seems to have been lifted lock, stock and barrel from one of the glossies, it is so luxurious. It seemed only about ninety seconds later that Hakim, another of the Commander's admirable staff, was in my midst with a cup off tea and, inevitably, the sun was pouring through the windows. He was followed in a matter of moments by my very cheerful host, looking wonderfully ornate in Pakistani dress – Arshad is not a big man, at least in height. He told me he would be leaving for the airport in just over an hour and a half for a flight to Rawalpindi where the First Test Match between Pakistan and South Africa would start the following day.

Pakistan cricket was in its usual state of semi-chaos. Majid Khan, a former captain of Pakistan and first cousin of Imran Khan, was the chief executive of the Pakistan board. The family effectively runs Pakistan cricket, whatever they may say, and in all probability Majid was hoisted to his present position by another first cousin, Javed Burki, also a former captain of Pakistan and now just about the top civil servant of all who just happened to be the then-President of Pakistan's cricket adviser. Majid replaced Arif Abbasi, who has twice held the post and is also a member of the same family, even if a slightly more distant relation.

Majid has been determined to bring back old-fashioned standards of decency and honesty to Pakistan's cricket. The team had just returned from Canada where they had been playing a series of five one-day matches against India for the Sahara Cup. This is an annual competition which has been inspired by TWI and takes place each year in Toronto. Pakistan had had the worse of this 1997 tournament which is never a popular move when India is the opposition, and charges of match-fixing, which are for ever being made in Pakistan, were once again flying about all over the place. Salim Malik's name often seems to crop up here and he had now been dropped from the Test side, as had Ramiz Raja who had been the captain in Toronto. In Pakistan captains seldom survive defeat, especially when it is against India. There was a strong rumour that Salim Malik's Test-playing days were over and he was nowhere to be seen in Pindi. Ramiz Raja, meanwhile, became TWI's newest television recruit and did an excellent job. There was never the slightest hint that Ramiz had in any way been involved in any match-fixing. It was being said, though, that there were other well-known players on whom Majid had his eye and that as soon as they gave the selectors the chance, they too would be out. The chairman of the selectors, the affable Salim Altaf, known to all as Bobby, is very much Majid's friend.

On the first morning of the First Test Match, I had been deputed to travel to the ground in Geoffrey Boycott's car. Mercifully I was in the foyer of the hotel in time, for suddenly the Great Man swept through looking neither to the left nor to the right and barely acknowledging my greeting. He was followed by Ramiz who was half running to keep up. Boycott kept saying 'shit hotel' to anyone who wanted to listen while looking at his fiercest. He was heading for the entrance and it was just as well I decided to follow in his wake. The Great Man was in a huff and a hurry. He made straight for the front door, sat down and reclined the seat as far as it would go, saying to the driver, 'Is this as far as it goes? What about my back?' Ramiz and I climbed into what was left of the back seat as quickly as we could with a horizontal Boycott urging the driver to get a move on. The driver received an unending stream of instructions in a tone of voice that brooked no misunderstanding. Conversationally, the half-hour drive through rough and teeming streets was orchestrated by the Greatest Living Yorkshireman. Anyone would have thought he was under the impression that the British Raj was still up and running. He was exceptionally unhappy with the hotel and broke off in his condemnation of it only to be exceptionally unhappy with the standard of the driving, the condition of the streets, the behaviour of the pedestrians and the occasional hesitancy of our own driver. He spared us no detail about the 'shit hotel', which I am bound to say I found adequate enough although it provided rather less than five-star comfort, and he told us with a triumphant grin that he had made arrangements to move to an infinitely superior billet in neighbouring Islamabad.

The pitch at Rawalpindi was the usual flat nothing where it is almost impossible to get batsmen out and only a great disparity between the two sides or divine intervention will produce a definite result. After winning the toss Pakistan's frontline batsmen systematically threw away the advantage that had given them with some dreadfully careless batting. If it had not been for Ali Naqui, a nineteen-year-old opener from Karachi with a precocious temperament, the South African bowlers might effectively have won the match on this first day. Opening with Saeed Anwar is always likely to give a newcomer an inferiority complex. Seeing the ball fly off

Saeed's bat from those flashing strokes at the start of the innings either makes his partner feel hopelessly inadequate or that he must join in. Naqui, in his first Test match, was one of the latter and, to his credit, he not only joined in but went on to outplay his illustrious partner. His driving and cutting were as much a delight as his determination to play his strokes whenever he had the chance. There was a lovely moment just after he had reached fifty. He survived a furious appeal for lbw against Allan Donald, who had beaten him with a splendid yorker. Naqui did not look in the least ruffled and, when Donald raced in to bowl the next ball, he drove him with impertinent ease over mid-on for four. Even a bowler of Donald's class and experience will have been deflated by that one. By the time he skied Donald to cover after batting almost six hours for 115, Naqui's unquenchable spirit was more than apparent. On a surface which allows the bowlers any movement his lack of footwork and technique must surely get him into trouble. Nonetheless it is extraordinary how Pakistan continues to produce these teenagers who are able to make such an immediate impact on cricket at this top level.

Ten runs before Naqui was out, he had been joined by Azhar Mahmood, another playing his first Test Match but at the ripe old age of twenty-two. Defending sensibly, he saw Pakistan through to 216 for 6 at the end of the first day, which still meant that the honours had gone to South Africa. They will have been even better pleased when soon after the start the next morning Pakistan had fallen to 231 for 8. It was now that Waqar Younis came out to join Azhar, who had so far looked composed enough in defence but had attempted little else. They had put on twenty-two without incident and without suggesting what was to come when suddenly the day and the innings underwent a sea change. Waqar, who can bat competently enough if he is bothered, took to Pat Symcox's off-spin, swinging him away to the legside boundary and driving him straight. The batsmen were now looking for runs. Azhar began to pick his bat up higher, cutting and driving with power and timing; there was about his batting a compelling flair and runs started to come at a great rate. These two had put on seventy-four for the ninth wicket when Waqar was hit on the toe and given lbw to a yorker from Shaun Pollock. He limped painfully away. He was passed by Mushtaq Ahmed who came cheerfully out to do the honours as the No. 11.

Now there are a great many No. 11s who know much less about batting than Mushtaq. At first he defended stoutly while Azhar continued to play his strokes and they had put on forty by the end of the day. Mushtaq is a comical figure. There is about him an underlying impishness and an overlying rotundity, a cheerful smiling face and a cheeky moustache. It is as though God intended him to be a leg-spinner. As he bounces up to the wicket and his arms twirl like a couple of demented windmills it is as if all the mysteries of the Orient are tucked up in his right shirt sleeve. With a bat in his hand he gives the impression he is playing the part of a clown who is pretending to take it seriously. At the other end Azhar, a slight figure who looks taller than he is, with a moustache which has not done much more than poke through the surface, rather like recently sown grass, was the student going to war. They were a mildly improbable and yet curiously complementary couple and what a lot of fun they gave us.

Mushtaq did not attempt to do a great deal more than survive but Azhar, after getting the flavour towards the end of his stand with Waqar, continued to hit the ball extremely hard, especially off the front foot. His judgement of length was good, his sureness of stroke was impressive and he was in control of both himself and the bowling. In the first over the next morning he played Donald off his legs through mid wicket with a stroke which made everyone sit up and take notice. Then, with another, he hooked Pollock for four and reached

61

his hundred soon after without any fuss or nonsense. Mushtaq now decided that with that out of the way it was time for him to join in and in one remarkable over from the off-spinner Pat Symcox, he pull-drove for three sixes over mid-on and swept for four off successive balls. When their stand had reached 151 and equalled the world record for the tenth wicket in Test matches held by Brian Hastings and Richard Collinge for New Zealand against Pakistan at Auckland in 1972/73, Mushtaq slogged at Hansie Cronje and dragged the ball into his stumps. Azhar was 128 not out at the end of a remarkable innings which had begun when Pakistan were struggling at 196 for 5. He had watched while they sank to 231 for 8 before he, Waqar and Mushtaq almost doubled the score, steering them to 456 on a day when the Queen, who was on a state visit to Pakistan, came to watch the cricket. South Africa also reached 400 and the Test was drawn.

While Ali Naqui has not been able to build on his first Test innings, Azhar has acquired a habit of scoring hundreds in Test matches and making a useful contribution with his seam bowling. He not only has a rare talent but also has the composure and the intelligence to go with it. Many of the young Pakistanis get into trouble when they find themselves playing for their country overseas because there is no one willing to tell them how to cope with the new conditions. Azhar showed in the three-match Test series which followed in South Africa, when he made two more hundreds, that he is able to adapt his game. While his strokeplay was refreshing and spontaneous in Rawalpindi, it was his ability to cope with the pressures that big stands at the end of an innings bring with them that was so impressive. Of course he was lucky to have two such old campaigners at the other end as Waqar and Mushtaq but he had, for all that, to protect them when they first came in. While he was doing this for Waqar his own first Test fifty was approaching and in your first Test Match it calls for character to be selfless at a time like this. Later, with Mushtaq to shield, he was approaching a hundred which is an even harder target to ignore in your first Test, and yet Azhar managed to do this. His game never changed as he neared this landmark; he was always composed, he never made the mistake of thinking to himself, 'If I don't get them now, the chance may have gone' and, as a result, having a wild and fatal heave across the line of the ball. When Azhar completed his hundred it was the first time in Test cricket that two players from the same side had made a hundred in their first Test innings in the same match, let alone the same innings.

Rain ruined the Second Test Match at Shekhupura, a town about an hour up the road from Lahore and the most memorable part of those five days was the car journey each morning, which allowed Geoffrey Boycott to get more off his chest about the Pakistan transport system and the need for a Highway Code. He would have been a tough Viceroy. We then all foregathered in Faisalabad after another entertaining drive with the Greatest Living Yorkshireman which I have described near the start of the book when Traffic Warden Boycott did much to uplift our spirits. The Third and final Test of the series turned out to be one of the great Test matches. The grounndsman at the Iqbal Stadium had helped raise our spirits too, because he had prepared a pitch which had a fair covering of rye grass and promised a much more satisfactory balance between bat and ball than either of those in Rawalpindi or Sheikhupura. The Pakistanis were so puzzled by the appearance of the pitch that the evening before the match began, when the umpires had left the ground, Wasim Akram and Mushtaq Ahmed, both old enough to know better, bowled a couple of overs on it to see what it was likely to do. This is strictly not allowed but what the two bowlers had not catered for was the presence of one of the South African Broadcasting Corporation cameramen, who filmed this entire practice session. I have dealt with this incident, which was seen on television in South Africa, in detail in the chapter I devoted to the scandals which cropped up during my cricketing year.

South Africa won the toss and batted on a pitch which had lost some of its grass when it was cut on the morning of the match. Cronje decided to bat, a decision he was soon to regret because there was some early moisture in the surface, the ball was moving around in the air and off the seam and Wasim and Waqar caused chaos with some brilliant bowling in the opening overs. They shared the first four wickets before Mushtaq, who was able to make the ball turn and bounce, took another three and South Africa were 98 for 7 at lunch. During the interval the Commander, who always came to the first day of the Test matches to make sure the sponsors were happy and the advertising boards were in the right place, was in buoyant good health. He was a little deflated when Symcox and Gary Kirsten put on 120 for the eighth wicket during the afternoon but he picked himself up when South Africa were finally out for 239. Pakistan lost two wickets that night. The Commander went jauntily to the airport but when, rather mischievously, I called him at home the next morning, Pakistan were 80 for 5 and I have known him chirpier. He need not have fretted yet, for Inzamam-ul-Haq, at his most upstanding and impressive, and Moin Khan now batted rather as Kirsten and Symcox had the day before and in the end Pakistan reached 308 and a lead of sixty-nine which looked as though it would be enough, especially when Kirsten and Bacher were out before the close of play.

In spite of another brave fifty by Symcox South Africa were bowled out for 214 just before the close of the third day, predominantly by the admirable leg-spin of Mushtaq and the off-spinner Saqlain Mushtaq. This left Pakistan to score 146 for victory and I doubt there was a single Pakistani in the country who thought that this would be anything more than a formality. They were 4 for none at the close and the Commander will not have needed to reach for the sleeping pills as he tucked himself up in Karachi that night. But I am afraid he did not enjoy the next day. The first gasp of pain came from the South Africans though, when, in the third over Amir Sohail turned Pollock off his body to square-leg where Bacher unaccountably dropped the catch, two-handed, in front of his face. Bacher was given the chance to make amends in the very next over, however, when Sohail played a wild hook at a wide bouncer from Donald. The ball screwed up to cover where Bacher dived to his right and came up with a beauty. Sohail's nerve had failed him, which was strange for such an experienced batsman.

In the tenth over Saeed Anwar, before he had scored, flashed at one from Pollock which was too far up to him and was caught behind. Ijaz Ahmed took his place and moved far across his stumps as he tried to turn his first ball to leg. It kept low and he was palpably lbw in front of the middle stump. The pressure had got to him too, for it was an absurd way to get out in that situation. Two overs later Ali Naqui, who had not looked up to it in either innings on this pitch, thrust forward at Pollock with his bat away from his body and was caught at first slip. In the same over Inzamam pushed at Pollock from the crease without trying to get his body behind the line of the ball and he was superbly caught by Brian McMillan, two-handed, diving to his left at second slip. Pakistan were 31 for 5 and it was all I could do not to ring up the Commander and tell him the score even if he would have considered it to have been a treasonable offence.

Nothing much happened for a few overs after that except that Symcox took over from Pollock, who had taken 4 for 27 in seven unforgettable overs. The score had limped to 68 when Azhar glanced at Lance Klusener and was caught behind down the legside off the glove. It then became a question of how long Wasim could restrain himself against the spin of Symcox. The answer was not for long and, at 85, he swung violently at a ball which pitched outside the off stump and was turning away from the left-hander and Kirsten gratefully accepted the skier at mid-on. Then it was all over in a matter of moments. Saqlain was comfortably caught at short-leg off bat and pad, Waqar received a dose of his own medicine when he was brutally yorked by Pollock and finally Moin swung Symcox into Donald's grateful hands at square-leg. Pakistan were all out for 92 and South Africa had won a wonderful Test match by 53 runs. The Commander's telephone was engaged. Then it was time to share a car with Geoffrey Boycott for the drive back to Lahore and to listen to another sort of commentary on the way.

We had four days before the start of a quadrangular one-day tournament in Lahore which turned out to be a waste of time. All the matches were played at the Gaddafi Stadium where each evening the ground was soaked by the heaviest of dews. The side fielding second had little chance because by then, under the floodlights, the ball closely resembled a bar of soap. It was not the most cleverly thought-out competition and in the circumstances of the dew, how much better it would have been if it had been played elsewhere in the country. In fact, South Africa won the final, batting first, because they scored over 300, a total they were able to defend against Sri Lanka in spite of the wet ball. This was just another in the interminable line of one-day competitions and it was not one of the best. It meant another dinner or two with the Greatest Living Yorkshireman who had taken to calling all the waiters 'George'. When they failed to listen to his master's voice as carefully as they should, they were told firmly, 'George, you've got brains of chocolate mouse'. It was perhaps as well they did not entirely understand him or, indeed, pick up the implications.

At the moment, cricket is enormously popular in Pakistan and this is the direct result of their recent success on the world stage which goes back to their extraordinary victory in the World Cup in 1991/92 when Imran Khan was still captain. Every small boy in the country wants to play cricket and the enthusiasm for the game is much as it used to be in the West Indies. Everywhere I went in Pakistan impromptu games were being played with total commitment. Any open piece of ground was being used, and the open road too in some places, although the usual traffic congestion makes this a less than secure venue. I wonder if Geoffrey Boycott's Highway Code would allow for cricket. Three sticks or an upturned box would be used for stumps and the next generation tore in to bowl, claiming to be Wasim or Waqar, to batsmen who were Inzamam or Saeed Anwar and now, I daresay, Azhar Mahmood. This is how children are introduced to the game all over the country. There are no facilities as such; everything has to be improvised and yet the Laws of cricket are roughly applied. The facilities at the top end of the game are also sensationally inadequate. There are probably not more than thirty turf pitches in all of Pakistan, and that figure includes the Test grounds. For these makeshift games, if an old bat cannot be found, a piece of wood of approximately the same size will be used and the ball will, more than likely, be an old tennis ball with sticky tape round it.

It is from these simple beginnings that the present generation of Pakistani Test cricketers have emerged. Even in these humble circumstances they have been able to develop their natural talents to the point where they can be recognised and taken forward to the path which leads to Test cricket. Tennis-ball cricket is where fast bowlers learn their skills. If they are to control a ball which has so much bounce, they must learn the appropriate arm action. As far as batting is concerned, these youngsters are quick to realise that the best way to succeed is by playing straight and therefore they learn to play orthodox cricket strokes. There is no coaching and so it is all a completely natural process. Another influence which makes these children anxious to make the most of what they have been given is a powerful socio-economic factor because they know that, if they are successful at the top level, cricket will bring them a marvellous livelihood as well as turning them into national heroes.

The path which eventually leads the most talented of these boys to first-class and Test cricket is straightforward. Almost all the present Pakistan side have begun life in the country areas where they will have progressed from street cricket with a tennis ball to a more organised form of the game still played in the most rudimentary conditions. As they have made their marks at this level, they will have been noticed and, with financial help from their families, will have travelled to the nearest city where the local cricket association will expect them. The next step is to play for one of the associated clubs, for club cricket thrives in the cities although again the facilities are woefully inadequate. Regular success at this level will then bring a youngster to the notice of those who select for the first-class teams. If all continues to go well, the next people to take an interest will be the Test selectors.

A young cricketer, like many of the teenagers or those just into their twenties who have played for Pakistan in the last few years, may then find himself selected to go on an overseas tour. When that stage has been reached he will still never have seen, let alone been taken in hand by, a coach. Ramiz Raja, who played in more than fifty Test matches, told me that he, like most other Test cricketers in his country, did not learn the game until he had become a Test cricketer. It was only then that he became aware of the importance of being able to play 'tight, compact cricket'. Ramiz was luckier than most too, because his brother, Wasim Raja, also played more than fifty Test matches as a batsman and Ramiz will therefore have received more advice at home than most.

The lack of coaching is not a problem when it comes to the initial development of these young men but it poses problems later. A youngster may thrive in his home conditions but when he has been selected to tour overseas he will find that there is no one to help him adapt his game to suit the needs of foreign conditions. That this should be so, argues a remarkable lack of organisation on the part of the Pakistani authorities and it is also a dreadful indictment of the selfishness of the established players if they are not prepared to help these young men with their problems. One notable exception here was Imran Khan, even if he tended to have his favourites. Over the years no Test side has been better at beating itself than Pakistan. They have had sides full of wonderfully talented individuals who have no idea of how to pull together. So often, personal success has been more important than collective success. This accounts for the alarming inconsistency of so many Pakistan sides who, although they seem to be better on a man-to-man basis, end up by losing. The importance of having a coach or two with a touring party, not least as a unifying influence, cannot be overstated.

Another adverse side-effect of the lack of coaching is that players who lose form do not know how to set about recovering it. They have been carried along on a wave of natural talent and, having been consistently successful, they have never had to stop and try and work out how they did it. They have never needed to strip down the mechanics of their art into its various component parts and then to reassemble them making sure that each is working in relation to the next link in the chain. The game has no predetermined infrastructure in Pakistan but this does at last seem to have occurred to those in charge as a national coach has been appointed and steps, admittedly hesitant first ones, are being taken to try to harness perhaps the greatest supply of natural talent in the world today. As it is, there is not a single bowling machine in Pakistan, let alone a cricket academy.

After hearing about the development of the rich stream of talent and seeing for myself the results when Ali Naqui and Azhar Mahmood made those hundreds in their first Test, I was extremely surprised one evening in Lahore soon afterwards to hear from Majid Khan how concerned he is about the long term future of the game in his country. We met at the house of his cousin, Javed Zaman, in one of the Zaman Park mansions. Majid is the most charming and gentle of men who is a stickler for standards although it is a moot point whether he is the best man to get this across because the modern generation of cricketers might find him a touch anachronistic to say the least. There is something delightfully old-fashioned about Majid just as there was when he batted for Cambridge, Glamorgan or Pakistan wearing an elderly yellowing wide-brimmed sun hat which his father, Jahangir Khan, might well have worn when he played for Cambridge before the war. It was Jahangir who killed the sparrow which sits stuffed in the museum at Lord's, when he was bowling for Cambridge against the MCC at Lord's in 1936. Majid himself is a double member of the Zaman family for he married his first cousin, the sister of Javed Burki, who is a formidable cricket lady. I had dinner in their house, also in Zaman Park, one evening when she electrified me with her understanding of the rules concerning the reallocation of overs in a rain-affected one-day match. No one else in a distinguished cricket gathering came near to the answer.

Majid is worried about the state of the game in his country and its lack of depth. He told me about the frightening shortage of decent grounds and turf pitches and the state of decay of many existing facilities. His principal worry was that the upper-middle-class boys in Pakistan who had the luck to go to schools like Aitchison College in Lahore, which has been such a wonderful nursery for cricketers, were no longer interested in playing the game. These schools have excellent facilities and yet nowadays the standard of what little cricket is played is alarmingly poor. The result is that the natural leaders are no longer coming through to take charge of the first-class and ultimately the Test sides as he and his two cousins, all products of Aitchison, had done. The consequence here is that at the top level of the game, cricket is being run by young men who come from humble origins and have no innate feel for the game or its traditions. Increasingly, there is no one to check the declining standards of behaviour on the field and round the periphery of the game. This has provided Majid with the motivation to try to get rid of the sharp smell of scandal which has been following Pakistan cricket for quite a while now.

He felt this lack of a natural leadership to set the example for the young to follow would, before long, damage the game irreparably in Pakistan. If the national side is no longer winning consistently, he was afraid that interest in the game would rapidly wane. Because there is anyway such a shallow base to cricket and the facilities are so scarce and inadequate and there is no money to improve them, the young would lose their enthusiasm and find something else which was more accessible. The supply of Ali Naquis and Azhar Mahmoods would dry up and the game would be doomed. It would have been interesting to have heard Imran on this subject but he and Majid still do not speak after Imran left his cousin out of the Pakistan side to play England in a Test match at Leeds in 1982. Imran and Jemima and family lived in the house exactly opposite Javed Zaman's and after dinner, as we were leaving, Imran walked across, carrying his baby son, and spoke to some of us before we climbed into our cars.

It had been an evening which had made rather a fitful start. Geoffrey Boycott had also been asked to dinner and our host had promised to pick us both up at the Pearl Continental Hotel at about a quarter to eight and eventually his son turned up for us. He was very definitely on Pakistan time for, by then, it was half past eight. Now, Mr. Boycott does not approve of unpunctuality and nor does he approve of the Pakistani habit of eating dinner very late. When attending a dinner party given by the Commander in Karachi he had insisted on being served dinner by himself at half past eight, some two hours before the scheduled eating time. The Duke of Wellington could not have been more chuffed after winning the battle of Waterloo than the Great Man was to have won this particular battle. When our host's son had arrived at our hotel to pick us up he was given a pretty sharp lecture of the 'I don't know what time you call this, then?' nature. It continued in the car and on our arrival our host himself was left in no doubt as to the great man's feelings, and for a time it was in the balance as to whether the dinner party would be honoured by the presence of the Greatest Living Yorkshireman or not. In the end he stayed, but finally left in a huff when one of the distinguished guests appeared to have the temerity to disagree with him over some point from his cricketing lore. 'I'm not going to waste my time talking to you', was how it ended.

When Majid and I met again, he told me he had expressed his fears to the ICC and his fellow chief executives had been astonished to hear them. But I only hope they take note of them. It is one of the duties of the game's governing body to do all it can to spread the game around the world and, if possible, to introduce and nurture it in places where it has hardly a toehold. Jagmohan Dalmiya from Calcutta, who is currently the president of the ICC, and Ali Bacher from South Africa who did so much to ensure that cricket was preserved at a high enough level during South Africa's years of excommunication, are both heavily involved in spreading the gospel. One problem which has faced ICC has been a shortage of money to spend on giving the game greater publicity and taking it to new countries. For years the ICC has watched as a series of lucrative one-day competitions have been held all round the globe although they have not yielded a single cent piece for its own coffers. As an organisation, the ICC moves at a pace which would make a snail look fast but at last it is now actively engaged in trying to raise money which will enable them to spread the game further and help improve the standards of the burgeoning nations in the hope that one day some of them will be admissible at least to the ranks of those entitled to play one-day international cricket. I can only wonder, after hearing Majid's fears and then visiting the West Indies for the England tour early in 1998 where a situation similar to that in Pakistan is developing, if the ICC has got its priorities quite right. One would have thought it should be using more money and influence to protect the game nearer to home. Of course, it will be a great bonus for cricket if the game is spread more widely round the world. But the creation of competitive cricket at club level in, say, Japan and Thailand is not going to count for much if cricket is going to sink below subsistence level in Pakistan or the West Indies. This may sound far-fetched, but the situation is such that if a careful eye is not kept on it, great damage could be done.

The main problem in the West Indies seems to be the proximity and influence of the United States. For many years cricket has been a unifying and all-pervading factor in West Indian life. It has been a game which has appealed to the West Indian temperament and in all those lovely islands and in Guyana on the South American mainland, it has been played with the same enthusiasm which I had found in Pakistan. By all accounts this is no longer so and when I was there I saw fewer visible signs that cricket had the Caribbean in its grip as it used to. The young have switched their allegiance to American sport which is so readily available on television while, because of the costs involved, cricket is hardly ever on the box. Handball, basketball, volleyball, netball and baseball all capture the West Indian imagination. It is natural that the West Indies should be drawn more to America than to the far distant part of the world which colonised the islands all those years ago and which has handed down its own traditions which may now seem increasingly out of place. America is more with it and of course attracts the Caribbean youth. It is a natural progression. To cope with this, West Indian cricket needs to be more structured and one hopes that those who run the game in that part of the world are aware of what is happening and are not just sitting back happily waiting for the next fast bowler to run off the beach.

At Test match time the grounds in the Caribbean were always packed out but now, as in India and Pakistan, it is only the one-day internationals that guarantee full houses. The young in the West Indies must also be aware of the greater financial rewards the top players in American sports take home with them. It would be no surprise if the youngsters are beginning to look upon cricket as an old-fashioned sport. At the moment the West Indies side is not the power it was a few years ago and the danger must be that, if West Indies cricket goes into decline at the top and they are forced to go through a lengthy period where success is hard to come by, interest will fall away ever more sharply and they might suddenly cease to be competitive. Of course this is some time away from happening but the mere fact that it is up for discussion which it never would have been ten years ago, shows that the authorities will ignore the present signs at their peril. As long as they are aware of what might happen and do not take their eye off the ball there is every chance that nothing of the sort will occur and that there will be remedies to put into place as the warning signals light up.

Added to this is the same problem Majid Khan is faced with in Pakistan. The well-to-do children, who go to the good West Indian schools like Lodge and Harrison College in Barbados, are no longer playing cricket either. The natural leaders are not, therefore, coming through and cricket is being increasingly controlled by those from a lower class background who do not have a true appreciation and understanding of the innate standards and traditions of the game. On the recent England tour of the West Indies we had a good glimpse of how standards have begun to slip. The pitches overall were a disgrace with Kensington Oval, Barbados, the one shining exception. If the great West Indian batsmen of the past, Walcott, Weekes, Worrell, Sobers, Kanhai, Nurse, Greenidge, Lloyd, Richards, and the rest, had been brought up on pitches where batsmen had to graft to score runs, we may never have seen their true genius. If anyone could have transcended poor batting conditions it was they, but only because they had already learned their job on excellent pitches which had, above all, the true bounce which is so important for the development of the full art of batsmanship. The facilities, too, on some of the grounds had been allowed to become too run down. Financially, West Indies' cricket has always been a poor relation principally because they do not make significant money from tours of the Caribbean which are so expensive to put on. Hotels are highly priced in an upmarket holiday setting, vast distances have to be travelled and the grounds are small with three of them, Guyana, Barbados and Antigua, holding less than 10,000. There is also a limit to what can be charged for tickets in a part of the world where the per capita income is small. With the sale of television rights and the increase in advertising, rather more money has come into their cricket, but one is left wondering if the best use is being made of it. I am not trying to scaremonger but West Indies cricket is more brittle than it should be after so many years of such dramatic success. It is sad that circumstances have not allowed them to cash in on this success and safeguard their future.

In the last decade the impact of television on the financial viability of international cricket has dramatically increased. Television audiences seem to have an almost insatiable appetite for the game, especially the one-day variety, and most particularly when India and Pakistan play each other. More and more one-day competitions have sprung up to satisfy the hunger of the television audience. Whenever a new competition is devised or the television rights in one of the main cricketing countries come up for grabs because a contract has run out, there is an ugly rush by the prospective buyers to try to win the rights. A fair amount of skulduggery goes on as the TV moguls try and gain the inside running for whatever competition is on offer. Endless clandestine meetings and telephone calls, the promise of personal favours, whispered threats and insults, frantic aeroplane dashes to get in ahead of the opposition, not to say good old-fashioned blackmail, are all a part of it. This is a clear indication of the value of the rights for modern cricket. There is, too, any amount of personal vendetta, for these television moguls mostly hate each other. It is dog eat dog.

I have seen some of this at first hand, having been involved for a short time in trying to help TWI acquire the rights for cricket in India and then assisted WorldTel in Mark Mascarenhas' initial surge to acquire the rights for anything going. I have seen some of the infighting and need hardly add that the Queensberry Rules do not apply. I was with Andrew Wildblood, of TWI's TV cricket arm, in Poona when, tense, snatched meetings in coffee shops, hotel bedrooms and the odd corridor stretched on until well past midnight before the deal was done whereby TWI won the rights to televise England's series in India in 1992/93. They took place in the Blue Diamond Hotel in Poona where the Indian Board of Control had gathered for their annual meeting which was held at the house of the president of the board, Mavradhao Scindia, the former Maharajah of Gwalior. Wildblood was most impressive, never letting the conversation slip away from him in spite of having to make telephone calls to Bill Sinrich in TWI's office in London when he needed to ratify new terms. In the end, the committee the board had appointed to deal with the rights were satisfied with our offer and hands were shaken. I remember being electrified the next morning after breakfast when one most influential member of that committee, Jagmohan Dalmiya, now the president of the ICC, had the temerity to suggest that negotiations still might be reopened with TWI's main rivals who were on that occasion Michael Watt's CSI. I have no idea if it was a leg-pull or not but I am glad to say Wildblood and I were able to hang on to what we had won that night.

A couple of years later I flew to Barbados on what turned out to be a much less agreeable trip. I was summoned by Mark Mascarenhas along with Chester English, one of his American partners who was himself more involved with boxing than cricket. I flew to New York, spending the night in Chester's splendid apartment, and the next day we flew down to Barbados where Mascarenhas was already ensconced in the Sandy Lane Hotel. Mascarenhas himself met us at the airport and the news was bad, for it looked as if the West Indies Cricket Board had closed ranks, presumably at TWI's behest, and it was unlikely that we were going to be able to see the right people. Mascarenhas was angry and in that mood is unlikely to win friends but he does have the happy knack of winning battles for television rights. His object in coming to Barbados where West Indies were playing a Test match against India was to try and persuade the West Indies Board to do business with him and not TWI. There was also a side-issue about the rights for the current series on pay-per-view in America, which TWI appeared not to have thought about.

It was not until TWI came along that the WICB understood that its own television rights were a massive unrealised asset. It sold them to TWI in the late 1980's when Sky television first came on the scene in England, and were anxious to show England's series against the West Indies in 1989/90. TWI formed a close and profitable relationship with the Board who, reasonably enough, were determined to remain loyal and to refuse all Mascarenhas's blandishments of more money which they never quite believed. During the 1994 summer in England, Mascarenhas, English and I had taken Steve Camacho, the chief executive of the West Indies Cricket Board, and Pat Rousseau, the Jamaican who was then Treasurer of the Board and was to become its next President, to dinner at the Club in the Dorchester Hotel. Much money was spent and plenty of propaganda was pushed across, but I am sure it made no impression on the two West Indians. Obviously, in their job, they were duty-bound to listen to any proposals or overtures made by TWI's competitors. Looking back on it, I doubt if there was ever the slightest chance they were going to do business with Mascarenhas and I fear they were not overimpressed by his bluster and swank.

Back in Barbados the three of us drove from the airport to Steve Camacho's offices on the Savannah and after a long wait, Camacho turned up but, knowing him as I did, I could see how embarrassed he was and knew full well we were the last people he wanted to see. To his credit, he was never flustered and was scrupulously polite throughout. The next day we went to Kensington Oval where the Test match was being played and I found this highly uncomfortable too, since I knew personally a number of the West Indies board, but in the circumstances they too will have felt I was an embarrassment. We were pushed into the box of the Barbados Cricket Association presided over by the President, the charmingly urbane Cammie Smith who made us more than welcome. When things are going against him, Mascarenhas does not come across well. The three of us talked in hushed whispers at the back of the box and messages were constantly sent through to the board's box next door in the hope that someone of importance would come and talk to us. Eventually, Rousseau's deputy as treasurer came to see us – Rousseau himself was flying to London, probably to sign a new deal with TWI – and it was quite clear that Mascarenhas had no hope of winning anything. There was one rather rich moment when Bill Sinrich left the board's box and walked past the open door of our box and down the outside stairs. Chester English saw this, shouted his name and rushed after him and had an animated conversation with his fellow American on the stairs. Of course, Sinrich was not going to give a single millimetre. Why should he have done? One could sense, too, a built-in antipathy to Mascarenhas who in adversity is let down by his bedside manner.

It was a few days after this abortive trip that I was summoned to lunch at the Halcyon Hotel and told effectively that he had squeezed me dry and, apart from my commentary, had no further use for me. I had been warned by Chester English that this might happen. Mascarenhas finds it helpful to be able to blame his own shortcomings on others. He is at the moment embroiled in a tussle with the Board of Control for Cricket in Sri Lanka. He had a Memorandum of Understanding to televise cricket in Sri Lanka for three years from 1997 but the issue has been blurred by allegations of bribery as a senior official of the board has been paid a significant amount of money and has apparently demanded more. It was said that the money was destined for the Government

Minister concerned, which he has denied, and the Bribery Commission in Sri Lanka took over. In the end, the Sri Lankan Board took the contract away from Mascarenhas although they allowed him the chance to bid again for it. It was at much the same time that Mascarenhas had problems with the renewal of his contract for the rights to international cricket in Sharjah. In both countries TWI was his principal opponent although perhaps Mascarenhas will again make an enormous and irresistible bid for cricket in Sri Lanka. He is a formidable operator.

After watching Mascarenhas, TWI and the others coin it in for years from all these one-day tournaments in Sharjah, Toronto, Singapore and Colombo not to mention the rest in India and Pakistan where a new limited-over tournament seems to find its way on to the statute book each year, the ICC have at last acted themselves. In order to raise money for the ICC, they have put on a one-day tournament for all the Test-playing countries in October 1998. The original idea was that ICC would be able to do a deal with Disneyworld whereby Disneyworld would build a stadium and put on the competition. It then transpired a Mr. Billy Packer (no relation to Kerry) with whom Mascarenhas had gone into business in another venture, was able to block the deal whereby ICC played its competition at Disneyworld. There are two governing bodies for cricket in America and they seem to be at each other's throats. Mascarenhas and Packer had dealt with the one which has control of the game in Florida and only cricket organised by these two could be played there. It is mildly ironic to say the least, that in another venture, Mascarenhas and Dalmiya are partners, yet here Dalmiya, as Chairman of the ICC, appeared to have been blocked by his own business partner from trying to further the ICC's interests.

The competition was then hastily rearranged so that it

could be played in Sharjah before another little local difficulty cropped up. Dalmiya, wearing his ICC hat, had persuaded Will's to come in as the name sponsors for this one-off tournament, but tobacco advertising is banned in the United Arab Emirates and Wills's offer was too good to let go. So, just before Christmas in 1997, Dalmiya announced that there would be another move and the tournament would now be held in Bangladesh, where they are less concerned about their people's health. It stinks.

I returned to London in the middle of November and after spending Christmas and the New Year in Norfolk it was time to pack the bags once more and head for the West Indies. I could hardly have anticipated the dramas that were so soon to take place in Kingston and Port of Spain.

CHAPTER FOUR

Atherton's Farewell

The excitements of Queen's Park Oval, Port of Spain, would never have happened if it had not been for the fiasco of the pitch at Sabina Park in Jamaica. The respective events are so intertwined that they must be dealt with together. I first saw the pitch for the Sabina Test, which had been relaid only in October, three days before the start on 29 January and I could not believe my eyes. The more I looked at it, the more sure I became that someone had slipped a sizeable whack of brandy into my coffee that morning and followed it with an even bigger shot in my second cup. Looking up the pitch from the George Headley Stand end it was exactly like a super-enlarged piece of corrugated iron with the corrugation running across from left to right. I then stood with my back to the old pavilion which is now at square leg, looking across the pitch. The effect was identical as another corrugation was running across from left to right even though I was now square on. So it was corrugated both ways and was truly a pitch of hills and valleys and, not only that, but in the deepest valleys an attempt had even been made to roll in some mud or clay to try and level it out a bit. I have never seen anything like it in all my life.

Trying to work out from this description what it really looked like is about as impossible as I feared it would be, but you have got the gist of it: it was a disaster and how any game of cricket could be played on it, let alone a Test match, was beyond belief. You did not have to be a genius to know that several people were going to be badly hurt. Yet such notables as Wes Hall, chairman of the West Indies' selectors, and Jackie Hendriks, president of the Jamaica Cricket Association (JCA), both of whom had played plenty of Test cricket, not only saw no cause for alarm, but went as far as to say publicly that they thought it would play all right. The only local alarm was tacit and had come from the groundsman when he had tried to roll in that extra mud which had only helped make it look worse.

On the morning of the match, I was at Sabina Park more than two hours before the start when the mountainous nature of the pitch was made to seem even more pronounced. The groundsman put a metal stake in the hole for the middle stump at each end with a string drawn across the surface between the two. The string touched the pitch only on about six of the high points and the shadow it cast when it was in the air between these high points told a most damning story. The participants, the umpires, the match referee and countless others were bewildered, and yet lack of pre-match activity confirmed that the ground authority, the JCA, appeared to be wholly unconcerned, which was backed up by what Jackie Hendriks said later. There had been a bad pitch which had also been recently relaid for the first Test Match I saw at Sabina Park, in 1967/68, when Cowdrey's and Sobers' sides drew an extraordinary match, but in appearance it had not been a patch on this. I can still remember the eerie silence which greeted Sobers' first ball, from John Snow, which ran along the ground and hit him on the ankle in front of middle stump. Even Umpire Cortez Jordan could find no way out of that one. This time at Sabina Park I wondered if we were all being fooled and someone knew something the rest of us did not.

Mike Atherton won the toss and batted on the reasonable assumption that the pitch could only get worse. After fifty-five minutes play when ten overs and one ball had been bowled, the England physio found himself in the middle for the sixth time that morning and England were 17 for 3. As the drinks came out at this enforced interruption, Alec Stewart, who would not have weathered more physical punishment in any single week, let alone hour, of his career, had waved on his captain. Atherton walked out looking as he often does, an apologetic figure, and spoke to Lara, his opposite number. They were then joined by the umpires, Srini Vankataraghavan from India and Steve Bucknor from Jamaica and, finally, by the match referee, Barry Jarman from Australia. They were soon all in obvious agreement that the pitch was unfit and walked back into the pavilion signalling the players to follow them. The decision had been made for the first time to abandon a Test Match because the pitch was unfit for play.

Now, the talking, not to say the shouting, began. Barry Jarman as match referee could not have handled the situation better and he met with Pat Rousseau, the President of the West Indies Cricket Board, who is a lawyer-cum-businessman and not a cricketer, Steve Camacho, the Chief Executive of the Board and Jackie Hendriks. The two Jamaicans told Jarman that he could not abandon the match. He replied that he had already done so. By then he will have spoken to David Richards, the Chief Executive of the ICC, in London, and, anyway, Jarman was not for turning. Both Rousseau and Hendriks had had plenty of time to do something since

October when the pitch had been relaid. Hendriks should have pitched his tent at Sabina Park ever since. Both will have complained to Jarman that no one had been hit in the face to which the South Australian will have replied that he had abandoned the match after fifty-five minutes to be sure that no one was hit in the face.

The next step was a hastily called press conference in one of the pavilion dining rooms. The media crammed in and eventually Camacho, Rousseau and Hendriks fought their way through. It was hot, humid and extremely cramped. Camacho sat on Rousseau's right and looked, for all the world, like the 'ashen-faced Ron Knee', *Private Eye's* mythical supremo of Neasden FC who, on a weekly basis, presided over one unmitigated disaster after another. Camacho never spoke. Rousseau, for all his lawyer's imperturbability, was quietly seething with discontent above and below a vibrating moustache, badly wanting to blame someone but, as yet, not quite sure whom he should have in his sights. He started things off and you could hear the time bomb ticking. He apologised, unwillingly I felt, told us that it would be impossible to arrange another Test Match in Jamaica and assured us that when the schedule had been gone through, another Test would be fitted in somewhere else in the Caribbean. Hendriks, on his left, was still bemused and I daresay the consequences had not fully sunk in. He managed a brave smile when I greeted him as he came into the room but it would not have been surprising if he had been feeling at least mildly apoplectic. When Rousseau had finished, Hendriks said, almost as a throwaway, that he thought that in spite of what the pitch looked like, it would play all right. Which may be more of a comment on his oculist than himself.

All this happened at lunch-time and within an hour of that meeting breaking up, Steve Camacho had, with great speed and skill, arranged for an extra Test Match to be played starting on the following Thursday in Port of Spain. The match originally planned for Port of Spain would start as it had been scheduled, on Friday February 13. So, with West Indies and England so rudely ejected from Sabina Park, the scene was set for two back-to-back Test Matches at Queen's Park Oval, Port of Spain.

The fallout was heavy for the next two days in Kingston. That evening I walked across the Knutsford Boulevard from the Liguanea Club, where I was staying, to the Pegasus Hotel where the England players were billeted. The Liguanea is a sort of super country club in New Kingston and was, I suppose, in the old days just about the centre of the universe. Even though the old golf course has now been largely built over, it has splendid facilities for tennis and squash and swimming, with a gym and several other things I am sure I missed. It is presided over by quite the most urbane and delightful of men, Colonel Ken Barnes, a Trinidadian who has lived his adult life in Jamaica and who was the top, bottom and sides of the Jamaican army and who is also the father of one John Barnes who has played a bit of football for Liverpool and now Newcastle, among others. I can still taste the wonderful ackee and swordfish I had each morning for breakfast with Harry Belafonte's' words ringing in my ears: 'Ackee rice are nice and the rum is fine any time of year'. For us it was Jamaica farewell and it was when I reached Trinidad I was able to discover for myself how far calypso has travelled since Belafonte burst upon us all those years ago in the fifties.

At the Pegasus, I met West Indian indignation in the distinguished person of an old friend, Lance Gibbs, the Guyanese off-spinner who took 309 Test wickets to beat Fred Trueman's 307 — he is the only spinner to have reached 300 wickets — who now lives in Florida. He was angry the match had been called off as early as it had and said, while wagging his finger, that no one had been hit higher than the hands, although the hands could have been up by the face and he ignored the ball from Ambrose which went off a length over Stewart's head.

As Perfidious Albion was getting it in the neck once again, I counter-attacked by saying that the three men most instrumental in calling off the match had been an Australian, an Indian and a Jamaican. Pause. Well, what was Atherton doing out there anyway? I replied that it was a drinks interval and Stewart had beckoned him out, which a batsman is allowed to do. Perfidious Australia took a bit of stick too, but Barry Jarman never wavered for one instant in his belief that he had done the right thing in standing by the umpires in spite of all the problems the decision would cause. There were many West Indians who thought they had seen a great chance of giving England a bloody nose get away from them. The West Indians love to beat England more than anyone and, of course, the old business of England having once colonised most of the cricketing West Indies is at the bottom of it.

The build up to Carnival which is held each year on the Monday and Tuesday before the start of Lent and strongly rivals the sister foundation in Rio, was in full swing when we arrived in Port of Spain, a couple of days before the start of these back-to-back Test matches. I must get one point straight before I go any further. The ICC had decreed from Lord's that although the First Test had been abandoned when England were 17 for 3, the scores would stand and count in the career records of the players involved. The aborted Sabina Park game would, therefore, still go down in history as the official First Test of the series. The two in Trinidad would become the Second and Third and not the First and Second. It is most confusing, but cricket has a genius for these things.

Queen's Park Oval is, for me, one of the three loveliest Test match grounds in the world and also one of the liveliest but we will come to that. The other two in the beauty stakes are Newlands in the shadow of those glorious oaks – now mostly

cut down – and Table Mountain in Cape Town, and the
Adelaide Oval with the cathedral and the lovely sweeping
views away to the Mount Lofty Ranges. Queen's Park Oval's
beauty comes from the unromantically named North-Eastern
range of mountains which lie behind the ground at the northern end. The best view of them is from the Pavilion end,
where the mountains look both intimate and distant. They
descend in sweeping layers to the suburbs of Port of Spain and
are covered by the most luxuriant foliage in every imaginable
shade of green. It is sad the cricket is not played when the
scarlet flowers of the flamboyant trees are in bloom. These
mountains are always changing. When the dark, misty rain-
clouds sweep in, as they did in both matches, the peaks are
suddenly hidden in the swirling mists and then they seem to
be drawn much closer. In contrast, when the skies are clear,
they stand back, proud and slightly aloof and become more
distant. The foothills are flecked with red and green tiled
roofs as the well-off have inched their way ever higher to an
even better view. You can look at these hills six times an over
and each time you will see something slightly different. They
are an endless fascination.

The Oval itself is neat and well ordered with stands going
most of the way round the ground. In order to make way for
the new stand next door to the media centre at the northern
end, the small group of palm trees and a magnificent spreading samaan tree have had to go, although there are still two
big samaans behind the stands on the western side which rise
over the roofs like two giant spreading green mushrooms.
There is just enough greenery to lessen the impact of the vast
flower mill which rises satanically in the middle distance
behind the pavilion, itself the product of modest, no-frills,
timber and corrugated-iron late-colonial architecture. The
steeply cambered cycle track which circles the ground in front
of the stands where spectators roast their bottoms if no other

vantage point is available, is a mild eyesore even though long usage has blunted its impact.

The Second Test was to be played on a pitch the ground-staff had had less than a week to prepare. In the preceding days it was subjected to a constant and largely unsympathetic scrutiny by a never-ending army of self-appointed experts. I could not help but wonder how many had the slightest idea of what they were looking for, lending weight to my long-held belief that as much bullshit is spoken about the likely behaviour of cricket pitches as it is about the likely behaviour of most unopened bottles of wine. Even Geoffrey Boycott's obiter dicta about the former are occasionally wide of the mark. The groundsman had now made it even more confusing by leaving on a thick covering of grass which, of course, he took off at the last moment but which had caused a wide range of forecasts. There was still enough thick grass to suggest the seam bowlers would find some sideways movement but more worrying were the cracks and craters which argued that the bounce would be alarmingly uneven. It most certainly did not look a good one but it looked an angel in comparison to what we had seen at Sabina Park.

The fast-approaching Carnival grabbed us all by the throat at the media centre end. It was about five years ago that the Trinidad Posse came on the scene as a sort of West Indian answer to The Barmy Army, the highly articulate young lawyers and accountants who go round the world following England's cricket and make such a wonderful job of pretending they are yobboes. The Trinidad Posse travel only in the West Indies where they also make a lot of noise and have a great time. As Trinidad is their home, they made a special effort to make their presence felt at the Queen's Park Oval. They have taken over the bottom section of the new stand next door to the media centre at the northern end. They buy all the tickets for that section and sell them on to those of like-mind at a price which includes drinks and perhaps even some solids as well.

They hire a calypsonian each day who never has a microphone out of his hand. Whenever a four is hit or a wicket falls or between overs and at the intervals, calypso music blares out of the speakers in this segment of the ground and the singer does his best. He may have only sixty seconds or even less because the music is turned off before play restarts and yet he makes the most of it. During these two Tests they consistently sang calypsos about 'Captain Lara' and there was another which started 'Brian Charles Lara'. It was all great value but it was difficult at times to broadcast against it. It was good to see so many of the English visitors taking part and it really lent a great atmosphere to the proceedings. The calypso dance, the jump up, went on almost all the time and when the music was not blaring out of the loudspeakers, the locals were still making rhythm by tapping knives or forks against empty bottles. They really can get a beat going out of thin air. On the Sunday of the second Port of Spain Test, the Trinidad Posse even organised a special lunch behind one of the stands for the media.

Mike Atherton won the toss and batted which is what he likes to do, while Brian Lara let it be known that he would have fielded first. I always think there is an element of gamesmanship in this. Anyway, why didn't they have a cosy chat in the pavilion and not bother with the toss? The atmosphere before the start was tense. The previous day I had bumped into Adam Hollioake in the lift at the hotel and he told me the England side were focused and teed up to perfection on the first morning in Kingston and how difficult it had been to do it again so soon after that enormous letdown. There were doubts all over the place.

Thanks to some lovely strokes at the start by Alec Stewart which included a classic pull through mid-wicket played with a dismissive certainty off Kenny Benjamin, and five-and-a-half hours of trench warfare by Nasser Hussain who seemed to spend most of that time in no-man's land, England reached 214, a more impressive total than it may have seemed. While no wickets fell to the grub or the larynx ball, there were enough of both to colour the batsman's thinking and to play on his mind from thereon. After a good start – England were 70 for 1 at lunch – the innings fell away all too predictably. Only two of the wickets were of any great interest. Atherton had been out in the morning and two more fell in the afternoon which brought in Graham Thorpe shortly before tea. England had been lucky that the West Indies slips had had a violent attack of butter-fingers soon after lunch when Lara and Hooper both dropped catches.

In his first four overs, while scoring eight, Thorpe had hit the ball with more confidence than anyone including Stewart and had made everyone sit up a fraction. There was one over left before tea and Lara threw the ball to Hooper, his off-spinner, who had had one over right at the end of the morning session. He was bowling to Thorpe and it should have been the merest of formalities for the left-hander to play out the over before shuffling off to enjoy a cup of tea or whatever. The first ball was only just short of a length and not more than three or four inches outside the off stump. Thorpe went across with his back foot and launched himself into a violent square cut and little David Williams behind the stumps almost threw himself into the air with the ball as he exultantly claimed the catch of the top edge. UGH! If ever a situation cried out for discretion this was it. In some ways I suppose it gives us all something to hope for when an experienced Test cricketer makes this sort of abject howler, which would have been unforgivable in a fourth-form game. Yet, how intensely irritating. Modern players are all too willing to tell us that cricket today is a more professional game than it has ever been. Really?

The second interesting wicket came soon after tea when Jimmy Adams was brought on to serve up his first over of occasional left-arm spin. Off not much more than two strides he bowled to Hussain who cut a most amiable offering to backward point and set off for a run. His partner, Adam Hollioake, seemed to be filled with doubt and was much slower in leaving his crease and it was clear well before he had reached halfway that he was going to be run out. Shivnarine Chanderpaul's accurate throw homed into Williams's gloves and he whipped off the bails but Hollioake, who was well out, had obviously seen something and before he departed he had a quick word with umpire Venkat at square leg. Venkat immediately signalled that he wanted the third umpire to look at the replay and confirm that everything was in order.

The third umpire was not on his toes for he should have realised at once that the doubt was not over whether Hollioake had made his ground. He was not much more than halfway down the pitch when the bails came off and we could all see that. He should have understood that he was being asked to look for something else and the most likely thing to have happened was for Williams to have knocked the bails off with his pad or glove before the ball had arrived. The third umpire appeared to have watched only one replay which will have told him nothing he did not already know for it was the replay of what Venkat had already seen. All he was able to see was wicketkeeper Williams's bottom which completely obscured the stumps. The third umpire should now have asked the television director for the replay from different angles and Venkat in his original communique, should have made it clearer what it was he wanted the third umpire to look for. He would then have seen that one bail had almost certainly been removed before the ball arrived in the keeper's gloves and when the TV technicians had blown the picture up even further, this would have been confirmed and Hollioake would not have been given out. As it was, after looking at the one replay, the red light was turned on and Hollioake had to go. Barry Jarman, the Australian match referee, should have been given a medal for diplomacy to go with the one he received in Kingston for being resolute of purpose, when he issued a statement which said that from the available evidence, the third umpire had had no alternative but to give Hollioake out. The third umpire, he said, had been faced with an unplayable lie. I can't help feeling that Sherlock Holmes would have wanted to explore a few more possibilities.

England began the second morning at 175 for 8 and got as far as 214 only as the result of an admirable stand of forty-two between Hussain and Angus Fraser who should play all his cricket to a background of martial music. He had not played for England for two years, having been one of those kicked into touch by Mr. Raymond Illingworth when he was the all-powerful supremo. Illingworth had been miscast in that role and his subsequent misjudgements and handling of certain players were rivalled only by the excuses which followed later. A fine player, a great captain, but a manager? No! Even though Fraser now scored seventeen priceless runs, I can promise you that I am not blaming Illingworth for not wanting to stick with him as batsman. But Fraser is a priceless cricketer of the sort found all too seldom these days. He desperately wants to win, will never be happy to settle for second best and will sell his soul for his country. He knows he has a job to do and gets on with it as best he can. It was his job now to make Hussain as good a partner as he could. As we were soon to discover, the batting was all part of a warming-up process for Fraser. When the West Indies began their innings later that morning, Fraser was left for sixteen overs to click his heels while Headley and Caddick did their best to disrupt the early batting with the new ball.

But before we continue to study Fraser's extraordinary

progress on this second day, we are going to go off on the sort of digression that cricket more than almost any other human activity seems to lend itself to and which, in this instance is hardly relevant, but is a bit of fun. To enjoy fully the skill of Fraser in Port of Spain and the effects of that skill, it is necessary to acquire some slight knowledge of the art of spread betting. Spread betting is a relatively new phenomenon and I am sure it will, as it were, be a closed book to many readers. Before the series, Sporting Index, the leaders in the sporting field for betting who are also great friends of mine, offered Fraser, the bowler, to their clients at 10-11. This meant that in their view they thought that Fraser was likely to take around about ten or eleven wickets in the five Test Matches. If you, the punter, expected him to take fewer than ten wickets, you would have sold Fraser at ten for any stake you wanted. If it had been for a pound and Fraser had finished with eight wickets in the series, you would have made two pounds.

If, on the other hand, you expected him to take more than eleven wickets, you would have bought him for whatever stake you wanted at eleven. If your stake had been a pound, you would pick up one pound for every wicket he took in excess of eleven. The interested clients, an admirable body of men and extremely knowledgeable about cricket, had no doubt that he would take comfortably in excess of eleven wickets and bought accordingly. Of course, Fraser was only one item on a particularly extensive spread betting menu but the weight of support for Fraser meant that his performances were likely to cause the bookies considerable anxiety. There's nothing better than to get the betting industry on the run and that's what made Fraser's bowling performances such particularly good news. Also one of our number in the media had let it be known in a series of stage whispers that he had bought Fraser at no less than £100 a wicket at twelve for, by the time he struck his bet, the spread had moved out a fraction, to 11-12. When Atherton threw the ball to Fraser, there were a good many people in England and Port of Spain who were taking an unusual interest in his wellbeing.

In his size twelves, Fraser now began to pound in under the unyielding, relentless Trinidad sun. Headley and Caddick had bowled short and wide, the West Indies were 31 for 1 and England's total of 214 was not much more than just round the corner. Fraser marked out his run studiously and precisely like a schoolmaster who is steeling himself to teach the same lesson for the umpteenth time. In he came, down that angled run up with those familiar slightly world-weary strides and settled at once into a length and line that could only be described as immaculate. In no time at all, Stuart Williams had pushed at him and only survived an appeal for a catch behind because the third umpire found the ball had bounced before Russell caught it. But that was a temporary respite. In Fraser's next over, Williams aimed to whip him of the back foot wide of mid-on, was deceived by a change of pace and the ball skied off the leading edge to Atherton at mid-off. I doubt if any of us, let alone the lucky punters, had any idea what they had just seen the start of. To make sure we none of us missed the point, Fraser, in his next over, bowled a big off-cutter just short of a length and outside the off stump. Carl Hooper moved right across his stumps and was staggered to find himself bowled behind his legs.

Fraser had five overs in his first spell in which he took two wickets and then just one over at the Pavilion end before tea and he was as accurate and testing as ever. In sharp contrast, Caddick's three overs afterwards produced twenty-seven runs and then Fraser tried again when the score was 99 for 3 and Lara and Chanderpaul were threatening to put the West Indies on level terms before nightfall. He was, at once, a calming influence. Then, in his fourth over, he persuaded

Chanderpaul to drive without moving his feet and he was caught by Thorpe at first slip. In his next over he took the most important wicket of all when Lara, whose answer to the situation had been to play his strokes from the word go, tried to drive him over mid-wicket but played a fraction too soon and the ball skied off the leading edge to Atherton at mid-off. At this point those buying spread betters really did begin to think they had a bargain on their hands. This was reconfirmed in Fraser's next over when Jimmy Adams played no stroke at one which cut back into him and he was lbw. Fraser had taken 3 for 5 in thirteen balls and 5 for 41 in all so far. Sporting Index were going hesitantly to an urgent meeting with their bankers while our illustrious chum in the press box was greeting his friends with the smuggest of knowing smiles.

His smile had developed into a broad grin the next morning when Fraser picked up the last three West Indian wickets and finished with the remarkable figures of 8 for 53. I am not sure our macho journalist did not also go on some sort of triumphal tour of the press and broadcasting boxes. England now had a precious lead of twenty-three which was such an important psychological boost for them. By the close of play that evening they had increased this to 242 when they scored 219 for 4 in their second innings after Atherton and Stewart had put on ninety-one for the first wicket. All the first five in the order had contributed and now that West Indies were going to have to make the largest score of the match to win, it looked as if England had as good as sewn up the match. The most surprising aspect of England's second innings was Lara's decision to open the bowling not with Curtly Ambrose or Courtney Walsh but with Kenny Benjamin and Nixon McLean. Atherton and Stewart could hardly believe their luck and got away to a wonderful start before Lara had to call up Ambrose and Walsh to restore some sort of order. It had been an extraordinary decision by West Indies' new captain and may have been the product of arrogance which had effectively made him say, 'I am in charge now and I will captain the side as I want'. It was a decision which made no cricketing sense and, like one or two others Lara made in the field during these two matches, it told of a surprising immaturity or perhaps a dangerous obstinacy. I felt then that there was something rather brittle about the swagger he had acquired and the assumed confidence which went with it. He had had the luck to play his first two completed Test matches as the official West Indies captain in front of his home crowd in Port of Spain. I wondered how the swagger would travel.

On the fourth day of the Second Test cricket was seen at its unsurpassable best. The England players will have had a good night's sleep while the West Indians will have tossed and turned, but not Curtly Ambrose. He hates to lose, and to England in particular, and he will have gone to bed hell-bent on stopping them the following morning. He had been the principal architect when England had been bowled out for forty-six at Port of Spain four years earlier. He will have psyched himself up now to do something similar. He ran up in that tersely stilted way of his as if determined to put the world to rights in the very first over. It was a ferocious and most meaningful run up. In his second over of the morning, Hollioake could make nothing of one that bounced and left him. Russell played back soon afterwards to what was a horrid leg-cutter to the left-hander which scarcely bounced and was lbw. For what it is worth, Ambrose had a bit of luck there for umpire Venkat had failed to spot that the ball had pitched outside the leg stump, as was confirmed by the television replay. By now, the supercharged Ambrose was in overdrive and he was spurred on even more when Thorpe nibbled at Walsh and Lara did the rest at first slip. Walsh was stealthily hostile; Ambrose was vibrantly demonic. Caddick, Fraser and Tufnell were brushed aside in a moment and England's last six wickets had fallen for thirty-nine runs, Ambrose having taken 5 for 16 in 7.5 overs that morning. The West Indies now needed 282 to win. It should have been beyond them but, yet again, the psychological advantage made a dramatic shift.

There was time for six overs before lunch and in the third, Sherwin Campbell reached for Headley outside the off stump and Stewart obliged low down at second slip. Instructed or inspired by his captain, Stuart Williams now decided to go for his strokes, which is anyway his inclination. He pulled and square cut and hooked and Lara was content to watch his partner with evident enjoyment and satisfaction. The score had passed sixty when Fraser came up from third man to bowl the eighteenth over. For a brief moment in his second over, when he came up that steadfast run of his to bowl to Lara, time stood still. The ball was just short of a length outside the off stump and Lara was drawn quickly across his stumps and, opening the face of the bat, tried to run it to third man. It flicked the outside edge of the bat and this was one that Jack Russell did not drop. Sporting Index quivered; our venerable friend in the press box who had become rather good at the 'I told you so' shrug of the shoulders, did it again and, of course, England felt that they were well on their way. Even so, the West Indies were 104 for 2 at tea and 282 may have seemed just over the North-Eastern range of mountains, but it was some way short of being over the horizon.

The good and faithful Fraser came back at the Pavilion end after tea and suddenly Stuart Williams played him firmly off his legs and straight into the hands of John Crawley at square short leg, who held on to an excellent reflex catch. One run later Chanderpaul aimed to pull a ball from Tufnell that was probably not short enough and bounced an extra inch or two and Thorpe celebrated the gentle skied catch at short extra cover as if he had just heard that he had won the lottery. After that Fraser, a man not known for his emotional excesses, ran in to bowl like an animated schoolmaster. When he found the edge of Adams' back stroke as he shuffled across his stumps and the ball sped low into Stewart's hands at second slip, he may have felt on reflection that punching the air together with a broad smile was rather overdoing things. West Indies were then 124 for 5 and in their wicket-taking huddle England must have been confident that victory was theirs.

Two mildly curious things had happened. At one end, Carl Hooper whose batting had never been hallmarked by an ability to concentrate for long periods, had decided to establish squatters' rights on the pitch in his newly-adopted home town. He was now showing the concentration which one of the best techniques in the contemporary game deserved. If Hooper was one curiosity, Tufnell was the other. As the match had progressed, it had looked increasingly as if Tufnell would be the man to bowl out West Indies in their second innings. It was simply not happening. Cheerful, cheeky, rebellious, enthusiastic and floppily fair-haired, he bounced in from the northern end with that familiar little skip in mid-run which seemed to emphasise his keenness to get at the batsman. He started bowling round the wicket to the right handers which was where he should have begun, continued and ended. He found some turn, albeit almost in slow-motion, but his direction was no longer faultless and he began to stray down the leg side and there was the odd short one too. He cannot be blamed, though, when Hooper came down the pitch and drove him past cover for four. It was a glorious stoke but Hooper's reaction was to go back into his crease looking like a Trappist monk who had forgotten himself.

Atherton, who finds it difficult to trust spinners, spoke to Tufnell and the latter, rather grudgingly, marked out his run over the wicket and ran in aiming into the plentiful supply of rough outside the right-hander's leg stump. There is no more excruciating way of playing cricket. With the ball pitching outside the leg stump, the right-hander is fully entitled to kick it away with his pads for he can never be lbw. It is a situation of near stultifying stalemate, yet is within the Laws and cannot be prevented. This really is one for the Lawmakers to get their teeth into – as they are. Of course, it is a different kettle of fish when he is bowling over the wicket to a left-hander for the ball is then pitching outside the off stump and the batsman can be lbw. In making Tufnell go over the wicket to the right-handers, which I have no doubt was against the bowler's own instinct, Atherton showed that his thinking had undergone a sea change. He, too, will have been hoping that Tufnell would have been his trump card in this final innings, but the evidence was now firmly against him. He had taken only one of the first five wickets, and that with a short ball, and Atherton now decided it was his seam bowlers who were going to take him to victory, from the pavilion end, and that it was Tufnell who had to block up the game from the northern end.

Except it did not work. For the final session of the fourth day (this session always lasted for about two and a half hours because the over rates, with ninety having to be bowled in a day, were slow) the light held for about forty minutes after the scheduled close at five minutes past five and there was the chance to make up some of the backlog. During this last session, after Adams was out, I got the definite impression that England felt they had won and were as much as anything going through the motions as they waited for the wickets to fall. They did not seem to realise what they were up against. Hooper batted like the smartest of Guardsmen on duty. There were no frills and his drill was exemplary. At the other end, David Williams flitted about like a butterfly, improvising here, hiding behind some outrageous footwork there and being thoroughly tiresome and impish in a way that Alan Knott, or even Jack Russell, would have envied, and there was a relentless supply of runs.

When the umpires decided that the light was too bad to carry on, they had put on fifty-seven and, at 181 for 5, West Indies needed 101 more to win. In the bar at the Hilton later that evening Atherton shrugged his shoulders and said in that inconsequential way of his, 'How to make hard work of an easy victory', which was fair comment. He will not have admired the exceptional view of Port of Spain from the long window in the bar that evening. Every England supporter talked a good game over dinner that night trying to convince each other, if not themselves, that what lay ahead on the fifth day was nothing much more than a formality. The more blasé amongst us tried to convince ourselves over our hamburgers and tomato sauce that it did not matter very much one way or the other. Not half, it didn't! The next morning we were even inclined to listen to our driver, the redoubtable Rollo, who spoke with such a broad Trinidad accent that it made comprehension almost impossible but even we could understand that he was picking England to win. We were grateful for his support.

The schoolmaster was on, first up, at the Pavilion end and the tension at the start was almost unbearable. It was to grow worse before the end. Fraser's first ball was up to the bat although it may have been a trifle slower than Williams expected. He drove without getting to the pitch of the ball and it flew back to Fraser's right at just above knee height. As he pulled up in his follow through, Fraser stuck out an instinctive right hand and the ball, which had not been hit as hard as he thought, struck him on the heel of the hand and bounced away to the ground. We were hardly in our seats and yet one had already got away. Fraser has held harder return catches than this and I wondered, if it had been off the second ball of the morning, he might have held on. It is not the sort of thing you expect from the first ball of the day, in the politest of circles. We all looked at each other. Was it an omen or did it not matter? It was a pity, there was no doubt about that. We had been joined overnight by Compton, a good name if you enjoy cricket, Hellyer, the chairman of Sporting Index who had flown out with a fellow director and aide-de-camp, Nick Pocock, a former captain of Hampshire. They had let it be known before the start of play that every wicket Fraser took in the series from now on would cost their firm £3,000 taking into account their overall position on the schoolmaster. When that first catch went down, they suppressed their feelings with admirable restraint – after all, it would have been a bit like laughing in church. Our persevering journalist gave us the 'seen it all before' nod.

An unbelievably tense first hour produced fourteen overs and twenty-five runs and, at 205 for 6, Fraser took the new ball. And, would you believe it, in his first over Williams aimed to glance a short one which flicked his glove and a difficult catch was dropped by the diving Russell. Dinner on Compton that night. Our newspaper friend was busy putting a brave face on it. As so often happens, the hardness of the new ball helped increase the run rate as it sped away faster over the grass. The hundred stand arrived and both batsmen passed fifty. The Englishmen had been unable to get back into the groove on this last morning and were paying the penalty for ignoring the old truth: the game is never over until the last ball has been bowled. They had relaxed on the fourth evening and, try as they did, they could not get it back now. There was just a brief flicker when the West Indies still needed twenty-nine to win. Williams played back to a ball from Headley which bounced on him and Thorpe held the catch at first slip. He and Hooper had put on 129 in 220 minutes and had effectively won the match. Immediately after Williams was out, Hooper, like a parson at play, advanced and drove Tufnell back over his head for four. Hooper did not quite time the shot but survived because he swung the bat straight through the line of the ball and most certainly deserved his luck. In the next over Ambrose pushed firm-footed at Headley and was caught behind, but the England bowlers could do no more.

There was a sad little footnote. With eleven runs needed, Fraser bowled to Benjamin. The ball skidded through low outside the off stump and bounced again before reaching Russell, who had had a dreadful match in awkward conditions. It went through Russell's legs and cannoned into one of the two crash helmets lying on the ground behind the wicket-keeper as they always are when the fielders do not need them. The Laws state that, if the ball hits a crash helmet on the ground, the fielding side forfeits five runs. Umpire Steve Bucknor made the appropriate signal, West Indies needed six to win and poor Russell looked an awful fool. West Indies won by three wickets and it was in a silent and still England dressing room minutes after the end that Crawley said through clenched teeth, 'That must never be allowed to happen again.' It is hard to come back quickly when you have lost a close match like this and which, in your heart of hearts, you know you should have won and yet in three-and-a-half days, England had to be back at the Queen's Park Oval for the Third Test. I am glad to be able to report that Compton Hellyer pushed out the boat to no mean tune while our intrepid hero in the press box found himself on the horns of a dilemma. The schoolmaster was now being quoted at 22–24 which meant our punter could sell at 22 and make a cool grand or he could hang on and hope that Fraser would do it again and he would then have an even better option. The problems some people have.

It was with a distinct sense of foreboding and unease that we all foregathered again at the Queen's Park Oval on a day which, with dark irony, described itself as Friday 13th February. West Indies played the same side which had won the week before while Hollioake's back ruled him out and an attack of flu prevented Mark Ramprakash from taking his place, so Mark Butcher was called in at the last moment. Atherton won the toss and I am sure it will have gone against his instincts not to have batted first. Hovering over his shoulder, however, was an ever increasing weight of opinion which said that England's best chance of victory was to bowl first. Atherton was undecided that morning when he arrived at the ground. How did he make up his mind? Was it something which was said? Did he see something new in the pitch? Was it a hunch? Did he have a sudden vision of the golden-armed schoolmaster in full flow? As Lara spun the coin, did he know for sure what he was going to say if it landed as tails? It was tails and Atherton held his nose and took the plunge. Wouldn't it be fun to know exactly how these things happen?

At lunch Atherton will have kicked himself for not following his instincts. Headley and Caddick, who will have been all too well aware of what England expected, got it wrong again and even Fraser was driven through the covers for four. He almost made up for such insulting treatment when he was within a millimetre of having Lara lbw as he shuffled across his stumps. Atherton will not have enjoyed his lunch. At the end of the first over afterwards he will have put suicide on the agenda. In the most dreadful over of the Test match, if not of the whole series, Caddick was hit for nineteen runs. How can an experienced seam bowler have so little idea of, or control over, what he is doing? Four fours came in that over. What was Caddick thinking as each one raced away to the boundary? Surely a Test Match bowler who has been about as long as he has, should be able at least to fall back on a fail-safe mechanism. It was all as unbelievable as it was frustrating.

But all was not lost. The schoolmaster marked out his run at the pavilion end, Campbell drove at his third ball and Thorpe took the catch gratefully at first slip. In the schoolmaster's second over Carl Hooper played a languidly elegant cover drive at a ball which may have been held back. He got underneath it, although he still hit it out of the middle of the bat with excellent timing, and it flew fast over Butcher's head at cover. Somehow Butcher, with both feet off the ground, managed to hold on to the ball in his right hand above and behind him. It was a staggering catch. A bemused Hooper slowly began the long walk back, Fraser allowed himself a flicker of a smile as he joined in the multiple congratulations which had submerged Butcher, the blood drained from Compton Hellyer's face and the fortunate hack struck his Napoleon Bonaparte pose.

Now it was Lara's turn to face Fraser. The ball was short and outside the off stump, but not short enough, and Lara, who enjoys walking on water, swivelled without moving his feet across and pulled vigorously. The ball flicked the edge and Russell claimed the catch. The umpires met and made that ludicrous sign which is, I suppose, meant to indicate a television screen in order that the third umpire should decide if the ball had carried to the wicketkeeper. Replay followed replay and in the agonising wait every eye in the ground was fixed on the two lights outside the third umpire's box in the media centre. Even the Trinidad Posse held their breath in eerie silence. At last, the red light glowed and Lara set off, a trifle reluctantly, for the pavilion. The schoolmaster had taken 3 for 4 in eighteen balls and his overall tally of wickets in the series so far to fourteen which he was to increase to sixteen when he later brought one back which had Chanderpaul lbw on the back foot and right at the end, he persuaded McLean to slog him to deep mid-wicket. The West Indies' last six wickets had fallen for twenty-seven in forty-three balls and they were all out for 159. After that horrendous first post-prandial over Caddick had smartened up and finished with 5 for 67. But why can't he be more consistent? While Atherton buckled on his pads, he may have felt that he should risk this sort of thing more often. His happiness was short-lived, however, for in the fourth over of England's first innings he played back to Ambrose and was lbw when the ball kept low. Before the end Ambrose had bowled Crawley off his pads and by then Stewart had been dropped by Lara off Walsh. England were 22 for 2 that evening and most apprehensive.

Ambrose probably regards night-watchmen as nothing more than an inconvenient irritation it is not worth wasting time over. To make his point, he knocked Headley's middle and off stumps out of the ground with his sixth ball the next morning with the obvious satisfaction a man gets from having a really good scratch at an itch. Hussain then pushed at Walsh and was given out caught behind by Mr. Edward Nicholls who seemed to have become unsettled by a concerted West Indian appeal. The replay showed about one and a half acres of daylight between bat and ball. Hussain lingered long enough after being given out to attract the attention of the ever-vigilant match referee, Mr. Barry Jarman. Stewart, as always, and Thorpe then fought hard before they both succumbed to the off-spin of Hooper who, from the way he spun round and looked at the commentary box, must have thought that Geoffrey Boycott was still telling the world that Hooper couldn't bowl his grandmother out. They were soft dismissals. After that it was only brave left-handed resistance by Butcher which took England to 145. The way in which Caddick ran himself out for a duck is best forgotten. West Indies, who set off at speed in their second innings, were 60 for 2 at the close. Fraser picked up his second wicket when he had Campbell lbw on the back foot. This sent Sporting Index scurrying back to their safe deposit boxes at the Hilton to see how many travellers cheques they had left and our gambling pen-pusher, I hope, to the bar to buy the first round of drinks.

The pitch had played better than the one for the Second

Test but this was the pitch which the groundstaff had had months to prepare; the other Test had been thrust on them at a week's notice. Paradoxically, this second pitch had produced a low scoring match. The ball had behaved much less dramatically but it was still not easy for batsmen to play strokes. Both the Port of Spain pitches would have come in for more criticism if they had not followed immediately the Sabina Park disaster which was so completely unfit for human consumption. The first faces I saw at breakfast the following morning were those of Lord and Lady MacLaurin. His Lordship, having just flown in, was as cheerful as ever and in his first unofficial communiqué was optimistically hoping that England would dispatch West Indies for not much over a hundred.

He was only a hundred runs out and, needless to say, it was the schoolmaster who started it off. He accounted for Benjamin, the night-watchman, in the third over of the day, not as conclusively as Ambrose had dealt with Headley but a skied catch to backward square leg was better than nothing. Ten runs later he bowled to Lara, who played back to a ball which came in to him on pitching and was lbw. Fraser allowed himself another triumphant punch of the air and then looked a trifle guilty. Compton Hellyer muttered something about 'in for a penny, in for a pound' and rang up to see if he could book himself an earlier flight home while our scribbler scribbled like mad to work out his current profit which was a minimum of £700. Only Chanderpaul and Adams prospered with the bat after that although McLean and Walsh stayed with Adams while fifty-one runs were added for the last two wickets. Adams became the first batsman in the match to pass fifty before the schoolmaster had him caught at mid-off. I am glad to say that Compton was on his way to the airport by then and would not have felt a thing, and our newspaper correspondent was able to congratulate himself on his sound investment judgement without fear of embarrassment. At lunch that day, the Sunday, the media had been entertained by the Trinidad Posse behind one of the stands. A good many of the Posse said they thought England would win. None of them meant it.

West Indies were all out for 210 and England needed 225, the largest score of the match, to win. I was in the forefront of the band of pessimists who felt it would be way beyond them. 'Oh ye of little faith.' In thirty-five years of watching goodness knows how many Test matches, I cannot remember a situation which left me as tense and nervous as I was now. I hoped I had outgrown all that. If England left Port of Spain two matches down, there would surely be no way back. The interest in the UK would disappear, Test Match Special would have a couple of old drunks and a dog as their only listeners and it would all be so depressing. But, I must come clean, I desperately wanted England to win. When Atherton and Stewart came out to face twenty-five overs that evening, there is no doubt that the nervous tension of each ball can only have shortened my life. The only two people who were apparently unaffected were Atherton and Stewart. It was with consummate nonchalance that Atherton started things off by playing Walsh off his pads behind square for four and Stewart then drove the same bowler off the back foot through extra cover with what can only be described as panache. Soon afterwards Stewart slashed Ambrose through extra cover and Atherton ran him to third man. At the close of play I climbed limp and exhausted into a taxi hardly daring to believe that England were 52 for none, needing 173 more to win. But what a mountain that seemed. When the stand had reached forty-six it was a significant landmark for England. Four years before, needing 194 for victory, they had been bowled out, principally by Ambrose, for that very score. It just shows the state we were in looking for any omen we could find. My Swedish wife assured me on the telephone that evening from London that England would easily do it. It takes a Swede . . .

If anything, it was even worse watching the next day. But out in the middle, Atherton and Stewart were amazingly composed. Stewart shook off the morning mist with a lovely on-drive for four off Walsh and then forced Benjamin through the covers for another while Atherton was more uneasy than he had been the night before. He almost ran himself out taking a second run to McLean, who has a powerful arm, at deep square leg and made his ground by barely an inch. He cut the next ball hard into and out of Stuart Williams's hands in the gully. A thick edge for four off McLean brought Stewart to fifty and England to 103 without loss and when rain brought the players off five minutes before lunch, England were 122 for none, needing 103 more. No wonder the West Indians respect the opening partnership of Atherton and Stewart as they do.

It may seem that as England had ten wickets in hand, there should not really have been any worry but with Ambrose and Walsh about and a new ball due later in the day, the tension was nail-biting and heart stopping, and caused frequent loo visiting for a nervous one. England's openers went on after lunch and the target was down to ninety-six when Atherton, who was forty-nine tried to run Walsh to third man and was caught behind. I am afraid that John Crawley is a health hazard at No. 3 at this level and suddenly Stewart found that he was unable to locate the middle of his bat. The score had crept most painfully to 144 when Crawley played Hooper to Benjamin on the backward point boundary and came back for a second run. It did not seem to occur to him that there was any great urgency and he never really stretched for the crease. The throw came in to David Williams and it was left to the third umpire to confirm that Crawley had not made his ground. Seven overs later when only seven more singles had been gleaned, Stewart followed a short ball from Walsh and Hooper, to global West Indian dismay, dropped a gaper at second slip. Stewart's touch had deserted him and later in the same over he played a similar stroke and this time there was no escape as the ball sank into Williams's gloves. When, four overs later, Hussain came down the pitch and lofted Hooper straight for four, it was the first boundary England had scored for thirty-one overs. An off drive by Thorpe in Walsh's next over produced another but in the one after that, Hussain played back to a ball from Hooper which rolled along the ground and he was lbw. No one could have played that one and England were 168 for 4 needing fifty-seven more.

Two more runs had been scored when the issue was complicated further by rain, which had been building up in the mountains over our left shoulders for some time. It was almost two hours before play could restart and in the ten minutes which were then possible, Thorpe and Butcher added eleven invaluable runs for England with Butcher slashing a long hop from Hooper triumphantly through extra cover for four. Then, with forty-four needed it began to rain again. This time it was only twenty-five minutes before the players were back and Ambrose and Walsh took the second new ball. There was time for five overs and another six runs accrued. Then, Butcher hooked at Walsh and the ball lobbed to Hooper at second slip. The West Indies players thought Butcher was out and so did I on Test Match Special but umpire Darell Hair, from Australia, saw that the ball had come off Butcher's elbow. That incident persuaded the umpires that the light was no longer fit for play. With one day left and wet weather about England still needed thirty-eight more runs to win with six wickets in hand.

In the Hilton Hotel that night, the *déjà vu* atmosphere was unbearable. But the next morning found Rollo still on England's side, not that I am afraid his views did much to soothe our nerves. Thirty-eight runs with six wickets in hand may not sound too difficult but, when Ambrose and Walsh are the bowlers and the ball is only five overs old, it is no pushover. The two Surrey left-handers, Thorpe and Butcher, set off again after rain had delayed the start for forty-five minutes and stretched our nerves a fraction tighter. Lara found himself in the age-old dilemma. He needed wickets but could not afford to give away runs. He had to compromise and he started off with a third man and a fine leg and no gully. Thorpe and Butcher came out with a plan to run short singles and immediately the ball was played gently towards gully and they were off. Walsh and Ambrose were magnificent, just as they had been when they destroyed England's second innings on the fourth morning of the previous match. Walsh, from the pavilion end, was a model of controlled and disciplined pace. His length and line were impeccable and he bowled eight overs straight off for four runs. Ambrose was more overtly hostile, taking 3 for 22 in nine overs although his line was upset by having to bowl at the left handers. He bowled too much at their pads and both Thorpe and Butcher are extremely adept at picking up runs off their legs. One ball flicked Butcher's pad and went away fine for four leg byes. For England's supporters every ball was a nightmare, every run an ingot of solid gold and four leg byes like a gift from heaven. The 200 came up. Just twenty-five were needed with six wickets left. Surely there was no need for the prevailing spectator anxicty.

Another single was scored and then Thorpe nibbled at Ambrose outside the off stump, and David Williams, tumbling in front of first slip, came up with a fine catch. Enter Jack Russell, whose form with the bat had disappeared as mysteriously as his form with the gloves. He helped Butcher add twelve in nine overs of acute discomfort before he, too, felt outside his off stump for Ambrose and again Williams held the catch. Caddick came next, looking horribly insecure, and all too predictably he was blown away first ball. His bat was instinctively drawn to a lifter he should have ignored and Williams held his third catch that morning. With three wickets left, England needed twelve more. Butcher and Headley somehow scrambled five of them and seven were needed at lunch. England could still have lost with the greatest of ease and lunch in the commentary box was not an enjoyable feast. The clouds were gathering and it was getting dark when play restarted. Butcher took a quick single from Walsh who, for Headley, brought his mid-on in to silly mid-on. He bowled a good-length ball on the middle and leg stumps and Headley, pushing forward, timed the ball so well that it sped past the close fielder and the batsmen were able to run three. It was arguably the most important stroke he will ever play. Headley can rabbit on in the bar and David Lloyd told him later that he would be prepared to listen to the story of that stroke as often as he liked to tell it. When Ambrose began the second over after lunch, England wanted three. Headley took a single to third man. This was followed by a no-ball and then Ambrose fired one down the legside, Williams dived but could not take it cleanly and the batsmen raced through for the bye that took England to victory. PHEW! It had been a close one and within seven minutes it was raining in torrents.

At the end of the two Tests in Port of Spain Compton Hellyer and his friends could have been forgiven for making a wax model or two of Angus Fraser and sticking every available pin into both of them, while our prosperous hero left the press box with a spring in his step and took off for a few days well-deserved R & R. He breasted the tapes again just before the start of the Fourth Test in Georgetown contemplating another rich haul on another moderate surface. The bookies were now offering Fraser at 29.5–31. He could have sold Fraser's wickets at 29.5 and made a cool profit of £1,750. A gambler to his socks, he decided to hold on. When Stewart dropped Chanderpaul at second slip off Fraser on the first morning, our punter pursed his lips and gritted his teeth. The schoolmaster took only three wickets in the match bringing his tally to twenty-three. Sporting Index mopped their collective brow and probably sent Stewart a bottle of champagne.

Fraser took three more wickets in the Barbados Test and only one in Antigua, which enabled him to draw level with John Snow's record of twenty-seven wickets in the 1967/68 series when Snow played in only four of the Tests. Tufnell dropped a catch and a clanger in Antigua, therefore, when he missed Hooper, who was six at the time, at mid-on from Fraser's bowling. The bet ended with our gallant punter who shall now be named as David Norrie of the *News of the World*, a mere £1,500 to the good. The last I heard was that Sporting Index were not only still in business, but about to post record profits. There's no holding these bookmakers.

Having got those three Test matches out of the way, I am going back to the start of the tour for a more leisurely look at the Caribbean before picking up the rest of the cricket.

CHAPTER FIVE

Caribbean Cricket

My favourite house in the West Indies is tucked away about ten miles west of Montego Bay and belongs to an old friend, Nigel Pemberton. I had not been to Bamboo Pen for more than twenty years because my life had sent me in different directions in the intervening time. I arrived on 23 January for a few nights, six days before the First Test Match began at Sabina Park in Kingston.

The drive to Bamboo from the airport told at first of the new, garish, downmarket nature of Montego Bay before the road emerged on the west side of the town. Hazy memories came flooding back. We could have turned left to the Town House where once we seemed to lunch on a daily basis; we passed the road on the right which led to the new shopping complex where, in the early seventies, I had bought two belts with Gucci-like gold buckles at a shop called, appropriately enough, Temptation, which was presided over by the daughter-in-law of David O. Selznick of Hollywood fame. There was the ridge ahead of us on which two unlikely bedfellows, the Duke of Marlborough and William Hill, both had houses. The winding road, still in need of repair, followed the coast and over the next few miles on the left, a number of smaller roads, several private drives, a signpost or two and a couple of houses set back in the hills brought back memories of parties, champagne, ladies in excitingly exquisite dresses, much nefarious nocturnal activity, glorious views and Johnny Kimberley, the fourth Earl, who would have been the life and soul of it all.

Then the road ducked a fraction inland and the well-policed entrance to Round Hill was on the right just before we came into the village of Hopewell where the world and his wife seem to be gathered in glorious inactivity on just about every corner. We turned left, up into the thickly wooded hills. The road winds and twists in dramatic and exciting style and after one hairpin the entrance to the long drive up to Bamboo glanced off to the right. The vegetation is lush, the palm trees and bread fruit trees was wonderfully alluring, just as they are at the start of *Doctor No*. Then, it was round a final sweeping bend and up to Bamboo Pen itself. Nigel's wife, Melody, and their splendid son Christie, who was then five, were there to greet us and in a moment a rum punch was in my hand, but sadly not put there any more by Sonny, the Jamaican Jeeves if ever there was one, who now plies his trade in New York on behalf of some Americans. The two Rhodesian Ridgebacks, Miranda and Cocoa, have long since departed this life and their places as guard dogs have been taken by a more plebeian assortment of large hounds of uncertain origin, capable of considerable noise and much ferocity should intruders appear.

Up the few steps, the big central room of the house looks out on to the most perfect view in the West Indies. The patio stretches out to the lawn and a heavenly swimming pool which beckons enticingly. Beyond that, more steps lead to a rough lawn which runs all the way down the hill to the trees.

The king palms that once stood on either side of the vista as one looks straight ahead have gone, victims of the hurricane in 1989, but their replacements are growing apace and are already handsome in their own right. In the distance and a little to the right, the wooded hills run down into the sea and Montego Bay sprawls across and away to the right. The town is far enough off to be silent and enticing and looking down at the sea, every now and then, a huge airliner glides in over the blue water like a great silver fish silently seeking out the runway. It is a view which never changes and yet is never the same and is always breathtaking. As I looked down on it that evening, I knew I had arrived in the West Indies.

Although I had not been there at the time, the England side had played their first match of the tour, against Jamaica, at Jarrett Park where they found themselves on the first of a series of bad pitches in a trail of devastation which led from Montego Bay to Kingston and on to Port of Spain, Georgetown and Antigua. Mike Atherton's men beat Jamaica in a game which was no earthly use whatever in the build up to what was going to be a tough Test series.

After four nights in a double bed which had been an old and trusted friend more than a quarter of a century before, I caught a small aeroplane which buzzed and vibrated its way down to Timpson Pen, a tiny airport not far from the centre of Kingston where a jumbo would not have dared to rev its engines, let alone take off. I spent a week at the Liguanea Club thanks to an old friend, John Bonnitto, who is usually there himself at Test Match time although on this occasion he was unable to make the journey from London. It was from my base at the Liguanea that I watched events unfold so sadly on that first morning of the Test Match at Sabina Park.

The most unfortunate aspect of it all was that a great many people had come to Jamaica from around the world to watch the match and some will have dipped decisively into their savings to do so. Small wonder at their disappointment and their avowed intention never again to visit the Caribbean. It was not only a story which reflected no credit on any of those concerned, it was also a body blow for cricket in a part of the world where it is anyway having difficulties in fighting its corner. Give a dog a bad name and hang him. The West Indies Cricket Board will have lost more than a million dollars and a lot of credibility too, while TWI, their business partners, who make and sell the television story, will also have suffered. It was, of course, a major local disaster. Advertisers lost out, so did the hotel trade; the airlines will have been caught on the hop and the ground authority, the Jamaica Cricket Association, became a worldwide laughing stock. The Jamaica Cricket Board have threatened to resign *en bloc* but I fear this may be a poisoned chalice no one will want to pick up, and Jamaican cricket will continue to be presided over by the same old lot.

Whatever the story in Kingston, at the bottom of the Blue Mountains, there is one marvellous piece of compensation waiting at the top of the foothills. The night after the Test Match had been abandoned, the drive out of Kingston up to the Blue Mountain Inn was as full of anticipation as ever. The old plantation house which has, in its time, been such a lovely restaurant, nestles into the side of the mountains beside a falling river with a magnificent sheer drop out of the dining room windows. You shouldn't sit in the window if you don't have a head for heights. It is an old stone house with the road winding past it with the mountains on one side and the cleft of the river on the other.

When we reached our table, I discovered that the Blue Mountain Inn was not unlike the modern Sabina Park. It, too, had been relaid and not necessarily for the better. When I first ate there thirty years ago, a five-course dinner of inspiring originality was rounded off with a Banana Flambé cooked at

117

the table. It was a dish in excelsis, beyond criticism and one I shall never forget. Now, it was ravioli with a crab filling and lobster sauce followed by an admirable fillet steak. Both were toothsome enough and the Mouton something or other was eminently drinkable but, somehow, it all lacked the finesse and the class of the old days. Everything had come a little too quickly, the table had not been laid with the same precision, the glasses did not gleam and the napkins were a trifle free range. I would go there again tomorrow; it has become a dinner well worth the journey up from Kingston but no longer the flight from Heathrow.

The flight from Kingston to Port of Spain takes you on a guided tour of the Caribbean, landing at Antigua and Barbados, which is an improvement because once upon a time it stopped at San Juan and St Marten as well. It was a long and boring day which began with two moments of great merriment which kept me going for some time.

One of the visitors to Kingston for the Test that never was, was Robert Atkins, who had risen to become John Major's Minister for Sport and was also a personal friend of the then Prime Minister. At Test Matches, Robert, resplendent as often as not in MCC tie and trimmings, was usually one of the first to come up to the TMS box. Once or twice the Prime Minister himself would honour us with a visit and we probably had Robert to thank for that. Unaccountably, at the last General Election, the electorate in the Ribble decided to dispense with his services and since then he has become a consultant to Vodafone who had taken over as the main sponsors of England's cricket. I bumped into Robert and his wife Dulcie, whom I had not met before, having a drink with my Vodafone chums at Kingston's Wyndham Hotel the night of the dinner at the Blue Mountain Inn. I put my foot in it in capital letters almost before I had sat down. Not having met her before, I referred to his wife in conversation as Mrs Atkins. Robert gave one of those small but meaningful coughs which was not unlike the noise Jeeves was in the habit of making when Bertie Wooster turned up in a particularly fruity cummerbund, and told me, with mild rebuke in his voice, that she was in fact Lady Atkins. Most charitably, he did not let this awkward moment hang in the air for more than a second as he went straight on to tell me that he had had a telephone call from John Major to tell him he was to be knighted.

A few days later we were in the same queue for the Port of Spain aeroplane and I was looking forward to talking to him on the flight. But, as I told him later, this became difficult when on boarding, he disappeared into economy class.

John Major himself had been in Kingston and had, by all accounts, made an excellent speech at an official dinner which launched the series a day or two before the Test Match. He did not forget to thank the British electorate for making it possible for him to be in Jamaica. He and Norma had just spent a few days at the Jamaica Inn in Ocho Rios where I once spent a honeymoon and the couple who had just vacated our suite so that we could clock in, were none other than Richard Burton and Elizabeth Taylor.

The other bright moment of the day concerned a newspaper story. One of the joys I have had over the years from touring with cricket teams is reading some of the remarkable crop of English language newspapers which one finds in different corners of the globe. The aeroplane I caught that morning from Kingston had begun its life with an early departure from Port of Spain and had brought with it a collection of the morning papers from Trinidad. In my vice-regal pew, not far behind the pilot, I laid my hands on a copy of the *Trinidad Guardian* and my eye was caught by a short piece called 'Oddspot' in the bottom left-hand corner of the front page. It was a gem and I must share it with you.

'A Honduran peasant castrated himself in a fit of rage

119

because his wife refused to have sex with him, a leading local newspaper reported yesterday. The *Herald* daily said Juan Pablo Valero, 47, cut off his testicles after his wife, Maria, lost interest in him. The couple have four children.

'Once he cut off his testicles he put them on a table, then grabbed them and went to a health centre to have them re-attached. The *Heraldo* said Varela was not in any danger but his chance of recovering full manhood were extremely slim.'

Poor chap. But advantage seldom comes from cutting off your balls.

The best headline of all was in the *Indian Express* and was shown to me in Calcutta on Mike Smith's tour, the first I went on, in 1963/64. The Chinese had been fighting in Tibet and the banner headlines across the front page of the paper read: 'Chinese General Flies Back to Front.'

When we arrived in Port of Spain, I found that Stephen Camacho had joined the aeroplane somewhere along the line and he now gave me a lift in to the Hilton where I later discovered we had neighbouring rooms, which was a health hazard as we both knew where the bar was. Trinidad was coming rather fiercely to the boil with Carnival about three weeks away. With two Test Matches to be played in those three weeks, it was confusion worse confounded. My strictures about the Hilton notwithstanding, and this is, after all, only a personal view, Port of Spain is a commendably gassy place. It is littered with good friends and my great sadness was that on the last leap before Carnival, which is on the Monday and Tuesday before the start of Lent, I was struck down convincingly by food poisoning and flu and was unable to see what went on. So much so, that by the time I left for Georgetown on the day before Carnival, on the Sunday, I was thoroughly fed up with the whole business. You would never believe that steel bands could be played non-stop for so long. My sickbed was strategically placed on the side of the hotel overlooking

Michael Atherton, with a knowing look and a final, winning throw, leads England to victory – at boules in Rheims, October 1997.

I suppose not too many people can boast that they have played in a first-class match with both Keith Miller and Denis Compton.

If a five-match Test series was played in Montego Ba
would spend three months with Nigel and Melc
Pemberton at Bamboo Pen. You can see w

Imogen Skirving. Owner, proprietor, licensee cellar
master and, if need be, general bottlewasher, outside
Langar Hall, where the sun always shines.

In 1998, Jim Swanton
was 91 not out, and in
every sense a Grand Old
Man of English cricket
whose contributions to
the game have been
enormous.

the Pelican Inn which has become a huge, fashionable and down-to-earth watering hole midway between a pub and a sort of elitist rum shop. Almost everyone drinks there. In the build up to Carnival, the music went on at such an unbelievable decibel content that it made Concorde sound like a nursery toy. It never drew breath until three o'clock in the morning. My head is still ringing.

In the old days, all the cricketers and hacks stayed at the Queen's Park Hotel on the other side of the Savannah, which was walkable to the Oval. This was a hotel of great character and dreadful discomfort for most things worked only on alternate Fridays. The redeeming feature was the large air-conditioned bar which was presided over by George who, in addition to being the best barman in Port of Spain, knew his cricket backwards. The hotel was owned by the Fernandez family who make rum and are some way from bankruptcy. In the end, they shut it down rather than spend a fortune on redoing it and it was eventually bought by an oil giant, rebuilding it for offices. The Fernandez family still own the Country Club, a mile up the road in Maraval and in that complex, John Fernandez has developed a high class wine shop. Excellent wine from all over the world can be bought there and at prices which are by no means outrageous. They look after it well and on my visits there I came away with some excellent Côtes-du-Rhône made by Paul Jaboulet and an armful of Louis Latour's Macon Lugny at around seven pounds a time which greatly eased the pain of three weeks at the Hilton.

The Hilton is one of those hotels you either love or hate and I am afraid I am one of the latter. It flatters to deceive without claiming blood relationship with Fawlty Towers. It has always been known as the upside-down hotel for the simple reason that you kick off at reception on the top floor where your car drops you and then you descend to varying depths to the rooms, as it is built down the side of a hill. It all looks good enough from the long, handsome entrance hall in which they have now most sensibly put a bar where the old reception desk used to stand, but one soon finds out that all that glitters is not necessarily gold. I had paid in advance for at least one more night than I needed and when I spoke to the lady concerned with these things suggesting the amount involved might be used against my extras, I was told in the most tiresomely schoolma'am-ish tones by someone who should have known better, that it was against company policy to give refunds. If that doesn't put your hackles up, nothing will.

As often as not, you have to undertake an interminable journey through dark, forbidding corridors to find what is barely three-star accommodation. You age visibly queuing for breakfast and then grow thin hoping a prehistoric toasting machine will respond to your blandishments. At the end of it, the bread is nicely warmed up but never brown which I always think is the purpose of the exercise. Whenever I want a meal I always seem to find that most of the restaurants in the hotel are shut, room service has a long way to come and the product is usually cold and prices are hiked hugely by a room service charge, service charges and tax. The sum total is presented in US and TT dollars, but you can only pay your eventual bill in TT dollars. I find it impossible to escape the impression that every time you sign for anything you are being ripped off. It is a hotel which desperately needs some really tough, hands-on management.

Having said that, it has a lovely swimming pool area, if you like that sort of thing, and the view from the huge window at the back of the bar on the first floor down, which looks right across Port of Spain to the Caribbean and one or two small islands beyond, must be as good as any in the world. The Hilton badly needs both but even so it is still in debt. Port of Spain urgently requires a billet which is a good deal more classy. Don't worry, the next person you run into will tell you it's one of the best hotels in the world. It's that sort of pad.

Soon after I arrived in Port of Spain, I was taken to a splendid dinner party up in the hills behind the Hilton and found myself sitting opposite an old friend, Michael de Labastide, the Chief of Justice of Trinidad. He asked me where I was staying and I replied cheerfully, 'At the worst hotel in the world. That dreadful Hilton,' and expanded upon it.

There was a certain amount of uncomfortable shuffling and a good deal of, 'Yes, yes, um-er-well mmmming.'

It transpired that the awfully nice chap sitting next to the lady on my left was the General Manager of the Hilton. Well, he knows now, doesn't he?

I cannot turn my back on Port of Spain and Queen's Park Oval without talking about two exceptional West Indian and Trinidadian cricketers who were later to become outstanding administrators. Jeffrey Stollmeyer played thirty-two times as an opening batsman for the West Indies between 1939 and 1954 and went on to become the President of the West Indies Board just as his equally famous opening partner, Allan Rae of Jamaica, was to do. Jeff was the pulse of West Indian cricket until he was brutally murdered in Trinidad by robbers in 1989 at the age of sixty-eight. Gerry Gomez, who was an all-rounder, played twenty-nine Test Matches between 1939 and 1953 and died in the middle of a game of tennis in Port of Spain just before his seventy-seventh birthday. They both captained the West Indies and it would be impossible to find two more gentle men. They were both a great influence for the good in the cricket world in general and in the West Indies and Trinidad in particular. Happily, there is now a stand named after Stollmeyer next to the pavilion at Queen's Park Oval and the new media centre has been named after Gomez, who holds one record which will never be beaten and which he enjoyed.

In 1964/65, the Australians played the Third Test of the

series at Bourda in Georgetown. One of the umpires, Cecil Kippins, who was a Guyanese, had withdrawn the evening before the match began at the insistence of the British Guiana Umpires Association, who objected to the appointment of Cortez Jordan of Barbados as the other umpire. There was no time to summon a replacement and Gomez, a West Indies Test selector who held an umpiring certificate although he had never stood in a first-class match, took Kippins's place. Each evening, after the close of play, Gomez went over to the commentary box to give his usual close of play summary and then he wrote a column about the day's play for a Trinidad newspaper. So, having helped select the West Indies side, he wrote and broadcast about the game and, for good measure, umpired it as well. He will have slept well each night. The Australian captain, Bobby Simpson, a hard man to please, was more than satisfied with his performance in the white coat although the West Indies won by 212 runs.

Stollmeyer and Gomez have each left huge gaps at the Queen's Park Oval and in the seventies and eighties I was lucky to know them both and to have shared a commentary box on many occasions with Gerry. I am indebted to Jeff, who was a brilliant dancer, for trying to teach me the rhythmical basics of the Jump-up, the Carnival dance. I was probably his only complete failure. He was also one of the stewards at the Port of Spain racecourse and at one meeting at the Savannah Racecourse in 1968, he tipped me the names of six of the eight winners. I wish I had trusted him.

The airport at Georgetown, which is an hour's drive from the city, is the old US wartime airfield called Atkinson Field. It is only fifty minutes by air from Port of Spain, quicker than the drive to Georgetown which, in the thirty years I have known it, has gone from bad to appalling and on to execrable before improving to atrocious in parts, which is where it is now. I landed at 10.15 in the evening and after an anxious search for my bag which had been removed from the carousel by an over-zealous tour operator, a taxi driver offered his services to drive me to the Pegasus Hotel, usually pronounced Pe*gas*sus, for a fee of twenty US dollars. I had no local currency and so in those circumstances you do as you are told. This is a journey which, even in the dark, tells you that you have left the West Indies far behind. I cannot put my finger on it, yet there is a different feeling about it all. In the daylight it is easy, as you can see the Demerara River on the left and at this point it is comfortably more than a mile wide. At night, maybe the wish is father to the thought. Round every bend you expect to come across a signpost saying Rio de Janeiro 2523 to the left and Caracas 428 to the right.

My driver set a cracking pace and it did not seem long before we passed on the right the huge state-controlled sugar factory which was in full swing, and soon after that we were in Georgetown. We passed the imposing cathedral which the Guyanese tell you is the tallest wooden building in the world. A jink left and then right and we were in Main Street with the Tower Hotel on the right and, I was happy to see, the Palm Court on the left two hundred yards further down the road. The Palm Court had clearly become something of a hot spot and I was to discover it had taken over from the Belevedere which had burnt down some years before. In its day, the Belvedere attracted just about the most beautiful collection of young ladies I have ever seen.

Thirty years before, on England's 1967/68 tour of the West Indies, I had planned to meet Jim Swanton one evening at the Palm Court for an unvarying dinner of rather tough steak and a bottle of Mateus Rosé. In my anxiety to be on time, I ran down the outside stairs from the Park Hotel where I was stay-ing, crossed the small road and fell straight into a badly-lit wide open concrete drain just by the restaurant. The drain was blocked and I had to return to my room and change before joining Jim, who was not especially impressed by my lack of punctuality. I was lucky I was not dining with Geoffrey Boycott. One evening this time when I dined at the Palm Court, I found the drain was in the same place and still blocked and, in fact, of all the items I have just mentioned, Jim Swanton was the only one not present thirty years on, but even he was not far away for he was holidaying in Barbados.

The final three hundred yards of my journey that night took me past the old Governor's house, over the now non-existent level crossing, past what was the Camacho family house and up to the octagonal Pegasus Hotel. It was past midnight and a relief to arrive.

Having said that, it suggests I felt unsafe, which could not have been further from the truth. It is just that when you arrive in a new country late at night, there is something rather comforting about meeting up with one's bed. In fact the Guyanese are just about the friendliest of all the people in the West Indies and although they live in an extremely poor country, their hospitality is wonderful. Georgetown itself has improved dramatically as I was quick to discover the next day. There are more restaurants offering a wider choice and better quality, the shops look smarter and it was more than possible to find a drinkable bottle of wine. Underneath the newly-modernised Park Hotel, a lovely Chinese restaurant called, most symbolically, The New Thriving, had just opened. The food was delicious, especially the squid cooked in ginger which was high on most people's lists.

There was one lovely moment at The New Thriving. I met Steve Camacho at the cricket ground at Bourda the day before the Test Match and he suggested I lunched with him there. On the short drive from Bourda, I asked him about the President of the country, Mrs Janet Jagan, the widow of the former President, Cheddi Jagan. She is a white American who is, like her late husband, an avowed communist and their party, the People's Progressive Party was once close to the Kremlin. When we were going into The New Thriving, Camacho turned to me.

'You asked about the President. She is at the table over there.' He nodded over to the left where an elderly grey-haired woman in a white blouse and blue trousers was eating with two girlfriends. The table was in the middle of the restaurant with other full tables all round. Mrs Jagan was relaxed and enjoying herself; there was not a single secret service man in sight and I could not see any suspicious bulges under the waiters' jackets either. Life went on as normal in the restaurant and there was not one jot of pomp or protocol. When they had finished they got up and walked out just like anyone else. It was all in sharp contrast to the days when Forbes Burnham ran his Marxist dictatorship. Whenever he moved about, the whole place bristled with weaponry and bruising great secret service chaps. If he had wanted to eat at The New Thriving, the restaurant would have had to be cleared and they would not have been given much warning either. In contrast, Mrs Jagan seemed to have enjoyed a disgustingly capitalist lunch.

There was a sad footnote to Mrs Jagan's lunch for her car was stoned later that day at the Parliament Building and three men were arrested by the police, who included Inspector Eddie Nicholls an umpire in the recent Third Test Match in Port of Spain. He had now been given the job of getting to the bottom of this incident. Apparently, an unruly crowd of 500 had broken down police barricades as the Presidential car was entering the Parliament Building compound for the official opening of Parliament. When the President left after a stirring address, some of the crowd threw what were officially described as rocks at her motorcade, injuring three female police officers. The next time The New Thriving will probably have to block off at least half of the restaurant for her and give her security guards free grub as well.

A notable visitor to the Fourth Test was none other than Mick Jagger who had interrupted a Rolling Stones tour of America and flown down to Georgetown in his private jet to watch a couple of days. On the third and fourth, the Sunday and Monday, Jagger, a raven-haired girlfriend and at least one bodyguard packed into a private box over the sightscreen at the Regent Street end. His progress was rather endearingly overseen by the former captain of Hampshire, Mark Nicholas, who has become to cricket presenting what Jagger himself is to pop-pickers, the world over. Nicholas's qualification for the role of ADC were the suavest of manners and close friendship with a member of Jagger's staff. He told me on the Monday morning before the start, in TWI's commentary box, in church-like tones, that he was hoping to bring the Great Man to visit the TMS box sometime during the day. I passed the word round and it was during the tea interval that Jagger arrived in a flowing pink shirt – pink is probably an old-fashioned description of the colour and Yves St Laurent and his chums would surely have had a more precise word for it, but it looked pink to me. Jagger joined Nicholas at the tele-vision interview point to the right of our box on the middle floor of what is just about the best media centre in the entire cricket world.

By the time Jagger and Nicholas had had their chat and had finished smiling at each other, play had restarted and I was at the microphone. Peter Baxter, our producer who makes non-stop action look like a still life, threatened to bring the Rolling Stone to an adjacent microphone. As I was commen-tating, I heard a surge of people behind me by the door of our box. I turned round and there was old pink shirt standing just inside the door listening and he gave me a beaming smile and a booming hello and I am not certain he didn't punch the air, which suggested he had been watching too much of Angus Fraser. Although he stayed where he was, I welcomed him to the box and got one more smile and then he was gone, for Nicholas was evidently anxious he should gather no moss. Jagger had only come that far because the intrepid Baxter had stood in front of him as he was about to leave our floor, and asked him if he would like to come and have a look at his investment. Jagger had bought the TMS commentary which he was putting out through his website on the Internet. Jagger was keen to have a look although Nicholas was reluctant to let him out of his grasp and was also dismayed to hear that he was taking the TMS and not the television commentary as he had done from the tournament in Sharjah before Christmas. It obviously made sense to take the TMS as the television commentary is geared to the picture while TMS has no visual aids and tells the story as it is.

Rather touchingly, Nicholas seemed to feel that too much exposure to the world of radio might not be good for Jagger and he was quick to spirit him away upstairs to the presumably cloistered calm of the television commentary box. Nicholas's single-minded devotion to duty was again most impressive later that night when he burst, somewhat flustered, into The New Thriving restaurant to make sure Jagger had not attracted undesirable company. Shrewdly, he did not waste a single moment to greet or even recognise several old friends as he rushed through to the back of the restaurant looking distraught. What a relief it must have been for him to find that the Great Man, although understandably concerned about Nicholas's absence, had not allowed himself to fall among thieves.

There were two notable re-arrivals in Georgetown. On the morning of the Fourth Test, Lord and Lady MacLaurin were among those present in the entrance hall at the Pegasus Hotel. I reminded his lordship of his words of hope at breakfast in the Hilton at Port of Spain before England's victory in the Third Test Match. He said now, 'I have never seen them lose.' Which could perhaps explain why when I next saw him in the entrance hall of the Pegasus soon after eight o'clock on the Sunday morning when England were 87 for 6 in reply to the West Indies' 352, he had just come back from early service in the Cathedral. He will almost certainly have felt that if he was to maintain his unbeaten record, he was in dire need of divine intervention. When the West Indies won by 242 runs, I was not altogether sure what the moral of this story was.

To go from the sublime to the ridiculous, Geoffrey Boycott, who has never put Georgetown especially high on his visiting list, had once again joined the party. Maybe his presence had something to do with a pretty healthy contract with the *Sun*, at least that was the general gist of the gossip at the time. He spent a good deal of the match pacing up and down and around our commentary box before disappearing off to write his learned dissertations in which as usual he pulled no punches. He was in good voice even by his own high standards as an ear-bender. Always has plenty to talk about, our Geoffrey, even if the subject seldom varies.

The West Indies won the toss and the match with it. England played both spinners, Philip Tufnell and Robert Croft, and it was imperative, therefore, that they won the toss in order that they would be able to bowl last when it looked as if the ball would be turning square. Of course, Sod's Law decreed that Brian Lara won the toss and Lara himself and Chanderpaul then proceeded to bat England out of the match on the first day taking the score to 271 for 3. Thereafter, thirty-seven wickets fell for 585 runs on a surface which looked like a combination of a minefield and a dirt track which had been closed for repairs. Having said that, it did not play as badly as its appearance suggested it would, but nor did it play anything like as well as its many protagonists claimed who, most surprisingly, were all Guyanese.

Bourda is the most delightful of cricket grounds. It is small but built in proportion so that it is, in effect, a big ground in miniature. I always feel I need to look at it through a magnifying glass. Sadly some of the facilities are rather run down. Guyana had a bad attack of the endemic West Indian disease too, which is a lack of punctuality. A new stand, named after Rohan Kanhai, was being built between the pavilion and the sightscreen at the southern end and it was intended to have it ready for this match. Only feverish activity in the forty-eight hours beforehand enabled it to be used at all and it cannot have been the most comfortable of vantage points. When it is finished, it will be a handsome tribute to a wonderful batsman and will provide excellent viewing and some plush hospitality suites. The outfield which was the best in the Caribbean for fielding, had also been let go, although this almost certainly had a lot to do with the severe drought caused by El Niño, which had gripped Guyana for nine months when the Test was played.

Those runs on the first day proved to be decisive and raised the question of whether England's selectors were justified in taking a line the success of which relied upon a fifty-fifty chance: ie, the toss. Sod's Law has a way of pricking up its ears on these occasions and I do not think they were justified.

The match contained a number of interesting points. In the first of the Port of Spain matches, Lara had opened the bowling in the England second innings with Benjamin and McLean and not Ambrose and Walsh, and it was a mistake for Atherton and Stewart put on ninety-one for the first wicket, a stand which should have led to an England victory. Now, at Bourda on the third morning when England were 87 for 6, the West Indian captain ignored Ambrose in the two hours before lunch, putting him out to pasture at deep third man and other exciting places. England needed sixty-six more to avoid the follow-on and surely it would have been ideal for the West Indies to wrap up the innings quickly and to have them in again before lunch. Ambrose and Walsh could have had a few overs with the new ball before the interval and then some more afterwards. It would have been the best possible scenario.

As it happened, Mark Ramprakash, in his first Test innings of the tour, played with the composure I had begun to feel that we might never see from him at this level of the game, and he found a resolute partner in Croft. They took their stand to sixty-four and although England were nine wickets down at lunch, they needed only three more runs to make the West Indies bat again. The follow-on was saved when Ramprakash steered Hooper along the ground to Lara at first slip, who should have stopped it easily but only got a finger to it. His nail was torn and so he had to go off for repairs, leaving Hooper in charge. Hooper's first decision was to bring on Ambrose, his second was to call for the new ball and in his second over with it, Ambrose had Tufnell caught at cover. The irony of it all may have been wasted on Lara. Later, he was questioned about his decision not to bowl Ambrose and he answered, a trifle smugly, 'It was just my plan.' Which, I can only assume, was to let England avoid the follow-on. By way of justification, it was being said that Ambrose cannot bowl flat out two days in succession and that Lara was keeping him for the supreme effort when England began their second innings on the fourth day. It is seldom difficult to be wise after the event. It may be that Lara was determined to show everyone he can do it his way or it may be that he has genuine blind spots. So many people are so anxious to tell me what a good captain he is that it almost convinces me they are worried about him. As in that Trinidad Test Match, victory allowed Lara to get away with it and he did not have to account for his decision. Similar doubts might be expressed by the Warwickshire committee.

The Fourth Test was enlivened by what I considered to be some brave and admirable umpiring by the Australian, Darell Hair. Cricket has had to put up for too long with the bullshit forward defensive stroke. The batsman thrusts the front foot forward with the bat tucked in behind the pad. There is never the slightest intention to play a stroke but the bat is pushed forward behind the leg to give the impression that a stroke is being played. In which case, if the ball strikes the pad outside the line of the off stump, the batsman cannot be out lbw. Jimmy Adams, a left-hander, is a prime offender, particularly when playing Tufnell, who spins the ball into the left-hander. It is as much a form of cricketing stalemate as it is when an orthodox slow left-hander (Tufnell) bowls into the rough out-side the right-hander's leg stump. He will endlessly pad the ball away for he knows he cannot be lbw with the ball pitch-ing outside the leg stump. For his pains, Adams was given out lbw playing the bullshit forward defensive to Tufnell in the first innings and to Croft's arm ball in the second, while Ambrose, another left-hander, was similarly out to Croft. Of course, they were decisions which produced some agonised squeals that evening when there was just an outside chance of an England victory. Joey Carew, a former West Indian open-ing batsman who is now a selector, described that day's umpiring as the worst he had ever seen. He was not the only one but twenty-four hours later when the West Indies had won, it had all been forgotten. Umpire Hair deserves all the support he can get for if umpires generally follow his example, cricket will be a better game. I hope others show the same courage. I bet they will not.

Any account of events over those few days in Georgetown would be sadly incomplete without reference to the large and amiable mongrel of highly dubious parentage who decided on the third morning that not only was cricket a pretty boring game but also that he – if that was his gender, which we will assume it was – needed to stretch his legs on the outfield in front of the pavilion. The players and the umpires did not notice him for a while as he conducted a preliminary warm up in the shadow of the pavilion. As he felt more emboldened and the spirit of adventure increased, he thought he would go and see what was happening in the middle and so play was held up. The admirable groundstaff at Bourda do not apparently possess a qualified dog handler and mere novices appeared, one by one, and gave chase. The dog thought this was distinctly sporting of them for he had nothing to fear in a one-against-one contest. He enjoyed being chased hither and thither even though at first he was as reluctant as Inzamam-ul-Haq to break into even a trot. He left it late each time but then showed an acceleration which was not to be taken lightly. At one point he left his pursuers standing and, with the crowd largely on his side, he dashed across the ground to a wide long-on where, to pass the time until the chasers caught up with him, he proceeded to have a spectacular and faintly majestic crap which brought him the biggest clap of the day so far. The chase was then resumed until the dog decided he had had enough exercise for one day and it was time for a rest so he ran off through the open gate in front of the pavilion. But that was not quite the end of it, for a man now appeared with a pail and a shovel which had a very long handle and, to everyone's delight, scooped up the residue. He reminded me more than anything of one of the Crazy Gang, performing a similar function behind some man made horses all those years ago in The Crazy Gang at the Victoria Palace.

By and large, Barbados is perfection. Alas, the Grand Barbados Hotel fell just a tiny bit short. We had met by chance and it is enough to say we did not hit it off. They probably felt they had the interest of my liver at heart when they refused to pour me a drink after eleven o'clock at night. My feeling was that it was my liver and none of their business. They may also have taken the view that the quality of their food protected my waistline and perhaps they were of the opinion that the noise of the air-conditioning in my room merely added to the general excitement while a room service order, when it arrived, brought with it all the suspense and excitement of popping your hand into a lucky dip. You never knew what was there except that it was not what you had ordered. The hotel did not take easily to criticism either. A colleague of mine wrote a letter of complaint to the General Manager in the measured tones you would expect from someone who writes for *The Times*. He gave it to the hotel receptionist the next morning and, when he returned to his room in the evening, he found that the envelope had been pushed back under his door, unopened. Now, that's a way to deal with complaints.

For four days, it was an absorbing Fifth Test Match. The West Indies selectors had at last got over their fixation with Stuart Williams and Sherwin Campbell as opening batsmen. The thirty-six-year-old Clayton Lambert from Guyana got the nod and so too did the Barbados captain, Philo Wallace, both of whom liked to use their bats at the start of an innings as if they were medieval jousting weapons. England were put in to bat on the best pitch of the series so far, not a difficult accolade to acquire. It had pace and bounce at the start and, wonderful to relate, an even bounce. It was a tribute to its founder, former Barbados and West Indies fast bowler, Richard 'Prof' Edwards. In no time at all, supreme ineptitude by England's front-line batsmen took them into lunch at 55 for 4, at which point Graham Thorpe retired with back spasms. It might have been worse for Ambrose had dropped a return catch from Ramprakash when he had made only two. Ramprakash is one of my heroes of the year and I have written elsewhere about his remarkable innings of 154. He was helped, in the first stage, by a recognisable innings from Russell, who had kept wicket and batted for weeks like a man in a bad dream. When Russell was out, Thorpe returned and played much his best innings of the tour, making 103 and putting on 205 with Ramprakash, and England reached 403.

We then sat back and watched some of the most exhilarating batting of the series as Lambert and Wallace put on eighty-two fearless and at times derisive runs in double-quick time on the second evening. Strokes streamed from their bats as if they were putting on a personal firework display. It was all rockets and thunder-flashes, booming drives, massive pulls and cracking cuts rather than Roman candles and stately pushes and subtle deflections. Wallace is a big man with a barrel chest and huge shoulders who bats like a cultured blacksmith. Lambert is more of a surprise, partly because of his exaggerated open stance and partly because he looks as if nature meant him to be a pusher and a prodder. While they were creating mayhem and putting England's recovery into a different perspective, Dean Headley and Andy Caddick, who opened the bowling, played into their hands. They bowled a succession of long hops and full tosses and appeared not to have the slightest idea where the ball was going. They had been bad enough on occasions in Port of Spain, but this was worse and made me wonder what advice they were being given from within the dressing room and whether they worked at their game as hard as they might. One reason for wondering this was the way in which Headley continued to bowl no-balls. There is no better way of relaxing the pressure at the start of an innings than by producing a stream of no-balls. They help the batsman to adjust to the light and the pace of the pitch, they keep the scoreboard moving and it is all so horribly unprofessional. If a bowler who aspires to play Test cricket finds himself continually overstepping, one would have thought he would have done everything he could to put it right. Whenever I watched England practise in the West Indies, Headley seemed to bowl as many if not more no-balls in the nets without him or any of the coaches being in the least concerned. He grew worse as the tour progressed and in the Sixth Test in Antigua, he bowled twenty no-balls in thirty overs. During the series he made the West Indies the present of no less than sixty-one no-balls.

On that second evening at Kensington, Headley had an unnecessary run-in with Wallace who kept driving him back over his head for four. Headley seemed to lose his temper at this treatment and more than justified the nickname of 'Headless'. It all ended when Cyril Mitchley, the South African umpire who has never been afraid of getting himself into the game, gave Wallace out lbw playing well forward to Headley. It will be a while before Mitchley is offered the freedom of Barbados. Wallace's dismissal lingered for a while because it became apparent later that evening that Atherton had given him a V-sign when he was out and one did not have to be a lip reader to get the gist of the two words that seemed to go with it. Sometime after play had finished, rumour had it that Atherton had said he had thought at the time it was a gesture which would be more trouble than it was worth. It is not often that Atherton takes risks. A touch careless of an England captain, one would have thought, to give a West Indian batsman two fingers in full view of a phalanx of television cameras and a couple of platoons of press photographers. It was not the act of a man who had his mind on the job unless, maybe, he thought he was untouchable. Looking back on it, it is even sillier to try and walk on water when you are not making runs.

The business did not end here either. The photographer who took the picture of Atherton in mid-gesture, did not know he had taken it until a colleague looked at the negative sometime after the close of play. Of course, it was just what the doctor ordered for the tabloids. Towards the end of this Fifth Test, when it began to look as if England might win, the group of snappers he was with made arrangements for three of them to take photographs of the victory celebrations inside the England dressing room when the match was over. The press officer with the side later told the aforementioned photographer that while he would not be officially banned from the dressing room, he would not receive any cooperation from the players. In fact, how dare you do your duty if it does not suit us. An alternative thought might be: doesn't the captain of England have a responsibility to behave himself? All these little incidents point to an unfortunate attitude within the England dressing room. We will do as we want. If you question us, it will be at your peril. What we do is our affair and so bloody well mind your own business. It borders on the arrogant and so too does the way in which those in important positions around the players do handstands to protect them from the unprotectable. Do they ever pause and consider what messages like that received by the photographer send out to the rest of the world? There are, in these pages, other incidents not dissimilar to this one. Just think how much better it would be if the rest of the world was to hear that the culprits had actually been ticked off for overstepping the line. The England party in the West Indies took their policy of self-justification and self-protection to unacceptable levels. In so doing, they isolated themselves from the real world and a siege mentality developed. It was in operation in the final Test of the English season when Sri Lanka gave England an imperial beating.

On the third day of the Bridgetown Test, the England team bowlers mended their ways, the two spinners, Tufnell and Ramprakash, whose off breaks are serviceable enough and, with practice, will become reliable, did an excellent job and the West Indies were bowled out for 262 giving England a more than useful lead of 141. They increased this to 374 when they made 233 for 3 declared in their second innings and Atherton did well to declare when he did, leaving the West Indies to score 375 in 109 overs. Many captains would have gone on longer and most of them for too long. What Atherton did not take into account was that he would again be let down by Headley and Caddick who, one would like to think, would have learned the lesson from their bowling in the West Indies first innings. Wallace and Lambert now received an assortment of long hops and full tosses which were even more alarmingly succulent than those that had been on offer on the second evening.

The West Indies were 71 for no wicket from nineteen overs at the end of the fourth day and even had visions of pulling off a remarkable victory. But by then England had suffered from one piece of great injustice. When Wallace had made twenty-four, he accepted a call from Lambert for a single to Stewart at mid-on. Stewart threw the stumps down at the wicket-keeper's end and umpire Nicholls called for the third umpire to adjudicate. The first replay made it look as if Wallace had made his ground. The others showed that although his bat was over the line it was still up in the air and he was therefore out. The third umpire gave Wallace the benefit of the doubt after seeing the first replay and was then horrified to find out from the other replays that he had made the wrong decision. If the third umpire was obliged to look at all available replays before making any decision, this situation would be avoided. As it happened, it did not matter as it rained for most of the last day after England had removed both the troublesome openers.

One of the features of the annual Test Match in Barbados is the splendid media party given by Tony and Jillian Cozier at their beach house at Consett Bay on the Atlantic coast. The one problem about the day is finding the place. We are all issued with maps but there are many guests who are probably still driving round the island looking for it. I gave a lift on this occasion to an old friend, Geoffrey Nicholson, who spends his summers in fruitless pursuit of success in the deckchairs at Hove and then transfers his affections to the Pickwick Pavilion at Kensington Oval after Christmas. He is past his best as a map reader and, but for his help, I am sure we would have arrived in time for lunch. Much rum, flying fish galore, delicious dolphin, a wonderful view of the Atlantic and much excellent company were on offer. My abiding memory of this tour's party was of the match referee coming across a bottle of red wine which he cuddled under his arm for most of the afternoon refusing to give anyone a drop, only for him to discover sometime later that it was empty. It was that sort of party.

There was a lovely evening on a cruise ship, the *Sea Goddess*, where briefly we touched luxury not normally on offer for Grand Barbados guests. The ninety-odd punters were cricket lovers who had come out from England for the Barbados and Antigua Test Matches while sailing round the Caribbean. There were plenty of celebrities on board and the night I was there, Richie and Daphne Benaud were doing their stuff and the raffle prizes were presented by none other than Jim Swanton who has been a regular winter visitor to Barbados over many years. He and his wife, Anne, who was with him, built the most charming house on the Sandy Lane golf course in the mid-sixties and Bitten and I were lucky enough, on my return to Barbados for the one-day internationals, to have dinner there with the present owner, the restauranteur, Nick Hudson, and his wife. Jim is ninety-one and is quite astonishing. On this visit to Barbados he had a golf lesson or two at Sandy Lane and his memory would be impressive for someone half his age.

The Recreation Ground in St John's, the capital of Antigua, is the newest of the regular West Indian Test grounds. It first staged a Test Match, against England, in 1980/81, an event which coincided with the wedding of Viv Richards, itself a memorable occasion. Richards himself, in a double celebration, scored a hundred on the third day of his honeymoon. Like Barbados, the Antigua Test Match against England is heavily patronised by English visitors who come along to the ground, among other things, to enjoy the daily virtuoso performance of Gravy, one of cricket's most intriguing and entertaining characters. A small, lean man in middle age, he comes to the cricket usually in a lady's dress and sits on a narrow platform sticking out from the front of the two-tier stand to the right of the Viv Richards Pavilion. His adoring fans pack in behind him and between every over, at the fall of each wicket, sometimes between balls and throughout every interval, loud Reggae music blares out of the speakers. Gravy, who usually has a tie-on white beard, goes through innumerable routines. At the end of each over he jumps up and dances. Sometimes he clutches the girder above his head and performs rhythmical acrobatics. When the West Indies batsmen were doing so well, he arrived in pads with a bat and gave his own musical version of the forward defensive stroke. Each time the music starts, the stand behind him dances with him. There is nothing quite like it anywhere else. It's very noisy but strangely compelling and he provides non-stop entertainment for five days.

The Recreation Ground is a small, rather homely ground which is now ringed with stands. It has a most friendly atmosphere even though the building just across the road on the east side of the ground, is the island's main prison where Viv Richards's father was once the governor. The pitch had been relaid for the Test against England and, after Sabina Park, there was a certain amount of apprehension about its likely behaviour. The outfield, too, had been returfed with grass from America. There had been no outfield, just bare earth, when the England party had arrived in Antigua early in January and it had looked a dump, but now it was a picture. Sadly, the groundsman did not have enough confidence in his own ability and on the day before the match gave the pitch, which looked pretty flat, another watering. He was frightened that it would not last the full five days and would start to break up. The result was that there was far too much moisture in the surface when the match began and it gave the side bowling first a decisive advantage. Lara won the toss and it was only thanks to some extremely brave and skilful batting by Atherton and Stewart that England did not lose more than two wickets on a first day which rain kept to 21.3 overs. It was easier on the second day but England batted appallingly, especially against the Trinidad leg spinner, Dinanath Ramnarine, and were bowled out for 127.

Before the match, Atherton was asked about Wallace and Lambert. He replied that they had been strangers to his side in Barbados, but, he said with a wry smile, he did not think they would find it so easy now. Famous last words indeed. By now, the pitch was playing as easily as the prognosticators had originally told us it would. In the twenty-seven overs before the end of the second day, Wallace and Lambert had ravaged England's attack for a small matter of 126 runs without being parted. There was a moment of dreadful and, who knows, significant irony in the second over of the inning when Lambert flashed at the sixth ball of Fraser's first over. It flew quickly to Atherton's left in the gully at shoulder height. It was not much more than a regulation catch for a specialist gully fielder, but Atherton moved like a man who had other things on his mind, as we now know that he did, and dropped it. The very next over summed up the hopelessness of it all for England. First of all, Wallace steered a short one from

Caddick past gully for four, he then swivelled and hooked a long hop square for six before square cutting him with a murderous crack like an irascible admiral dispensing justice on the quarter-deck. Any comment on Caddick would be superfluous. Wallace's fifty came from fifty-one balls with eight fours and one six. It really was enough to make strong men weep.

Wallace is a cultured opportunist and he plays in such a way that, for me, all feelings of bias and partisanship disappear. He is such a joy unless you have the misfortune to be asked to bowl at him. There is something rather loveable about his partner too. Lambert bats a little like the Ancient Mariner. He shoots the albatross early in his innings and then disappears into a wearying display of crab-like left handed atonement. He had been given the chance of a second Test career at the age of thirty-six and, my goodness, he was going to make the best of it. He did too, with a first Test hundred which took all of five and three-quarter hours and which no one can ever take away from him.

When the opening stand was worth 167, Wallace gave way to Lara who was at his best, and one can say no more than that as a succession of bewildering and bewitching strokes raced wristily and exotically between the fielders to the boundary. His eighty-nine was a small, succulent piece of smoked salmon compared to the main course of lobster thermidor he had given us at the Recreation Ground four years earlier when he made 375. Even so, his batting now was such a joy that a great many of the Englishmen at the ground will have been sad when Stewart held a brilliant diving catch at mid-wicket to end his innings. The match referee later told England's coach, David Lloyd, that he needed to have a chat with Graham Thorpe who had taken an unforgivably long time to leave the crease after being given lbw to Ramnarine the day before. It had been a poor decision but no matter. Lloyd was less than pleased at the news and when his expostulations, which may also have caused the referee some concern, had finished, he told Lloyd quietly that he was putting Stewart on a charge of bringing the game into disrepute. Lloyd got all steamed up again and asked why and the answer, 'for catching Lara', did not raise even the glimmer of a smile. Lloyd's strangely overprotective manner when it comes to his players rebounds on him more than he realises. I doubt, too, that it sends out the right signals to the millions of youngsters who follow the game and love to imitate their heroes. If bad behaviour is seen to be condoned, there will never be an end to it and it will happen at every level of the game. The players love Lloyd because he makes a business of hiding them from reality and adds to their belief that the world has had a great bit of luck that it has been blessed by them in the first place.

After Lara came Hooper. For 215 minutes, he batted with a classical grace which has not been given to many in the game's history. Tufnell should have caught him at mid-on from Fraser's bowling when he had scored six, but Hooper went on to round off a hugely enjoyable West Indian innings. He is incapable of an ugly movement and each of his strokes, in attack or defence, is straight from the coaching book with some lovely personal touches which make his art come alive and gives it its irresistible individuality. When it was over, England had two days to avoid defeat. Atherton and Stewart made a reasonable start. After lunch on the fourth day, Lara allowed Ambrose one over at the pavilion end and then changed him round. His first ball from the Factory Road end came back into Atherton off the pitch as he shuffled across his stumps and he was lbw to Ambrose for the third time in the series. Atherton's body language now took over and it was easy to see that this exit was accompanied by real sadness, not to say desperation. It proved to be his last active walk during a Test Match as England's captain, although he did not confirm it until the following evening. It was a walk to the gallows.

Stewart batted well and what a wonderful series he had had with the bat. No challenge is too great for him; he is cheerful to the end and a century now would have been a fitting end to his tour. He was twenty-one short when he was caught off bat and pad. At 127 for 3, England were in obvious danger; at 295 for 3, in the middle of the following afternoon, rain having delayed the start until after lunch, it looked as if they were safe. Hussain and Thorpe had played wonderfully well, putting on 168, and although Lara had taken the new ball, it was weathered and both batsmen must then have been grateful that Lara delayed the reintroduction of his spinners for sixteen overs when the harder ball would have given them a little more bounce, Then came one of those extraordinary, unnecessary, foolish and pivotal occurrences which transform a cricket match and induce a sense of despair in those concerned. Thorpe pushed Ramnarine to square leg and set off for a run. Hussain responded, then Thorpe stopped and so did Hussain, before Thorpe set off again but this time Hussain did not get the message and was only just outside his crease when Thorpe went past him and Murray decorously removed a bail at the other end. It was Hussain who was run out.

Five runs later, Ramprakash played back to a leg-break when he should have been forward and the ball turned and hit his off stump. By now, Lara had called up Walsh at the Pavilion end and, working up a good pace, he swept through the England lower order taking 4 for 7 in thirty-two balls, the last three in just eight balls for four runs. England's last six wickets had fallen for twenty-six runs and the West Indies had won by an innings and fifty-two runs with 6.4 overs remaining.

These four wickets took Walsh's tally in Test cricket to 375, which leaves him one behind Malcolm Marshall whose

376 is a record for a West Indian in Test cricket. I wonder how many of Walsh's 375 have been bowled out and how many have been thrown out, because the more one sees Walsh bowl in slow motion on television the more certain it appears to be that at times there is a definite straightening of the right elbow at the point of delivery. There has been talk of this within the game for several years and yet I wonder if his action has ever been subjected to the close scrutiny which modern camera technology makes possible. If each frame of the delivery is frozen, it is easy to see when the elbow is straightened. When bowlers grow older and their actions become more open-chested the likelihood of throwing increases. Sometimes it is done knowingly while others, who are doing all they can to maintain the old speed, perhaps fall into it unwittingly.

This is an issue about which the game's authorities continue to pussyfoot. Law 24.2 says 'For delivery to be fair the ball must be bowled, not thrown.' This is so fundamental to cricket that chuckers should be ruthlessly exposed and put out of the game if they are unable to change their actions. Walsh is now thirty-five and nearing the end; there has never been a more whole-hearted trier whether playing for Jamaica, Gloucestershire or the West Indies, or a much nicer man, but that is not licence to throw. Because retirement looms, those in a position to do something are almost certain to shrug their shoulders and say that this is one which will go away, and do nothing. Spare a thought for the young aspiring batsman who has been dismissed at a crucial time by a bowler who does straighten his arm let's not pussyfoot here either, who chucks – and has lost his place in a first-class or Test side or whatever and his livelihood has been affected. Recently in India, the Australians have complained about off-spinner Rajesh Chauhan's reinstatement in the Indian side, whilst in August, David Lloyd had his say about the Sri Lankan Muttiah Muralitheran.

Those of us who were at the Recreation Ground to see England's defeat had hardly had time to recover from the griping belly-ache it had brought on, when Atherton came into the post-match press conference gripping a piece of paper. He announced his resignation from the England captaincy with immediate effect. He had come to the West Indies to win, a trifle reluctantly as we know, and had lost. He resigned his commission. Fair enough and, in all honesty, not too many tears were shed. The England captaincy, the Atherton debate and the choice of his successor have all been discussed elsewhere.

The England party trailed away from Antigua in two directions. Six of the players who were not needed for the five one-day internationals which followed went back to England; the other nine returned to Barbados where they joined up with the six newcomers who had been part of the side which had won so well in Sharjah before Christmas and had become the engine room of England's one-day side. Adam Hollioake who had captained that side and was originally appointed as Atherton's vice-captain for the one-day matches in the West Indies, now took over from him. The dramas and the disasters of Antigua had left little time to savour the joys of the island. There was no chance to visit that exclusive settlement at Mill Reef or to enjoy the St James's club, let alone English Harbour and Nelson's Dockyard.

Back in Barbados, we had two excellent one-day internationals, which can often be an anti-climax after a hard fought Test series. Nick Knight, full of joyful left-handedness and eager to win back his Test place, batted splendidly in both games, the lower middle order flourished, the bowling passed muster and the fielding excelled. England just won the first and the West Indies got up in the final stride to win the second by one wicket with one ball to go.

Away from the cricket, Bitten and I found Peter Odle's

Mango Bay Hotel in Holetown on the west coast a brilliant resting place not fifty yards from three of Barbados's best restaurants, Mews, Olives and Kitchen Corner, and less than half that distance from the Caribbean. One evening we were lucky enough to be asked to a large barbecue party at Robert Sangster's lovely house next door to the Sandy Lane Hotel. At least, I think it was Robert Sangster's although by the time we left we were not altogether sure that it was not Mark Nicholas's. When he took us round and pointed out the salient features of what had become his billet, it was with nothing if not a proprietorial air.

Then it was on to St Vincent, a delightful and beautiful island which is much more the general perception of a typical West Indian island. It is not so obviously a rich man's play-ground as the west coast of Barbados. The only blemish was the cricket. After their good start, the newcomers had managed to pick up most of the bad habits of the Test side and Hollioake's captaincy seemed to be more the result of consensus politics than his own fierce individuality. England lost both matches and the competition most dismally and the West Indies left the island three-one up with only one match to play.

The Royal St Vincent Police Force went around with the letters RSVP emblazoned on their shoulders which tickled me. My salt-of-the-earth taxi driver, a man in his sixties with a gruff, almost gravelly Vincentian voice which was exceedingly difficult to understand, gave me his card which solemnly announced that his name was Fuzzy. I asked him about this and he told me his real name was Harry but so many taxi drivers in Kingstown were called Harry that he had turned to Fuzzy because, as he said with a broad grin, 'There's only one Fuzzy.' He was charming and nothing was too much trouble. He gave us a good insight into Vincentian democracy too, one evening at the house of Sir James Mitchell, the Prime

Minister, who bravely gave a party for the Fourth Estate. Having decanted us there in the first place, Fuzzy promised to pick us up later. He was early and decided to pop in. When it was time to go I found him by the table where the drinks were being dispensed, having a chat to one or two people he knew with the PM nearby. I was reminded of W.S. Gilbert's lines in *The Gondoliers*:

> The aristocrat who banks at Coutts,
> The aristocrat who hunts and shoots,
> The aristocrat who cleans the boots.
> They all shall equal be.

If he had been in St Vincent, Gilbert might just possibly have added:

The aristocrat who drives and toots.

Sir James Mitchell, who hails from Bequia which looms large about five miles from St Vincent and where he is a considerable property owner, is the most friendly and affable of men. He stood on no ceremony whatever and was not in the least perturbed to find that he was on Christian name terms with one or two of his guests almost before they had shaken hands with him.

Another mild blemish in St Vincent was the Cobblestone Inn, in the middle of Kingstown, which I can only assume came into my travel agent's vision against the wind on a particularly bad day. The Karaoki Club across the street from my room was less than a delight, and when a chap with a voice like a demented chain saw, attempted, at 2.45 a.m. his eighth consecutive rendering of 'My Way', it was a great deal worse than that. Sunday dinner was another problem because there was none, but it would have been impossible to fault the breakfast omelette.

CHAPTER SIX

Cricketing Scandals

The dictionary says that scandal is an outrage upon morality or propriety and that it also embraces malicious gossip which ensures that in any cricketing year I am going to have plenty of material from which to choose. The decision still to be made is which scandals should be omitted or included elsewhere. Only in a very bad year, or good one if you prefer it, would there be room for all of them. I then had to decide whether to discuss them in chronological order or in the order dictated by the magnitude of the scandal. As that is a matter of opinion, I felt it was safer to start at the beginning and soldier on to the end.

My twelve-month period began with one of those rather curious scandals which, when it began, hardly seemed a scandal at all. When it was over, it did not seem much more than a minor scandal, but the more I thought about it, the more major it became and so here goes.

England's inability to compete against the best when it mattered had been made embarrassingly clear by the

Australians as the 1997 summer gathered pace. After England had gained an impressive victory in the First Test at Edgbaston the Australians pulled themselves together in no uncertain terms and for the next four Tests England were seriously outplayed and by the end of the Fifth, at Trent Bridge, Australia had taken an unbeatable 3-1 lead and, even more seriously, had hung on to the Ashes.

As the series progressed, poor old Mike Atherton's form with the bat had grown worse and his physical form, as in body language, was also down in the dumps. His future as captain was on the line although, as he had been appointed for the series, he was duty-bound to take charge for the Sixth Test at The Oval. This was not the first time his own form had failed him while England's captain, nor was it the first time his job was threatened. His tenure as captain now stretched past the previous record held by Peter May, who had captained his country forty-four times. Perhaps the main reason Atherton had continued in the job had been the lack of an obvious replacement. Against Australia, his captaincy had been, to say the least, uninspiring, his own enthusiasm for the job had been called into question and his form with the bat did not help.

He had let it be known, before the Sixth Test began, that, when it had finished, he was going to take himself off and go into a brown study before deciding if he wanted to continue in the job. The selectors, led by David Graveney, the chairman, had made it abundantly clear they wanted him to continue and, when asked, his players all showed him a fervent loyalty which bordered on blind faith. It appeared that in spite of his recent record as captain and opening batsman, there was never the slightest chance he would be replaced. England won the Sixth Test, Atherton disappeared and the world held its breath even if it did not come to a complete standstill.

When he had told the world of his intentions beforehand, Atherton had said that the result of the Sixth Test might influence him. England's splendid victory did much to re-kindle all our hopes with the tour to the West Indies coming up, even though Australia had kept the Ashes. If the Ashes had still been at stake when this final Test began, I have little doubt that the Australians would have scored the 124 they needed for victory for the loss of about four wickets. They were nothing if not a touch demob happy in the fourth innings. Nonetheless, at the time of this victory, it seemed to English supporters that the siege of Khartoum might have been relieved by less. In the last innings, when Australia were bowled out for 104, Atherton had handled things well and Phil Tufnell, his left-arm spinner, had never bowled better.

The jubilations at the end were a trifle muted because of the captain's imminent departure to goodness knows where, to decide if he wanted to continue in a job which, as a matter of accuracy, he had not yet been offered. I would like to think that in the best of all possible worlds, a good many people in his exalted position would have come off the field that day at the Oval, poured some champagne into the nearest glass, slurped it down, thrown their hat in the air and told the chair-man of the selectors in ringing tones that he could 'take the captaincy away from me over my dead body'.

For a week, we were kept in suspense while Atherton made up his mind. The selectors, on bended knee, implored him to continue – maybe they did not fancy the job of trying to find a satisfactory successor. I have no doubt that all or some of them will have made secret telephone calls to Atherton in his hideaway. Atherton had better luck than Prince Charles or Bill Clinton in that nobody bothered to listen in. I bet Atherton was closer to chuckling at the consternation he had created than he was to chucking it in.

I would be surprised if he did not make a few other hush-

hush calls to find out what his worth was likely to be in Civvy, if not Fleet Street should he have decided that the time had come. Eventually, the country was informed that the chairman of selectors and Atherton had fixed a meeting and that the following morning the world would hear at a press conference at Lord's what Atherton had decided. What a charade and the stakes were nothing less than the England captaincy. The chairman of the selectors has to bear some responsibility for this farce. It felt as if the night would never end and then, when we could bear it no longer, we were told, amid happy smiles, that Atherton would deign to continue as England's captain. It was not as if he had been anything other than a pretty moderate one either. When the chairman had heard the news the night before, presumably he pushed his chair back, shouted 'Yippee' three times, wiped his brow and asked Atherton in bated breath if he would consider captaining the England side in the West Indies. The two of them must have been like a couple of sailors on shore leave.

Under questioning Atherton was not dramatically forthcoming about the state of his fevered mind during his few days of isolation. The selectors had agreed to his request to miss the one-day competition in Sharjah in order that he should be fully rested to lead England in the Caribbean and score mountains of runs besides. The irony of this was that the captain's job for Sharjah was given to Adam Hollioake whose own form of extrovert and involved captaincy played a big part in England's victory in the Champions Trophy. As a result he became perhaps the first real challenger to Atherton which was, I suppose, a form of rough justice although Hollioake's challenge effectively blew itself out in the West Indies. But, by then, Atherton, after another runless tour, had resigned anyway.

The next scandal followed close on its heels. For the last two years, as we have seen, India and Pakistan have gone to

Toronto each September to play for the Sahara Cup. The event had been mildly disturbed in 1997 by the understandable refusal of some of Pakistan's best players to make the journey. Mushtaq Ahmed had preferred to stay with Somerset and bowl his leg-breaks at Taunton, while Waqar Younis showed a similar preference to stay with Glamorgan's title challenge.

If one is uncommitted, the interminable succession of limited-over tournaments around the globe impinge on the consciousness only if one's eyesight is good enough to read the small print at the bottom of the sports pages down among the croquet, the snooker and the ice hockey. In 1997 the Sahara Cup found a novel way of drawing attention to itself, however, and putting itself on the front pages. The majority of the spectators at that charming ground in Toronto – I must own up to not having seen it but the Commander tells me it is charming – were, hardly surprisingly, a mixture of ex-patriot Indians and Pakistanis living in or around Toronto. As happens in any part of the world when representatives of both are locked together in combat in a sporting arena, feelings run high. One spectator became badly carried away by his emotions. Sitting towards the back of a modest temporary stand, he spent most of one day while the Indians were batting yelling violent abuse through a megaphone at the large and genial Pakistani batsman Inzamam-ul-Haq who, for much of the time, was fielding close by on the boundary. It was a level of abuse which was high on the Richter scale of these things. It reached and maintained a level which was probably higher than that which persuaded Eric Cantona to leave the football pitch in a hurry at Crystal Palace and carry out a particularly nasty tackle on that loudmouth.

Inzamam is a gentle giant and, as a rule, it takes a good deal to persuade him to move at the double even when he is fielding. To start with, he shrugged off this verbal abuse, but eventually it got to him and he could stand it no longer.

Suddenly, he raced into the stand and began climbing over the seats to get at his tormentor. Inzamam was within a couple of rows of him when strong hands caught hold of him and pulled him back on to the field. It so happened, by the strangest of coincidences, that one of the Pakistani party who was not playing in that game had walked round to that side of the ground with a bat in his hand. Inzamam snatched it from him and ran back towards the troublemaker, who was now coming down the gangway of the stand, megaphone in hand, apparently ready to hit Inzamam who had raised the bat above his head as if he was the Lord High Executioner. They almost established contact before more hands pulled Inzamam back on to the ground, where he stood for a while with smoke pouring from his nostrils. He tried to break free from those who were holding him at least twice so that he could rejoin the battle but he could not get away from his minders. He was eventually shepherded back to the pavilion while the police arrived and took care of his adversary and his megaphone. In court a month or two later Inzamam was discharged in his absence, presumably because of extreme provocation. History does not relate what happened to his opponent when he faced the local bench.

The next piece of scandal was not long in coming – only a few days later, on the last day of the English season late in September at Chelmsford where, the previous month, Mark Ilott of Essex and Robert Croft of Glamorgan had briefly grappled in the closing overs of an exciting NatWest semifinal. On this final day of the season, when Middlesex had come off the field after a drawn game, Tufnell, their left-arm spinner, was instructed, when he was ready, to go to the physio's room for a normal, random drug test. Tufnell who has a record for somewhat irregular behaviour, failed to turn up for this test and not surprisingly there was a considerable outcry. In the past he has been known to dabble in these forbidden substances and there was a problem on England's recent tour of New Zealand, and yet being the end of the season, he may have been keener than usual to get away. In the hurry, it may genuinely have slipped his mind although naturally there were those only too keen to say that it was clear he avoided the physio's room on purpose. Or so the arguments went. In the end he received a suspended sentence and was put on a good behaviour bond. This leniency produced yet another argument which was that with his success in the Oval Test against Australia still ringing in most people's ears, it was felt he had now made himself indispensable to England and could have an important role to play in the West Indies.

I have just touched on the bribery scandal over the sale of television rights in Sri Lanka in another chapter. That particular market place is tough and a little rough too, and I just wonder if what happened when an official of the Board of Control for Cricket in Sri Lanka is said to have demanded a sweetener, half of which was apparently paid as a matter of normality by the company concerned, is the tip of the iceberg. There are some ruthless operators out there and I suspect we may hear of other incidents. One moment it will be the cricket officials, the next it will be the television moguls. Watch this space.

Pakistan cricket has had more than its fair share of scandals in recent years. Ball tampering, match fixing or bribery allegations seem unending and, as often as not, members of the Test side are all too eager to point their finger at former colleagues. I have, incidentally still to be convinced that reverse swing which is all the vogue these days, is achieved by strictly legal methods. I have asked a number of skilful reverse swingers how they do it and have never been given a satisfactory explanation. It may all be above board but, if so, why are they so unwilling to go into the details?

The Pakistanis like to complain that they get a raw deal

round the world and are always being accused unjustly of skulduggery. But rather than keep trying to justify their past actions, it would surely be more sensible to try to ensure in the future that they are squeaky clean. Yet they have the recurring habit of shooting themselves in the foot and my next scandal is a perfect illustration of this. In October 1997 Pakistan and South Africa came to Faisalabad for the Third and final Test Match in a series which had so far seen two drawn games played out on the dullest of pitches although the Second, at Shekhupura, was also ruined by rain. Shekhupura is about an hour's drive from Lahore, a journey we made each morning by taxi and it provided good net practice for Geoffrey Boycott who was later to make a name for himself on the much longer and infinitely more hazardous drive from Lahore to Faisalabad. On the Shekhupura run he put together his first draft of what he thought should be the new Highway Code for Pakistan.

The pitch at the Iqbal Stadium in Faisalabad promised to be a much more lively affair than either of the first two. It was firm and there was more grass on it and it looked as if the bowlers might for once enjoy themselves. The seam bowlers were likely to find some movement and the chances were that it would take spin later on. When I arrived at the ground the day before the match, I was told that interest in the pitch had been acute, so much so that Allan Donald, who had had no fun or success bowling on the blancmange surfaces which had so far been provided, and one of the other South Africans had been told firmly by the groundsman during their practice session in the morning that they were not allowed to bounce a cricket ball even on the ground immediately behind the crease.

The Laws governing the pitch before a match begins have been tightened up over the last decade, mainly because the international authorities felt the television experts were

157

taking too much of a liberty by walking on and prodding the pitch in their endeavours to find out how it was going to behave. Geoffrey Boycott invariably brought along his hotel key and stuck it in the surface to see how much moisture there was. The match referees, former Test cricketers from a third country who oversee each series, were not happy about this. I well remember Geoffrey having a huge argument at Jamshedpur in India with Cammie Smith from Barbados who used to open the batting in a very unBoycott like manner for the West Indies and had played in the famous tied Test in 1960/61 at Brisbane. Cammie, who was the match referee, would not allow Geoffrey to bounce a cricket ball on the pitch while doing his pitch report. The Great Man had stormed off and Cammie had won the day. Nowadays Geoffrey does not even bother to bring along his hotel key. He is allowed nowhere near the middle of the pitch and, although this has knocked a little piece of television gimmickry on the head, I think it is fair enough for it is more fascinating if the likely behaviour of the pitch remains an unknown quantity until the first ball is bowled. Besides, what can you really tell with a key?

As the day wore on at the Iqbal Stadium, the South Africans left the ground and their place was taken by the Pakistanis whose turn it was to practise after lunch. When their formal practice had ended, the television cameras had been put to bed for the night under their waterproof covers, the umpires and journalists had gone, only a few players and officials remained and, significantly, Cedric, the South African Broadcasting Corporation's roving news cameraman. He was standing virtually out of sight by the television commentary box at the top of the pavilion. The match referee, Ranjan Madugalle of Sri Lanka, whose almost baby-like features hide an admirably determined and forthright mind, was another who had returned to his hotel.

Among the Pakistani players who were still at the ground were Wasim Akram and Mushtaq Ahmed, both vastly experienced Test cricketers and there will have been no need to remind either of them about the laws concerning the pitch before a match starts. There were a number of Pakistan officials on the ground at the time, and it is not possible that Wasim and Mushtaq did not realise they were there. Yet under the full gaze of everyone present, they both bowled an over or two on the pitch which was to be used for the following day's Test Match. It was equally clear to all those watching what was happening and yet no one did anything to prevent these two bowlers from claiming an unfair advantage. As far as one knows, it was the first time in 122 years of Test cricket that this has happened so blatantly and they can have done it only to give themselves a head start over South Africa. They were hoping for evidence to help with the final selection of the side but they had their come-uppance when South Africa won a marvellous game of cricket by fifty-three runs.

Wasim and Mushtaq clearly expected to get away with it but they had not taken account of the lurking Cedric on top of the pavilion. He was not a newshound for nothing and, seeing exactly what was going on, he had his camera ready. Hiding the lens from view, he shot the entire performance and later that night his pictures electrified the television audience in South Africa. It was incontrovertible evidence. The two players had waited until they thought everyone who would object had gone home. The story reached Madugalle who watched the film and was on the telephone to the ICC offices at Lord's as soon as it had finished.

A good deal was made of it by the visiting media although the recording was not shown over the air in Pakistan. The Pakistan Cricket Board was TWI's client and they did not want to upset the hand that paid them although this was obviously a story of some magnitude. It provoked some interesting reactions and it caused me to come as close as I have ever been, which is still not very close, to falling out with the Commander who said in his most quarterdeck manner that he did not think it much mattered. I felt compelled to tick him off. Here was a proud alumnus of the Royal Naval College at Dartmouth, who had himself played for the Navy and the Combined Services in England, condoning behaviour which, if it had occurred under his captaincy, would have ended with the culprit being court-martialled and cashiered and probably tarred and feathered into the bargain. The Commander held his ground but I thought looked distinctly sheepish. We kept coming back to it over the next week or two but I was unable to budge him.

There are many areas of intriguing uncertainty in the game of cricket. One of them concerns the final selection of a side. On the morning of a Test match, the captain and selectors will mull over the pitch and decide whom, of the twelve or thirteen players they have brought to the venue, they will leave out. It is the condition of the pitch and its likely behaviour which affects that decision. If it is well grassed, they may decide to go into the match with an all-seam attack; if it is bare and dry, they will probably decide to play one spinner, if not two. This decision has to be made before the toss and it is only after play has begun that they will know whether or not they have made the right one. If they have made the wrong one it may easily backfire on their side before the match is over. It is one of the fascinating imponderables of the game. If bowlers are allowed to try out the pitch before the start, it would rob the game of one intriguing area of suspense and it would be the poorer because of it. As far as the Pakistanis are concerned, this incident was another black mark on their image. When cricket followers round the world read of what went on that evening at the Iqbal Stadium, they will have said to one another, 'there they go again'. It was monstrous and if it had not been for the admirably alert Cedric, they would have got away with it. One day soon I shall bring it up again with the Commander.

Geoffrey Boycott creeps recurringly into these pages but, as I am sure he would put it, you can not keep a good man out. The Great Man exploded into the headlines and our lives in the second half of January 1998 just as we were all packing our bags for the West Indies. Alas, it was not the tale of a comeback century which I daresay even Boycott would have been hard pressed to have turned into a scandal. At the age of fifty-seven, he had long since hung up those boots for good. The facts were simple. In his absence, a court in the South of France had given him a suspended prison sentence of three months and fined him £5,000 for beating up a girlfriend when they were staying at the immensely posh Cap D'Antibes Hotel towards the end of 1996. The original conviction was later withdrawn when asked for and was granted a retrial as Boycott had not been present at the first hearing. The lady, who had returned to England with Boycott soon after the alleged contest had plenty of photographs to prove that she had run into a bit of trouble. She said it was him; he said he had been gallantly preventing her from hurting herself and even from throwing herself off their balcony.

It was all big news at the time it happened just before the England tour of Zimbabwe in 1996 and there was an even more comprehensive slow-motion replay now, when the French court got to work on the case. Boycott had been advised not to go to the hearing and so her story was unopposed and the judge had made some caustic remarks about the Great Man's presence at a cricket match in South Africa rather than in his courtroom. As it happened, he had got the dates wrong and was back in England. Fiery, as he is known by those with whom he played cricket, held a self-justificatory press conference in the offices of the *Sun* newspaper, for whom

he is a columnist. He wagged his finger at the press as if they
had been a bunch of Pakistani waiters and told them a thing
or two about the way they should behave. On the way out of
the building, as arranged by the *Sun* he bumped into the lady
in question, who was carrying a photograph of her face when
it looked as if she had had a recent meeting with Rocky
Marciano. It all made for splendid photographs and excellent
copy but I doubt if it proved very much. She is apparently a
bankrupt and, according to some, extremely economical with
the truth.

If it had all ended there, it would not have qualified for this
chapter. But the Great Man was shortly to fly to Jamaica
where he was going to commentate about the First Test
between West Indies and England in Kingston for TWI,
whose principal client was BskyB television in the UK. He
had also been asked to work alongside Pat Murphy for Radio
Five Live in addition to writing his usual column for the Sun.
He had apparently been assured by TWI that they were sticking by him. His arrival in Kingston was a muted affair by his
normal standards and he did not, for the first few days at any
rate, venture far from his hotel room. A colleague of mine
found himself in the room opposite and for two days he
thought it was some irascible north country businessman
across the corridor. When he discovered who it was, he was
able to report that Boycott had been keeping the room service
staff up to the mark and making sure the best standards were
preserved.

It was two days before the start of the Test match that
Radio Five Live decided that it would be inappropriate to use
Boycott. The next day TWI were forced to jettison him, probably because of pressure from Sky, and so did BBC television
who were showing a highlights package each night which was
bound to involve his comments.

When you are on the look out for scandal, it is surprising

how often it creeps up on you. We were only just getting over Geoffrey Boycott's departure from Port of Spain to London on that worrying legal business when reports began to filter through of skulduggery in South Africa. Pakistan were about to start a Test series and, although my binoculars are not that powerful, it was clear that scandal was afoot. Just before the First Test in Johannesburg came the news that two of the Pakistani players had been mugged, not in downtown Johannesburg, where it is more or less compulsory, but in the wealthy, upmarket suburb of Sandton which is the home of all the posh hotels and department stores and a restaurant called the Linger Longer which more than lives up to its name and is as good as any in the country.

The Pakistanis, Saqlain Mushtaq and Mohammed Akram, were, according to their own story, out walking late one evening close to their hotel when a blue car drew up beside them disgorging sundry coloured gentlemen who mugged the two cricketers who had nothing on them except a little money which was taken. Both were left battered and bruised and they limped back to their hotel to tell the story. The Pakistani management were indignant and demanded increased security and also that the start of the First Test should be delayed. Naturally the South Africans were most embarrassed and fell in with all the wishes of their guests.

Muggings in Sandton were not going to produce good publicity for the Republic and newspaper headlines all round the world told the story. Not surprisingly the police became involved and obviously they wanted to interview the two victims, but the players were reluctant to grant an interview without their lawyer being present. The police made their own enquiries and were surprised by the few details of the incident the victims were able to give, and came up with a very different story. As a result of their researches, they discovered that the two cricketers had been visiting a night club enticingly named 'The 69', which was close to the team hotel, and where a certain amount of stripping was the order of the night. According to the police, the Pakistanis had got into a major argument and were thrown out, being roughed up a certain amount in the process. If this was so, a mugging story may have seemed at the time the best way of sparing the participants a good deal of embarrassment.

Meanwhile, in Barbados, the Greatest Living Yorkshireman was back with us living in vice-regal splendour at the Sandy Lane Hotel even if the white Rolls Royce was no longer an optional extra for him which may have been something of a relief as it did not come cheap. While there he will have found solace in the larger than life company of the ebullient head of WorldTel, Mark Mascarenhas. Between them, I bet they taught the staff a thing or two.

Scandal again burst on the scene during the Fifth Test at Kensington Oval, Bridgetown. West Indies were making a hash of it as they replied to England's 403, which had been inspired by a brilliant first Test hundred from Mark Ramprakash. England had worked their way through the bulk of the West Indies batting when they took the second new ball and Angus Fraser bowled the second over with it to Shivnarine Chanderpaul, who had just been badly dropped by Jack Russell off Phil Tufnell. Fraser's second ball was a full toss to the left-handed Chanderpaul. He drove and hit the ball on the full toss six inches up the bat on the edge. It had then hit the ground and gone to Stewart's right at second slip where he caught it in both hands and claimed the catch. Chanderpaul, who knew what had happened, stood his ground. Umpire Nicholls, the Guyanese police inspector, gave him out and Chanderpaul, to his everlasting credit, walked off without making any fuss. It required only the briefest of glances at the first available replay to see what had happened. It was abundantly clear that it was not out. All the world could see that on their television screens long before Chanderpaul had reached the pavilion. The third umpire must be allowed to intervene in such situations.

I have little doubt that the two slips, the wicket-keeper, the bowler and backward point, will have known exactly what had happened. Fraser was the only one not to appeal when Chanderpaul stayed. The England players will probably claim that they should have won both Test matches in Port of Spain and that only appalling umpiring in the first enabled West Indies to win. They will claim that David Williams, who made sixty-seven, was out lbw at least three times, the first time as soon as he had come in. In their view umpire Bucknor was the guilty party. After that Atherton's men were unworried by the niceties of the game; they decided that anything went and they would take what they could get. Of course, they could have drawn the umpire's attention to the fact that something was not quite right when Chanderpaul was dismissed at Kensington or they could even have called him back. They did not and celebrated the wicket as vigorously as any of the others. Modern cricketers will shrug their shoulders, say that it is one of those things and smile at those overcome with an attack of indignant morality. Cricketers of previous generations will say cheating is the only word for it. Both are the product of their times and both are probably right. What happens on the cricket field today is a reflection of contemporary society just as the cheating reaction is a reflection of different times. Two wrongs never make a right and it is a rotten philosophy to pretend that they do but in the modern world it is used as a justification. The bottom line must be that it is both outrageous and a disgrace to claim a wicket which the fielding side knows to be not out and which the world can, seconds later by way of the television replay and long before the batsman is back in the pavilion, see for itself is not out. Stewart was to blame again when, in England's first innings, he played a wild forcing stroke off the back foot against Walsh and hit the cover off the ball. When the loud appeal came for a catch behind, he laboriously took guard for the next ball and appeared unwilling for a long time to look at the umpire's raised finger. This is what Test cricket has come to and it is extremely sad. I wonder what view the selectors took before appointing Stewart as Mike Atherton's successor.

Scandal struck again when England were in Antigua although those sitting on one side of the fence, the offenders, will argue long and loud in self-justification. I include the incident in this chapter because it caused such hard feelings, it was extremely rude and would have been easy to avoid.

In November 1997 the West Indies Cricket Board let the ECB at Lord's know there would be four official functions during the tour of the West Indies and the dates were given. There was to be one in each territory staging a Test with the exception of Guyana. Cable & Wireless are the official sponsors of West Indies cricket, as Vodafone are in England, and it was Cable & Wireless who would host these functions. The West Indies Board received a reply from Lord's which queried only one, a boat cruise in Barbados. As a result the concept for that was changed and a party during the two one-day internationals in Barbados at the end of the tour, was switched to terra firma. So far, so good.

During late January or early February the England party was asked to go aboard Sir Paul Getty's magnificent yacht in Antigua for drinks on 18 March, the day of the Cable & Wireless party. The Getty invitation was accepted. A business friend of Steve Camacho, the chief executive of the West Indies board, heard about this and, when the England side was in Guyana for the Fourth Test, Camacho asked Bob Bennett, the tour manager, what was happening. Bennett told him that England were not going to the Cable & Wireless party as they had a firm commitment to Getty. Camacho told Bennett he was going over his head and spoke directly to Tim Lamb, his equivalent with the ECB at Lord's. Lamb came back to Camacho and told him he had spoken with Bennett and a satisfactory solution had been found. Bennett then told Camacho that the England players would go to the Cable & Wireless party for an hour before going on to Getty's yacht for a drink. Would that be OK? Camacho's answer was effectively, 'No, but I am not prepared to quarrel'.

It then became apparent in Antigua at another party a day or two before the Cable & Wireless bash that Bennett had thought it started at 6.30 whereas it had been scheduled to begin an hour later. The following morning Bennett made it clear England would be going to Getty's party and not to Cable & Wireless, and that is what happened. Camacho will have written a robust letter to Lamb at Lord's. Bennett's case was weakened when a further invitation came to visit the Getty yacht while they were in St. Vincent for two of the one-day internationals. If a few players had been detailed, as they should have been, to go to Cable & Wireless in Antigua, they could have caught up with the yacht later. In any event, my spies tell me they arrived at the Getty yacht an hour early.

The day after the official party Barry Jarman, who had been a guest, told me it had been beautifully organised with an English corner where typically English fare such as roast beef and Yorkshire pudding was served, and a West Indian corner where West Indian food was on offer. The only problem had been that not a single member of the England party had turned up and that the hosts were beside themselves. In an interesting comment on how times change, Jarman told me that, when he had toured England with the Australians in 1961, they went to nineteen official functions in the first two weeks of the tour when they were practising at Lord's before a ball had been bowled in anger.

I am sure some people will think this is pretty small beer, but these days sponsors provide the game with its life's blood. In England Vodafone have just taken over from Tetleys as sponsors of the England team, and are paying upwards of £13 million over five years for the privilege. For this they have every right to expect a good deal in return and, if it had not already been promised would not have been prepared to come in. Cable & Wireless have sponsored West Indies for many years and have helped provide the money which has kept West Indies cricket afloat. Is it too much for them to expect the visiting tourists to give up four evenings to them in the space of three months? When West Indies visit England, similar requests are made to them to attend functions hosted by England's sponsors. I wonder what the West Indies answer will be when they receive a list of evenings they are required to keep free when they next visit England.

England's reaction to this party in Antigua is just another example of the way in which players take no account of anyone and do precisely what they want. They do not seem to consider that they have responsibilities to anyone except themselves. Now, Bob Bennett is a reasonable man who is close to the heart of cricket and knows more than most how the game is organised and the importance to it of the sponsors. I cannot believe this was a decision he will have made on his own. In fact, I had to wonder whether he had his hand forced from within the party. It was wretchedly discourteous that Cable & Wireless were so slighted. This episode does not do English cricket anything but harm and is yet another illustration of the way in which it is run at this level. Surely, in the circumstances, a manager in control of his players would have said, 'Look, I realise you all want to go aboard the yacht but I am afraid that half of you are going to have to come with me

168

to the Cable & Wireless party. We will explain what has happened to Paul Getty and I am sure, if it is possible, he will enable those who do not do so now to go aboard at a future date. In the meantime this is how I have divided up the party for these two functions.' If the situation is that the manager is unable to have even this much authority over his party, things are considerably worse than I thought and the poor little darlings feel so terribly hard done by.

At the start of this chapter I did not say that the scandals had of necessity to be about cricket or cricketers, merely that they should have a cricketing background. It is for the reader to decide whether the following scandal was an outrage upon morality or propriety. It was most definitely an outrage although it may also have indicated that we had been away for too long.

Our final port of call in the West Indies was Port of Spain for the fifth one-day international. The dear old Hilton was bristling with security when we arrived for the US Secretary of State, Madeleine Albright, was holding talks there. My first effort when I got to my room was to order a large bottle of mineral water from room service. They told me it would take fifteen minutes. They were optimistic; it took twenty-five. There was then a slightly impatient rap on the door.

'Just coming,' I yelled jumping out of the chair by the window. I was no more than three paces away when there was another angry rat-a-tat-tat on the door. There is nothing that puts my hackles up more than self-important harassing and showing off by waiters. I opened the door and had a tray containing an ice bucket with bottle and a glass pushed into my tummy. I backed away and indicated he should place it on the top of the fridge. He did so.

'Sign this' was his only utterance as he waved the bill. I looked at it. It was in US dollars which made me wonder if it was for Madeleine Albright before I remembered that all bills at the Hilton are in US dollars and are only converted to their Trinidad and Tobago counterparts at the bottom line. The total cost when room service charges, government tax and something else had been added on, was 46TT dollars or almost five pounds.

'Too much money for a bottle of water,' I complained. 'You can take it back.'

'It's a litre,' he explained with hasty and indignant justification.

I ushered him to the door.

'You mean, you don't want it'.

'No thank you,' I replied, 'I'll get it cheaper somewhere else.'

It wasn't worth the trouble, though. Being in the upside-down hotel, I caught a lift up to the lobby to get a hotel taxi. An assortment of enormous and prehistorically old Cadillacs queued up outside the Hilton glistening in the way an undertaker makes a corpse look palatable. The drivers are older still. A small wizened man was the driver of the car which was next in line for a passenger.

'You want a taxi?'

'How much will it be for a return journey to the Hi-Lo Supermarket in Maraval?' I asked.

'Nine dollars US,' came the reply.

'I am afraid I don't understand that and I don't have any US dollars. How much is it in Trinidad dollars?'

'Nine times six,' was the evasive reply.

'All right. Fifty-fourTT dollars there and back?'

'Fifty-four dollars to the supermarket one-way,' was the unpromising reply.

'Tell me how much you charge for a journey to the airport' The airport is twenty-two kilometres away, the Hi-Lo just ten minutes.

'A hundred and twenty dollars.'

'And how much to the Hi-Lo and back?'

'Twice fifty-four,' he promised and then, 'but the wait will be free.' He allowed himself the thinnest of smiles at this as if he knew it was the clincher.

'I'll make other arrangements,' I said rather huffily and walked off.

I then arranged the equivalent of a mini-cab which cost a total of forty TT dollars to Hi-Lo and back. The Hi-Lo, an excellent supermarket, supplied me with three litre bottles of mineral water at 5.68 TT dollars apiece.

This sort of thing does not endear you to a hotel. The management will doubtless say that the mineral water is a special brew and that to enable the hotel to keep up its standards there has to be a big mark-up. A big rip-off might be a better way of putting it and, while I am at it, I wonder what standards they would have in mind. Of course, the prehistoric Cadillacs and the rather nasty, surly old dinosaurs who drive them, are out of the management's control but they do not do the reputation of the hotel any good either.

Anyway they were quick to get back at me because the air-conditioning in my room was missing on at least three cylinders and, when I woke up the next morning, it was to find a regiment or two of ants drilling most impressively on my bedside table. It was then I knew it was time I went back to England – the one point upon which the Hilton Hotel and I would have been in full agreement.

CHAPTER SEVEN

It's Better Than Working

When people come up and say, as they often do, what a wonderful life I must lead, or ask if I know how lucky I am, I have developed a stock answer which, if given with a smile, usually kills a line which can never lead to anything very much. I say, simply, 'It's better than working.'

Most weeks in my life end up being frenetic. Some start that way as well, but I did not consider the week beginning 17 May was going to be above average when it began. It was a perfect Sunday morning and on the way to Lord's I bought the Sunday papers and thought how nice it would be not to have to go to work. I had been entrusted with the job of watching Middlesex play Somerset in the Axa League on behalf of the *Independent*. It was my fifth day running at Lord's for I had seen Middlesex annihilate Somerset in the County Championship over the previous four. Just at that moment, Lord's was not quite the oasis it normally is because there was a lot of building going on, there is nowhere to park your car except for a distant car park rather nearer to Baker Street

172

Underground Station than the cricket ground. Although, on some of the more important occasions, there were buses to ferry you to and fro, whenever I turned up, the bus had either just left or was newly broken down. With a great piece of luck, however, I managed to persuade Stuart Weatherhead, one of whose jobs at Lord's is to mind the media, to ask his father, Ray, who presides most amiably over the Grace Gates, if I might be allowed to use the underground car park beneath the Tavern where the Lord's staff park their cars. They took sympathy on my recently operated-on knee.

Normally, when the sun shines Lord's has a distinctly Elysian look to it but the mass of scaffolding had put that on hold for a while. However, there was a new pleasure awaiting me. The MCC, in their infinite wisdom and generosity, had decided after, I am sure, lengthy deliberation, that from the start of the 1998 season, they would provide the Fourth Estate with free lunches. The menu was not expansive. Soup, a hot main course, cold salmon or a ploughman's was the batting order which was not altogether unpromising. As I remember it, the soup, the hot main course and the salmon were off on the Sunday but the ploughman's was worth the wait if not quite the climb up five steep flights of stairs.

I ate in the Press Box and, between mouthfuls, had a good look at what I could see of the new Media Centre which had been rising steadily during the winter at the nursery end which, as a result, bore a passing resemblance to Cape Kennedy. It had been driven up the motorways in sections from Plymouth and now it lay on its side absorbed into a mass of scaffolding like a beached whale breathing its last, straddled across the gap between the Compton and Edrich stands resting on two huge pillars. There was something vaguely Lilliputian about it especially when workers in white hats crawled across the scaffolding. But having said all that, I didn't find it offensive and when it's up and running it may

173

even grow on you. It's still possible to see a good many of the trees at the nursery end although I am afraid the St John's Wood church which Gubby Allen loved to look at through the Committee Room windows, especially when England were batting, is now more elusive.

To my left as I looked out of the Press Box at the top of the Warner Stand, the upper tiers of the new Grandstand were also encased in scaffolding and a good deal of work still remained to be done. Everyone assured me it would be at the top of its form by Thursday, 18 June, the first day of the Lord's Test against South Africa. It was too, although nothing much worked and a well-known cricket administrator got stuck for an embarrassingly long time in the ladies' loo. Then there was Father Time, whose temporary resting place after moving from the top of the old Grandstand, has been on top of the clock above the Tavern scoreboard. It had been decided that this is to become his permanent home and I don't think the news had particularly pleased him for he was looking more bent and careworn than usual. A bit like Michael Atherton taking a press conference when England had just lost a Test Match by an innings.

The Axa League is, from the cricketing point of view, the most spurious of all the one-day competitions, although as I write these words I can hear the defenders of the faith, otherwise known as the old farts, buckling on their swords and mounting their chargers. Just before two o'clock, the umpires appeared looking most fetching in their jackets, which were a little darker than Cambridge blue. They were followed, shortly afterwards, by the Somerset side dressed in pyjamas which were predominantly a robust terra cotta-ish colour and then came the Middlesex openers whose garb was predominantly light blue. About half the stands were open and they were pleasantly full with a crowd who saw a wonderful game of cricket.

On a pitch which had been used for the four-day match and was no help to stroke-makers, Middlesex, who had been put in, made 160 for 9. Somerset then lost their first three wickets for 14, two of them to the admirable Angus Fraser, looking at his most schoolmasterly. They recovered to 125 for 4 thanks largely to Richard Harden, who made the only fifty of the match and the second half of it with a pulled hamstring. Wickets then began to fall in a rush and with only two remaining, Somerset needed to score ten runs from the last over. When Mushtaq Ahmed drove Paul Weekes's first ball over cover point for six, that seemed to settle it but he ran himself out off the second. After playing one ball, Andy Caddick pushed his second for a single, whereupon Marcus Trescothick swung at the next and was caught at deep mid-wicket. The batsmen crossed while the ball was in the air and so Caddick was on strike needing three from the last ball of the match. A drive to mid-off brought a single and he was run out setting off for the second. You can't get much closer than that. Middlesex had won by a run and there was great excitement. The paying customers loved it and will come back for more and the old farts will have started the 'I told you so' routine. Not that any of it had anything to do with making England a better side.

While it had been chaos in the middle, it had been chaos in the Press Box too. These games start at two o'clock, unless they are lucky enough to be played in front of the television cameras when they begin an hour earlier so as not to interfere with the precious schedules, and end at getting on for half past seven, which is anti-socially late and can play havoc with dining arrangements. A close and unpredictable finish also gets in the way of deadlines for first editions. When Somerset were 14 for 3, some of us took what seemed a reasonable punt and began to write about a Middlesex victory. All this ever does is tempt providence and at 120 for 4 there was the sound of much furious scratchings out, muffled oaths and the hum of Tandys as new intros about a Somerset victory began to exercise the assembled minds. Of course, the flurry of wickets soon followed and a Middlesex victory was again on the cards until Mushtaq drove the first ball of the last over for six. By the time Middlesex had won, I had written a total of four intros, none of which would do, and I suppose the surprise was not that my piece was bad but that it was there at all. 'Marvellous finish,' a chap I knew shouted at me as I emerged grey and haggard from the Press Box having negotiated those five flights of stairs a trifle too recklessly for my knee. 'Yes, wonderful wasn't it,' came out like bullets from between clenched teeth. I didn't wait for the answer and hurried on thinking dark thoughts.

On Monday morning I had a date with London Weekend Television which was moved at the last moment from the Television Centre on the South Bank. The new venue was some studios in Thackeray Road off Queenstown Road in Battersea. The nearest I had come to Thackeray Road before this was to a neighbouring street some years ago to collect a case of 1982 claret I had bought in an auction. I remembered the journey well and now I found the studios at first attempt and was ushered upstairs by a chatty and well-upholstered young lady to a sort of waiting room which had seen better days. It was extremely dusty and a little grubby round the edges, which caused me to refuse the cardboard cup of coffee which I had originally intended to accept. My guide told me she thought I had made a wise choice.

Pondering this, I sat and waited with some of the morning papers I had spotted on a table on the other side of the room. After about ten minutes, Mike – his surname has vanished – with whom I had discussed the programme the week before over lunch at the Cooper's Arms in Flood Street, came to say hello and to tell me they were running half an hour late. I told him I was anxious not to linger too long and he left to find out if anything could be done. Another ten minutes went by before he returned and told me it was only going to be ten more minutes. My arithmetic is not very good but it seemed to me that his sortie into the inner sanctum had not achieved a great deal. Mike then told me he was going to interview me and he wanted to go over a few of the questions. I am afraid my goodwill was beginning to ebb and, rather tersely, I said, 'Isn't that what we did over lunch last week?' He agreed, looked disappointed and left. A few minutes later, a lady with her fairish hair in a band hanging down at the back and discreet dark clothing which suggested considerable pregnancy (which was later confirmed), introduced herself a Nell, the producer of the programme. She told me her husband, a barrister, had been junior counsel under Charles Gray when he acted for Ian Botham and Allan Lamb. They had sued Imran Khan for libel in the High Court in 1996 and had gone down to a famous and expensive defeat. We talked about it for a moment and then it was time for the studio, which I also thought a little dusty round the outside. I sat down, the microphone hanging above my head was positioned to the millemetre, and I heard Mike suggest to Nell that she do the interview. He looked highly relieved when she agreed and off we went for half an hour. Like so many of these things, you wait interminably for them to begin and get fidgety and a bit irritable if you aren't careful. Then, when everything is at last ready, you start and it goes like a breeze. Goodness knows how much of my piece they used, probably very little as they were interviewing such luminaries as Ian Botham and Bob Willis and several others and the programme was only an hour long. I never saw it.

I had a quick lunch at home and then it was on to Putney where I had been booked for a three-hour session with Paul Postle, a photographer who had been commissioned by Simon and Schuster to take the photographs that appear on the dust jacket of this book. It became mildly fraught because when I reached Fulham High Street I found I had left my wallet at home and only had £1.40 for a parking meter. I found a space near Putney Underground station but could not find the studio, which was on the other side of the New King's Road. I then made a bad decision, which was to sacrifice the £1.40 which I had put into the meter and to try and get my car closer to my destination. When I located the right address, I rang Paul on my mobile and rather nervously told him that he would have to lend me some parking money as I had no wallet. I half expected him to tell me to piss off and I wouldn't have blamed him but with considerable spirit he agreed. I mounted the pavement outside the narrow passage which led to his studio, he came running with the swag in his hand and I set off to find a meter. In the end, I had to settle for one which was only two away from the original one in which I had planted my £1.40 and I walked back to the studio feeling rather stupid.

It took three hours. Make-up first, then sitting, drinking tea and twiddling my fingers while Paul and his assistant worked out the lighting with the help of a polaroid camera. There was a most exciting and entertaining incident when a big battery, which he told me had cost him £1500, suddenly caught fire and smoke billowed all over the place. Paul made an admirable fire fighter and had the situation under control in seconds, saying in the most matter-of-fact tones that they had a habit of doing that but it was the first time it had happened to him. I had been there an hour when Paul took the first polaroid, which he pronounced too 'cold'. A long pause followed while a ring of yellow perspex was put round the extremely powerful bulb. The difference was remarkable and the next polaroid was perfect. We then got down to work. Paul flashed away like nobody's business and I looked wherever he told me and did my best to smile and not to look too awkward. Occasionally, the flash did not go off and Paul quickly carried out energetic first aid. I wore my panama hat. Then I took it off and wore headphones and finally I held a mike and away we flashed again. I looked at my watch. 'I've got to go in ten minutes. The parking meter runs out.' We had a number of 'just one more's' and I went haring down the stairs and beat the traffic warden by the shortest of short heads. He was peering at the wretched meter but had not begun to write a ticket.

The next day, Tuesday, it was Worcestershire v Essex in the Sunday, or Axa, League at New Road and back again in the evening. We were having a late dinner with some friends in the Chelsea Ram. One would have thought that only in Ireland would a Sunday League match have been played on a Tuesday but maybe that culture is creeping upon us more steadfastly than we thought. It was a two o'clock start and I meant to set off at half past ten. It was nearer half past eleven when I eventually got going and a vigorous motorway journey lay ahead. The Hogarth Roundabout and then the M4, the M25, the M40, the M42 but it's not all that bad. The Heathrow bit was pretty boring, then it was left and right onto the M25, which was jammed but not solid, and I proceeded at about 47mph to the M40. The M40 is my favourite motorway. It goes through some lovely country and somehow seems more informal than a fully blown motorway – after the first ten miles of roadworks that is.

First, it took me past Beaconsfield where the year before, on the most delightful of grounds, I had watched Buckinghamshire lose to Essex in the first round of the NatWest Trophy. The roadworks stretched to High Wycombe and then it was on to the Stokenchurch turn off with that huge television aerial on the right. If you turn left here you are within a couple of miles of Sir Paul Getty's magnificent ground. From the motorway, you would never begin to guess it. In a sweeping valley distantly hemmed in by wooded hills, I first saw this lovely ground in 1997 when Bitten, my wife, and I were asked by Sir Paul to watch his side play the Australians. The hospitality was supreme and there were some very important people there which made it a name dropper's delight. Some of the people I talked to had a frightful time peering over both my shoulders trying to decide if an Earl or a recent Cabinet Minister, not to say Prime Minster, should take preference. Testing moments, these.

The M40 crosses the Cherwell a couple of times and thereabouts on the left is an extraordinary structure. Shortly after the turn off to Blenheim, a small and imposing tower stands in the corner of a field overlooking the motorway. It is built on arches and has what looks like a red-tiled roof as well as a small balcony. What can it be? Perhaps the Duke of Marlborough keeps a colony of most noble bees and this is their stately home. It might also be the corner point of the Blenheim estate. It is too small to be a watch tower. While trying to puzzle this out, I swept past Banbury, Leamington, Warwick and Coventry and on to the M5. The Worcester South exit is heralded by the small, grass-covered hill on the right by the turn-off which always reminds me of that lovely old hymn, Ancient & Modern Number 137. 'There is a green hill far away, without a city wall.' Then, it was down into Worcester, up the hill past the cathedral and the newsagent's originally owned by Dick Howarth, the only man to have taken 150 wickets and scored 1500 runs in a season since the war, across the Severn and into New Road, the loveliest county ground of them all.

When I arrived, the Gestapo on the gate, employed by Worcestershire County Cricket Club who lease the ground from the Dean and Chapter, behaved at bit like a living personification of Christ's church militant here on earth, and they reluctantly accepted credentials good enough to have kept the KGB at bay. The present body of attendants, who are no spring chickens, uphold an old and presumably treasured tradition at New Road. Long years ago, a car park attendant there is reputed to have refused Jim Swanton permission to enter the ground and survived to tell the story.

After all the recent rain, the ground was green and lush, the weeping willows by the river were spectacular and so were the blossoming chestnuts and the cathedral rose in stately and solemn manner above them all, overseeing its domain from its perch on the hill. Looking across the ground towards the cathedral, it is impossible to believe there is a finer view in the cricketing world. At the moment, the Worcestershire side finds it hard to live up to the glory of its setting. They have some good players and some irritating ones too, like Graeme Hick from Zimbabwe, who for years has done his best to scupper an unusual natural ability. At the time of writing, he has just scored his ninety-ninth first-class century in the first innings against Sussex and his hundredth in the second.

On this Tuesday, they were also playing Sussex.? You may have gathered by now that I have lost what affection I may have had for the coloured pyjamas which are worn on these occasions. At New Road, I half expected the Dean and Chapter to appear on horseback, spears at the ready, in a processional protest. If ever a cricket ground needs white flannelled figures, it is Worcester. Nevertheless, a fair crowd watched the Axa League match even if it did not show off the competition quite at its best. But it did produce a moment or two of great puzzlement although this was not the fault of the competition. Sussex were put in to bat and, thanks to the Newell brothers, Keith and Mark, they reached 258 for 7 which, in a forty-over match, will give anyone an excellent chance. The brethren played some fine strokes against bowling which did nothing more than insult the view. Keith

Newell, who had opened the innings, was dropped three times and when he reached his hundred, as indicated by the figure on the scoreboard, the locals gave him a good hand. But when brother Mark had reached 72 brotherly love ran aground and he was run out. He walked off shaking his head and looking over his shoulder. It put one in mind of Cain and Abel. Keith perished soon afterwards and it was then that the trouble began. Not even the Sussex scorer could always be sure which Newell was which. After two runs had been subtracted from Keith's 103, because a blow which had been originally signalled as a six had been adjusted to a four but the scorers had not taken in the alteration, they decided to recount the brothers' runs. There was much scratching of heads before the returning officer, the Press Association's correspondent, was given the figures. When it came, the final verdict was that while Mark now clocked in at 77, brother Keith had to be content with a miserly 97. There is no end to these excitements in the Sunday League, even if the modern tendency to enact them during the week is to continue. Maybe, at New Road, it was divine intervention for no longer rendering unto Sunday the things that are Sunday's. Sussex won easily and on the journey back to London, it occurred to me that the noble beehive might just possibly have been a dovecote of great distinction.

In the settlement in which we live in the outer reaches of Chelsea, free range kids are very much the order of the day. The mutual car park is littered with the wrappings of instant food, the automatic gates are used for mountaineering practice and garden fences seem to be regarded as part of an assault course. One side of my wooden fence was listing like the Titanic on a particularly bad day. Nearby in the New King's Road, is the World's End Nurseries, presided over by that most benevolent of men, James Latery and a telephone call set his men on the trail. It was one of those 'little' jobs which at each turn become more complicated and ended up as a problem to rival the final tallies of the Newall brothers. Feeling rather useless, which is nothing new, I spent the morning after I got back from Worcester with a Merlot-induced headache watching a New Zealander and an Australian cope with the fence in a way which suggested, contrary to rumour, that the Tasman Sea was not always an antidote to friendship.

It was half past six that evening that a smart car, or limousine as they have a tendency to call it in the trade, arrived to ferry me to SkyNews at Isleworth. I end up there from time to time to discuss cricket matters on air with Mark Saggers. He is an old friend who, at his prime, kept wicket with distinction for Cambridgeshire in the Minor Counties Championship. Wicket-keeping runs in the family, for Mark is a kinsman of Ron Saggers who was the reserve keeper to Don Tallon with Don Bradman's 1948 Australians. We had first met in the mid-eighties when his first job at Broadcasting House was as a gopher for Peter Baxter, the producer of TMS. A few years later Sky spirited him away from the BBC sportsroom. On this occasion we nattered on, pretty inconclusively, about the one-day international to be played between England and South Africa the following day at the Oval. My judgement was as impeccable as ever for I backed England to win and they came second with some ease.

The car dropped me at about a quarter past eight at Brinkley's, a restaurant in Hollywood Road where our old friend Compton Hellyer was giving a pre-season dinner party for the cricket media and one or two others. Three eminent South Africans, Barry Richards, Graeme Pollock and Mike Procter, turned up. The England camp was represented by the coach, David Lloyd, or Bumble as he was universally known. It was a good dinner, although the downstairs room had something of the feel of a Turkish bath. The company's financial wizard, Lindsay McNeile, was sporting enough to place me next to him but had the misfortune to be on the wrong side of my deaf ear, which made life a little complicated for us both. All I gleaned from my left-hand side was an animated and enthusiastic hum. There were several speeches; some on my right side and others, mercifully, on my left. Towards the end of the evening, a messenger brought us the news that Real Madrid had got the better of Inter Milan by the only goal of the match – news which would not normally provoke outrageous behaviour in Hollywood Road, SW10. But it transpired that the bookies' clients had effectively put their shirts and any other garments they could find on Inter. Compton's company was something like a hundred grand better off and so the ensuing revelry was justified. Ian Botham summoned the wine waiter and made serious inroads on Brinkley's stock of magnums of noble claret. It was only a seven minute walk home for me but, like Agag in the Old Testament, I trod delicately.

The first day of the international season is a wonderfully exciting moment. I woke up wondering if I had forgotten how to commentate and mildly surprised that my state of health had not been kyboshed by Real Madrid. It was standing room only on the underground from Green Park to Vauxhall and a crowded walk along the Harleyford Road to the Oval. The eternally cheerful Shilpa Patel, our producer's maid of all work, was in the commentary box squeaking away like a box of puppies. Peter Baxter was looking altogether more serious as if the season had already got to him, while Bill Frindall, the statistical wizard, was more grey bearded than hitherto and largely benevolent. My fellow-commentator, Jonathan Agnew (nicknamed Aggers) was as full of it as ever while my other colleague, Chris Martin-Jenkins ('CMJ') was seriously late and so little had changed. Gerald 'Absolute' de Kok was with us too, bringing his inimitable South African vowels to the microphone. It was all the usual faces, therefore, and the first day of the season always has an element of Old Boy Day about it. For most of us though, it was little more than a month since we had been chattering away in the West Indies.

By Test Match Special standards, it was a reasonably, peaceful game. Apart from the joy of being able to ask CMJ to tell us about the problems he had with the traffic while trying to find the parking spot the Oval had managed to secure for members of the media at Covent Garden, there were no moments of high or even low humour when I was on the air. Before leaving CMJ and the traffic, and the occasions are many during the summer when the two become inextricably entwined, he gets his leg pulled unmercifully at the Oval because a few years before during a Test Match, he was identifying the various parts of south-east London we could see from our perch and he had a terrible time with Nine Elms which he had just located in the heart of Lambeth. It must all sound extremely trivial but it gives us the greatest possible fun. Brian Johnston kept saying when a batman played a stroke that he had hit the ball in the direction of what CMJ would say was Nine Elms.

At this first one-day international I was reminded how different it is commentating on a limited-over match compared to a Test Match. A one-day match is so much more intense and there are more details which have to be got in. It's no good giving the score without the number of overs which have been bowled and in the second innings there is the constantly changing equation of how many runs are needed in how many overs or balls. As a result, there is not the same chance to be discursive and to rabbit on about the red buses and the helicopters and the pigeons. In a way, it is not so much fun. The pace of the game is slower in a Test Match, it is statistically less demanding and there is a place for all the peripheral stuff. Listeners are not so forthcoming with the cakes in one-day cricket either.

The game at the Oval was not the most exciting I have ever seen and although South Africa won by the relatively narrow margin of three wickets, there was no great tension as I don't think anyone felt at any stage that England were actually winning the match or that they were going to win it. When they were put in to bat on a cloudy morning, the ball swung and the batsmen did not make much of a fist of it. There was the sad moment Hussain played Symcox to square leg, within range of Jonty Rhodes and called for a run. When the batsmen saw who the fielder was, panic set in. Hussain stopped running and Knight was unable to get back at the bowler's end. We hear so much about the intensive planning which goes into England's cricket, yet had no one been told that when the ball is played to within half a dozen yards of Rhodes on either side of him, a run is out of the question? Every batsman should have Rhodes's position firmly implanted in his mind before every ball. Knight's departure brought in Darren Maddy on his first outing for England. He is, by trade, an opening batsman but now, unaccountably, he was asked to come in out of position at number five and just as the innings was faltering. He managed a single and perished hitting across the line. Was it the selectors? Was it the coach or was it Adam Hollioake, the captain? Whoever it was, it was barmy. And what about Alistair Brown? He was in the squad and surely had to play at the Oval, a ground he knows so well playing for Surrey. Of course, he was left out. The recall of Chris Lewis was another mistake.

Then there was Hollioake's captaincy. In the West Indies it was as if the up boys and at 'em extrovert had been corralled and neutered. He now said that he realised the error of his ways and was about to convert to his old self. Sadly, it just did not happen. England's total of 223 for 9 posed the eternal one-day dilemma which the captain was unable to solve. He did not appear to be able to make up his mind whether to try and defend this total or to attack and try and bowl South Africa out. He was reluctant to attack new batsmen and when Rhodes came in towards the end, Hollioake kept his long-on and long-off in position, which meant that it was no great problem for Rhodes to push the ball around for singles. He was still far from the Hollioake of Sharjah. As I walked back to Vauxhall Underground station, I wondered if there was any point in splitting up the captaincy, for Hollioake is a marginal selection as a player while Stewart will always be an automatic choice. With Hollioake trying to captain the side like Stewart, it all seemed a mildly futile exercise.

Friday was the day I was introduced to the intricacies of the Internet. Ten days before, having dinner with my daughter, Suki, an old friend of hers, Rupert Saunders, had said, in conversation more than as a deliberate suggestion, that I ought to launch my own cricketing website on the Internet. Now, the thought of computers and the Internet and all the high tech business that involves scares me to death. I doubt anyone could be more hopeless than me when it comes to understanding and working all the newfangled equipment which has apparently been invented to lighten our load. I once had a highly primitive word processor with a memory which was so small I feared it had contracted Alzheimer's. Anyway, we struck up a working relationship over a number of years but it was unwieldy and too heavy, and whenever it broke down I had terrible trouble getting it mended. It was so out of date. I have to own up, too, to having carried a Tandy round Australia and then the West Indies without getting a single story back to my newspaper on it on either occasion. I told Rupert, a publisher by trade, that if he wanted to explore the possibilities, that was fine with me but he was not to expect any help.

He rang me a day or two later full of excitement, saying that he was halfway to setting it all up. I put him in touch with Johnny Sachs, my agent, and a meeting was set up at Johnny's office at a quarter past one this Friday afternoon, before I started the journey north for the one-day international at Old Trafford the following day. When I arrived, Johnny and Rupert were in conclave and I joined them and listened spellbound as the whole thing was set up. They were both extremely enthusiastic. Rupert had even prepared a paper headed 'blowers.co.uk'. By the time I left to negotiate the motorways for the second time that week, the financing, the initial advertising and the way in which the website would operate, had all been discussed and settled. To be honest, I was in two minds as I steered my car northwards. I felt rather buoyed and slightly one up to be almost on the Internet, but this was offset by a darkening realisation that I was going to have to learn how to operate a lap-top. Having seen various colleagues in press and commentary boxes going through agonising birth pangs when they first used their lap-tops, and people who were much more technically on the ball than me, I doubted I had a hope in hell of making mine work. I had said this at our meeting and both Johnny and Rupert had assured me that it was laughably simple. I was not so sure, although we had already come so far down the line I knew I was going to have to pull myself together.

My worst fears were soothed by a brimming glass of champagne when I arrived at another of my favourite hostelries, the Belle Epoque in Knutsford, where I have been staying for matches at Old Trafford for about twenty years. Keith and Nerys Mooney, my hosts, had recently turned the original La Belle Epoque from an upmarket and excellent restaurant with a rather solemn decor into a more cheerful brasserie. The 'La' had been deliberately dropped to help the new informality and it was being a tremendous success. When I arrived, the early diners were munching away and Keith and Nerys were near the entrance welcoming everyone in their inimitable way before shepherding them off to the appropriate tables. One of the features of the Belle Epoque is Keith's jackets. He always seems to have a new one and although not everyone would be brave enough to wear the bright and colourful checks, he carries it off in style. They keep it all in the family because their son, David, is the head chef and does a masterful job. That particular night I did not test his expertise too severely as I began with potted shrimps from Morecombe and went on to a steak with a delicious sauce. It was all washed down with a highly drinkable 1985 Cru Bourgeois from the Haut Medoc. By the time I put my head on the pillow, I had forgotten the very existence of lap-tops.

There was a little bit of a hold up in Barlow Moor Road the next morning but I still parked my car on the practice ground at Old Trafford more than an hour before the start. Each year the climb up the four flights of concrete stairs to the commentary box gets harder and by the time I reached the top, I was puffing as John Arlott used to do. We had three commentators, with CMJ sitting this match out as I was going to do the following day at Headingley. It was another most disappointing day for England, who put South Africa in to bat and would have kept them to fewer than 200 but for an heroic display of unbridled violence at the end by Lance Klusener which took them to 226 for 9. I felt that Hollioake's captaincy was still too indecisive while the futility of bringing back Chris Lewis was again underlined. Too often, he would bowl four or five good balls in an over and then a long hop or a half volley on the batsman's pads would come along and he would help himself. In one over, Lewis bowled four beauties to Daryll Cullinan and then came a long hop which was thumped to the wide mid-on boundary and a half volley on the leg stump which hit the fence at mid-wicket. It was exasperating. Matthew Fleming was the main victim of

Klusener's assault at the end and his medium-paced seamers, usually so effective in the closing overs, were just what Klusener wanted. England's batting was depressing and this time, when Stewart and Hollioake were pulling England back into the match, Hollioake played the ball to within reach of Rhodes and called his partner for a single. Stewart continued on to the pavilion. Why won't they ever learn? As had happened too often in recent years, England had played soft cricket at too many of the crucial moments.

During the day, I watched Aggers and his lap-top with the keenest of interest. He was supplying the Lord's website at regular intervals with his peerless prose. He has been Internet crazy for about a year and it was impressive to watch the way he had mastered his lap-top. The occasional frown as he sat in a chair at the back of the box, his machine on his knee, indicated a spot of bother with his clichés rather than the technical side of the operation. It all seemed easy enough but I could not avoid the sinking feeling that when my turn came it would not be anything like so simple.

At Old Trafford, there is a tented village on the practice ground at the Stretford end for the purposes of corporate hospitality, which has become such a part of big cricketing occasions. I was destined to have lunch with Chris Gent who had driven up that morning from Newbury with his youngest daughter. There was an impressive display of bottles on the table, for he had brought his own wine with him. The innings was opened by some Bollinger, some excellent Puligny Montrachet stood by, cold and waiting for the fall of the first wicket, and the middle order was looked after by some 1988 Chateau Kirwan which also went down a treat. Unfortunately lunch at a cricket match is much too short to enable one to do justice to such a notable gathering. I also had to try and make sense on the radio during England's innings. A state of reasonable coherence was therefore essential, I regret to say, and so sadly it was only a sip of this and a sip of that, but it had been a pleasant way to end what may seem a hectic week but was not really so very different from most of the others except, of course, for blowers.co.uk.

CHAPTER EIGHT

Tales from the Commentary Box

Strictly speaking, the story I am about to tell does not quite come into the twelve-month period of this book. However, as the criminal was not named until the Oval Test Match against Australia and the saga lingered on after that, until the NatWest final in September 1997, I feel a good case could be made for its inclusion. In the unlikely event that anyone still needs reminding, it will give a good idea of the prep-school hopelessness which sometimes spreads through our activities in the Test Match Special commentary box. I know it drives some people nuts but there are others who seem to find it reasonably jolly. Anyway, it is typical TMS.

During the Lord's Test against Australia in 1997, Jonathan Agnew arrived in the box on the first day with an old, trusted and well-used (not to say battered) umbrella. It carried the NatWest logo and, at a past NatWest final, one such umbrella had been given to each member of the media. For some reason, Aggers cherished the aged, woebegone relic and was much miffed when, later in the match, it had disappeared.

Being the tenacious fellow he is, he embarked upon detective work which, at another time, would surely have earned him his deerstalker hat.

He was alert enough to have remembered that on one of the early days of the match, we had been honoured by a visit from that supreme advocate, Bob Alexander, who had been turned into Lord Alexander of Wedon. On his retirement from the Bar, he had become chairman of the National Westminster Bank and had been instantly translated to the peerage. In the days when he had been plain Bob Alexander, he had acquired fame and notoriety, and I hope fortune as well, by appearing on behalf of Mr Kerry Packer and World Service Cricket in the High Court in 1977, in Packer's battle against the authorities. It was Alexander's skilful argument and oratory which helped persuade Mr Justice Slade, at the end of a long and often bitter case, of the selfish and tyrannical injustice of the cricket establishment's arguments. The verdict cost the game a fortune. Lord Alexander now came to the box to chat with solemn profundity to Chris Martin-Jenkins about his bank's cricketing plans for the future.

Remembering this, our sleuth came to the not unreasonable conclusion that the noble peer who, on his arrival, had been jovial to a point but completely umbrellaless, was so relieved his inquisition had ended, that he turned to crime. Seeing a vintage NatWest umbrella nestling in the corner of the box, his hand had been instinctively drawn towards it and he had left swinging it merrily, rather hoping that CMJ would ask him another awkward question. Aggers reckoned that the noble lord had undoubtedly vamoosed with the swag and TMS listeners were left in no doubt that when Lord Alexander of Wedon was next canvassed about his hobbies, umbrella stealing would be high on the list.

But none of this took into account the sinister Moriarty-like figure lurking in the background who was well known to us all and was, indeed, one of the longest serving and most respected members of TMS. As far as we knew, his lengthy career had been without blemish – of course, we later spent hours wondering what else he had got away with over the years – and our sleuth never had him down on his list of suspects and it had not occurred to him that it might have been an inside job. As we moved on through the summer from one Test ground to another, we had plenty of letters about the umbrella that had disappeared but, for a while, Lord Alexander kept himself to himself. As the finger of suspicion closed in on him, however, the former advocate wrote a letter to the BBC Cricket Correspondent absolving himself from guilt. He even quoted a fellow peer, long since deceased, Lord Bowen who, more than a hundred years ago, had written:

> The rain it raineth on the just
> And also on the unjust fella:
> But chiefly on the just, because
> The unjust steals the just's umbrella.

There was a lengthy period when nothing happened. Then, late-ish on in the summer Moriarty himself turned up at a charity cricket match carrying an aged, battered umbrella which bore the NatWest logo. Feeling, no doubt, that he was being hemmed in on all sides, he announced airily that he had no idea how such a scruffy umbrella came to be in his possession. He said, rather lamely I felt, that it had turned up one day in his house. Bill Frindall was one of those who heard this admission and instantly pounced. He took the news with him to the Oval Test Match and in that reticent way of his managed to spill the beans and reveal over the air to the entire TMS audience that he knew who had done it. It was a breathless moment as he confirmed that Moriarty's name, and it pains me even now to mention it, was none other than Trevor

Edward Bailey of Dulwich, Cambridge University, Essex, England and Test Match Special. He is not one of those chaps who finds it easy to dissolve into thin air and to reassemble the body elsewhere – he doesn't have the figure for it – but he had come into the box to pay us all a visit and with that sleight of hand which once dumbfounded opposing batsmen, had made the umbrella vanish. Maybe he had set up Lord Alexander as a decoy.

TMS has inevitably changed a good deal over the last twenty years, firstly with the departure, in 1980, of one of the founding fathers and the best-known commentator of all, John Arlott Then, fourteen years later, Brian Johnston died. On both occasions it was as if one of the pillars had fallen off the Parthenon: the show might go on but it would never again be the same. Of course, it never has been and it never will be because you cannot bring back the inimitable Hampshire burr of Arlott or the adjectives and the intense humanity or the japes, the jokes, the high jinks and the irrepressible good humour of Johnston. The programme survives because it still talks about a much loved game in an enduringly kind and typically English way. It has never been afraid of a joke and perhaps people like to laugh; it provides a faithful commentary of what is happening out in the middle; it is full of the unexpected and boils down into an unscripted chat show which goes on for anything up to eight hours a day when England are playing a Test Match and sometimes when they are playing a one-day international. Radio Four has still to be convinced about one-day internationals, especially those which are played abroad. The programme appears to be as popular as it has ever been.

Another important crisis passed in 1997, when the controller of Radio Four, James Boyle, who provides us with our home, visited us for the first time during the First Test at

Edgbaston. He assured us that while Radio Four long wave may not be the ideal spot on the dial for TMS, he would never let us go to the wall. It may have been more a promise of survival than of opulence but it was something, although it is still difficult not to get the impression that TMS is being increasingly marginalised. It may help our cause now England have begun to win the odd match or two. It may seem strange that a programme which is as popular as TMS should have such difficulty in finding and then keeping a place on one of the networks. In any one year, TMS will not be operating for more than seventy days and only that amount in an exceptionally good year. Whichever wavelength provides us with a home will have to appease regular listeners to its normal output, especially if they do not enjoy cricket and are unable to pick up Radio Four FM where they live or work. The boffins do not seem to have been able to work that one out but when digital radio has swept through the land, everyone will be happy. That is not going to happen until we are comfortably the other side of the millennium; and buying the equipment necessary to receive digital outpourings will, I believe, be expensive, so it will be years before it becomes a universal service. When it has, everything you want will presumably be there all the time at the press of a button. So, as long as James Boyle can put up with us in the meantime, there should not be a problem, except for those who live in parts of the UK which cannot pick up Radio Four long wave. But then life was not meant to be easy.

It is always a sad moment when we hand back to the studio from Lord's at the end of the final of the NatWest Trophy in early September. Another season has sped by, another winter lies ahead and who can say for sure whether we will be at it again before the one-day internationals the following May? An empty Lord's seems emptier than usual that night. For some of us, the outlook was cheerful enough after Essex's nine-wicket victory over Surrey in 1997. Most of us had some cricket to watch before Christmas. I was off to Pakistan for six weeks; England were going to Lahore for training and acclimatisation before the competition in Sharjah and there was plenty of cricket in Australia for anyone who felt left out. After Christmas we were all, except for Bill Frindall, foregathering in Kingston, Jamaica, for the First Test between the West Indies and England which was to begin at Sabina Park towards the end of January. TMS was covering the full series and these thoughts helped soften the blow that evening at Lord's.

It is rather like the start of a new term when everyone drops in from different starting points and we all want to know what the others have been doing. What was Pakistan like this time? Was Sharjah all right? And so on.

We had scarcely marked out our runs in the commentary box at Sabina when the match was over, abandoned after fifty-five minutes' play because the pitch was unfit. It was the sort of situation which should have produced moments of high humour or at least high excitement in the commentary box but as far as I can remember there weren't any. We were overtaken by events and all we could do was relay them as they happened. Peter Baxter had a frantic time with demands from Broadcasting House for interviews and pieces for news bulletins, and thus he and Aggers were constantly racing across to the other side of the ground to try and get the views of various of the participants on tape, to say nothing of the umpires and the match referee and the local officials and the chairman and chief executive of the West Indies Board of Control. The chaos in the George Headley Stand, where the dressing rooms are situated, was remarkable when we all trooped over for the inevitable press conference, which was held in what looked as if it started life as a committee dining room. It took a while for the enormity of the situation to sink in and that went for those of us in the media as much as it did for all the people I have mentioned.

Apart from the abandonment, I came away from Sabina that afternoon with the memory of one extremely bizarre occurrence. The gents' loo was situated immediately outside the door of our commentary box on the left. Play was going on, and it was the only place I could find where there was anything like peace and quiet so that I could do my first piece of the day through my mobile telephone to the *Independent* Cricket Line. I squeezed in – it was not a spacious loo – and half shut the door. Having got through first time, which is always something of a triumph, I was in mid-flow and thought it was going really well when suddenly the door was pushed open and in stomped the grinning Aggers. I am not sure he so much squeezed past me as stood shoulder to shoulder, undid his zip and went vigorously about his business while I was still on the air. For just a moment or two, I was mildly thrown and did a certain amount of umm-ing and err-ing while Aggers was in what I can only describe as mid-season form. I cannot remember whether or not he finally pulled the chain, but I do know that he had a devil of a job getting out because it was a loo built for one. I am still waiting to get back at him but I have not as yet come up with a good idea.

Then, it was on to the lovely Queen's Park Oval in Port of Spain where the two back-to-back Test Matches were played to make up for the Kingston fiasco. In the second game, TMS made history and used a lady commentator for the first time. One evening during the first match, I was sitting in the bar of the Hilton Hotel ruminating about nothing in particular over a glass of wine with Peter Baxter when Aggers bore down on us with that knowing look of his. When he had not been in front of a BBC microphone, he had been commentating for one of the local stations and one of his colleagues was a charming lady called Donna Symmonds, who has been commentating in Barbados for many years. In real life, she is a high powered barrister. She comes from a strong cricketing background and her family were close to that of the late Sir Frank Worrell, so she knows her cricket pretty well and is also the most delightful and attractive person. I had worked with her on a number of occasions on previous tours and so had Aggers, who had been most impressed with her commentary during this match. He now suggested we use her during the second of the Port of Spain Tests. She would be up to standard, it would be good publicity for TMS and it would help smooth over the feelings of those who think that TMS is a hotbed of male chauvinist pigs. It was an excellent idea.

The upshot was that she did a session of commentary for us every afternoon and, depending on her local radio commitments, another in the evenings. It provided excellent variety and, as summarisers, Vic Marks and Mike Selvey enjoyed working with her. There was a considerable knock-on effect and a number of other BBC programmes were keen to interview her, so it was all a great success. Peter Baxter presented her with a TMS tie which may not do her much good, but perhaps some fashion designer is even now working on a TMS blouse or whatever. I suppose she was bound to cause some apoplectic indignation among elderly MCC members who were later able to vent their wrath by voting to continue the exclusion of ladies from membership of the MCC. I hope it made them feel better.

It was just as well Geoffrey Boycott was not part of the BBC in Port of Spain. He was to have helped Pat Murphy on Radio Five Live. Pat was, as usual, perilously perched between two television cameras on the narrow balcony in front of our box. When media centres are designed, those in charge appreciate that television has to have commentators but they appear to think it is unnecessary to have cameras as well, since they seldom make provision for them in such a way that they are not blocking everyone else. I cannot believe Geoffrey would have been too happy sitting on a concrete step in between two cameras. He would probably have sought out the architect and given him some straightforward advice and a piece of his mind too, I daresay. After spending the first of the two Port of Spain Test Matches in the pavilion collecting the autographs of players, past and present, on about twenty miniature cricket bats, he returned to London, for important legal consultations, we were told.

There was one other TMS excitement in Port of Spain. On one day of the first match, I had worn a pair of khaki shorts and dear old Aggers found it about the funniest moment of his whole life. Whoever it was who said that all men's knees look like underdone rock cakes may have had a point. Now, Aggers is mad about the Internet and with a special camera he took a photograph of one of my legs (the other was hidden behind a door) and put the result on the Internet. Amazingly, it produced quite a response, lending weight to the argument that many people these days do not have enough to do. One reply which came from Toronto, of all places, brought the house down. A man said that he wanted a copy of the photograph of my leg to put on his mantelpiece, as he thought it would be the best way of preventing his children from coming too close to the fire.

As far as TMS was concerned, the Fourth Test in Georgetown was memorable for the two fruit cakes sent to us by the *Guardian* from London. They were the best ever although Aggers, to whom one was addressed, was forced to hand over the equivalent of four pounds to the local Customs and Excise before he could have it. His reluctance disappeared as soon as he had tasted it. The other notable feature was the Media Centre, which was as good as any in the world. Plenty of thought had gone into it and our commentary box was brilliant with a perfect view and masses of space. The people who looked after us were delightful. It was just a pity about the match.

We moved on to Barbados for the Fifth Test and by that time, poor old Peter Baxter had been lulled into a false sense of well-being by the way everything had been organised in Georgetown. He was pulled up with a start by the new facilities at Kensington Oval, where a media centre had been built at the far end of the ground, opposite to the pavilion. Kensington Oval was the one ground where he would have expected everything to have been in order. At great expense, the Barbados Cricket Association had employed architects who had gone ahead and built the new facility, apparently without asking advice from anyone in spite of the fact that the most travelled cricketing journalist in the world, Tony Cozier, lived on the island. There is no one who, considering his experience and expertise with the press, radio and television, would have been better placed to have checked that the design was satisfactory. Yet the architects, and presumably the BCA too, thought they knew best. It was an expensive mistake.

The first floor of the building is made up of hospitality suites while the Fourth Estate has, and by all appearances, somewhat reluctantly, been housed upon the second. The gently tiered Press Box meant that those sitting behind had to look between the heads of those in front in order to see, for only Curtly Ambrose would have had any luck looking over the top and even he would have needed a cushion. It was unusable. The commentary box which had been earmarked for TMS was situated behind the press but was not elevated by a single inch. It was a joke. Sitting in a chair looking out with the Press Box empty, it was possible for a tall man to see the top of the stumps, but only at the far end. When the Press Box was being used it was impossible to see anything. The television commentary box and those for local radio were equally

201

laughable. Only a genius could have come up with that design.

Thank goodness we have such a thorough, hard-working producer as Peter Baxter, who is a stickler for detail and stops at nothing to make sure we are in the right position. He had an awful lot of negotiating to do with administrators who were unable or unwilling to see his problem. So too, did TWI and in the end, and in the nick of time, an emergency platform was built on the top deck of the stand which allowed the cameras uninterrupted view and the commentators to see what was going on. For a time, the plan was that we should share a part of this platform with TWI. Then, in the morning, the day before the match, it was decided by no less a person than a government minister, that TMS should be allowed to use the old green commentary box, perilously placed on the roof of the pavilion. This was the best possible answer for us in that it provided a spacious, enclosed and happily situated home for us.

This was a Test Match which produced one of the better TMS stories, too. One morning before the start, I think it was the Sunday, I had been talking on the telephone to Bitten in Norfolk. She had been asked to ask me to mention a dinner I was speaking at in aid of our local church's roof, which was not in good order. Hoveton St John is the church in East Norfolk in which I was christened and, with any luck I shall be planted there as well. A dinner had been arranged at the Petersfield Hotel in nearby Horning, in April 1998, to try and raise some cash for the roof. When I returned from the commentary box at the other end of the ground, I joined forces with Everton Weekes and while one of the fast bowlers was in action, I told listeners about the dinner and exhorted anyone interested to get in touch with the Parish Council or whoever and come along. When I had finished, Everton piped up that he had known me for forty years but had not realised that church was a part of my life. I told him about Hoveton St John and how expensive it is to keep old churches like this in a state of adequate repair. I mentioned it was the roof that we were having the dinner for and then I paused slightly before going on with: 'And then there's the organ.' Heavens above, I thought, how is he going to interpret that and quickly I looked round at him. He was smiling broadly and then came that irresistible throaty chuckle which left no one in any doubt whatever as to how he had decided to take it.

My main memories from Kensington, besides those two, included the delicious pizzas we were sent each day for lunch from my old friends Theo and Margaret Williams. He was once the general manager of Tamarind Cove Hotel before a health problem forced him to give it up. He had now become a pizza king. He owns two pizza parlours with plans for more and, appropriately enough, both are called Pizzaz. One is in Holetown on the St James's coast where all the nobs stay and the other is in the quaintly named Fontabelle which is not much more than a good cover drive from Kensington. Each day about half an hour before lunch a huge pizza cut into about a hundred delicious pieces was brought up to the box and usually my greedy colleagues had scoffed the lot before I could get off the air.

There was also the trek which Aggers and I had to make about ten times a day. Two local radio stations were doing a commentary on the match; he was working for VOB, I was working for CBC, who also used Everton as a summariser. As soon as I had finished my twenty-minute spell with them, I strode round to the back of the pavilion in time for my next stint on TMS. On the way round at the back of the stands I always passed the same four police horses which were in lovely shining condition. One of them was a grey. Aggers was braver than me, and walked round the boundary – to the delight of his many fans. On the third morning, I was walking busily round the ground and was just about to go past the grey when Ian Bishop, the West Indies nightwatchman, was caught behind by Russell off Tufnell and a huge roar went up. The grey had not been expecting it and began to play up – or it may have been that he was a Jack Russell supporter and was celebrating because a catch had at long last stuck in Jack's gloves. Whatever it was, his rear hind leg scuffed my trouser leg and was within a whisker of smashing my knee.

Each morning when I completed the journey to the TMS box and was halfway through a cold glass of Coke, a good, healthy puffing announced the arrival of Everton and in no time at all we were at it again on Radio Four long wave. What fun it was. Trevor Bailey, in charge of a group of tourists from whom he took no nonsense, was with us for the Barbados Test and his form could only be described as inimitable. We had a visit from Brian Johnston's widow, Pauline, who was keen, as usual, to present the magnum of Veuve Cliquot champagne which goes each match to the winner of the Brian Johnston Champagne Moment. Most of the last day of this excellent match was rained off and while Radio Four understandably went back to their regular programmes, they showed a remarkable reluctance to bring listeners up to date with what was happening in Barbados and there were hundreds of angry calls from listeners who had turned on hoping to hear about the Test Match which was so tantalisingly poised, and were amazed not to be able to tune in. Apparently, there was some problem about breaking into the programme without getting permission from on high. Anyway, poor old Peter Baxter's hair went considerably greyer and I am not sure it did not stand on end, in his frustration.

The Antiguan Test Match was another that England will want to forget. It was not the happiest of matches for TMS either because our commentary box was impressively small and did duty as a passage for the guys with Sky. Their commentary box was on one side of ours and their interview room on the other. The door between their commentary box and ours could not be shut without our summariser having to get up and move away because the door opened inwards, directly on to him. Our box cannot have been much more than two and a half paces across and it was quite a test for our patience and endurance. Two intrepid visitors who came to pay their respects were Sir Robert Fellowes, the Queen's Private Secretary who was a flighty off-spinner in his day and was in the Eton Eleven with me when I was captain in 1957, and Lord Vestey, who is President of Gloucestershire and has a beautiful private cricket ground of his own. Their families were holidaying together in the island and the two of them, with various children, had escaped for a day at the cricket.

It is a fun ground to commentate on as something always seems to be happening in the crowd where the noise is tremendous and Gravy keeps us all entertained in a raucous manner. Viv Richards was with us as one of our summarisers and we also had Chris Cowdrey for the only time on the tour. Richards was in great form and is always interesting to listen to; he is not afraid of a laugh, either. My final memory of the Recreation Ground this time was of Aggers in a panic trying to do all his post-match broadcasts without missing his flight back to England later that evening. Heroically, he managed to achieve both objectives, but all the British will have left the Recreation Ground that evening downhearted and depressed after another dreadful batting performance.

TMS at home and TMS abroad are very different. When we are overseas, the technical side of things always seems more likely to go wrong. We don't take our own engineers with us – just the ubiquitous Baxter – and the local guys, although willing to a fault, are often working to a different plan through no fault of their own. There are occasionally frantic moments when the line goes down and Peter Baxter goes ballistic and is hard pressed not to publicly execute some local engineer who, beaming with goodwill, has pulled out a pretty important plug for no very good reason. Then, there is the pioneering spirit which comes through strong when, in Antigua, for example, you are positioned in a large and rather deep cupboard. It brings you sharply back to those unforgettable days in the forties and fifties when the atmospherics, or whatever it was, produced all that buzz and crackle and hissing which so distorted those pre-dawn commentaries from Australia, but helped to make them infinitely more exciting than today's. You only had to listen, to feel you were breaking new frontiers.

At home, we have platoons of highly qualified and delightful engineers to cope with the technical side of things and our equanimity is disturbed by nothing more exciting or dramatic than having to hand over to the shipping forecast at the appropriate time of day, although there have been occasions when to do that is both exciting and dramatic. By and large, it only requires a little extra concentration, although judging by Peter Baxter's footsteps, I am not sure that we do it as efficiently as we might. There are many different barometers of success and failure and most people know their own. If our splendid producer becomes a trifle agitated in the box behind us, his immediate reaction is to quicken his step from point A to point B. If this agitation develops into full-blown anxiety, he breaks into what the purists would undoubtfully call a trot but always has the sound effect of a troubled gallop. You can hear this developing behind you as you commentate and it tells you that, when the time comes to hand over to your successor, it is better to slink away undetected. Having said that, our producer is normally silver-haired amiability itself. I would hate to get on the wrong side of him but just occasionally he allows himself to become worried.

Another big difference in England is Bill Frindall, our

inestimable scorer, who was born during the famous timeless Test Match in Durban between South Africa and England in March 1939, which may account for it. After ten days of play, the England side had to catch a train to Cape Town to make sure they made the boat home and the match was drawn. So, Frindall popped up in a welter of indecision. Besides his immaculate scoring, Bill will always be known for his snort which greets anything he finds amusing or erroneous. On those not infrequent occasions, he makes a grampus feel sadly inadequate. He is a stickler for accuracy and when, for example, I speculate about a player's height and have the temerity to be an inch (or maybe only half an inch) out, he throws the book at me. But as he writes all the record books himself, he may secretly regard me as a good advertising medium as well as a mathematical nincompoop. Bill is a devoted Lord's Taverner although these days he is less exact about his own bowling and batting averages than he used to be.

Since I first met him, in 1972, he has always been bearded and the present edition, now that it has bowed to the advancing years and become completely grey, gives him a distinguished look. Of course, it was Brian Johnston who nicknamed him Bearders. He is not only a brilliant scorer but he also set the trail which contemporary scorers follow. He developed the system which was handed down by Arthur Wrigley, who was his immediate predecessor with TMS. It tells you everything in one line, at a glance, and is about as different from those classical scorebooks which we were brought up with, as a leg-break is from a googly. Bill succeeded in 1966 and is the longest-serving member of TMS. He has extraordinarily neat italic handwriting, a lowish level of patience and a great penchant for half bottles of Australian white wine which help him to while away the lunch interval in company with his food, which is dutifully and elegantly prepared, usually by Debbie, his wife. There are times when he puts the fear of God into me as he reaches for the microphone because I know he is about to draw the world's attention to some frightful howler I have just made. He descends upon you, a bit like the hosts of Midian. Occasionally, I am brave enough to retaliate and ask him to supply me with a fact which even his army of reference books may not be able to come up with. The glare I get is a little like the one Fred Trueman once gave to batsmen who snicked the ball to the wicket-keeper and did not walk. Bill's statistical researches in the winter do not often leave him free to tour and when we are abroad we are usually in the commendably safe hands of the completely clean-shaven and rather more demure Jo King.

Brian Johnston was often the first to arrive in the commentary box, invariably wearing his brown and white co-respondent shoes and since his departure, no one has taken on this mantle although, in reality, the first to arrive has always been the luckless fellow who has been deputed to do the early shift and answer a couple of questions on the *Today* programme followed by two more on one of the early Five Live Sports Desks. You have to get to the commentary box at about eight o'clock unless you are CMJ, who often arrives in the middle of the next programme. If the match is being played at the Oval, I find the journey from the Chelsea borders just about OK, but if I am staying at the Belle Epoque in Knutsford, it is a good thirty-five minutes to Old Trafford and it's debatable then if it's worth going to bed. Jonathan Agnew draws this particular short straw more often than anyone else which, he may feel, is the one downside of being the BBC cricket correspondent. Aggers bustles about the place at a pace which suggests he would not lose to Peter Baxter by more than the shortest of short heads in the walking stakes. He is always busy, on the telephone or on the Internet or conducting an in-depth interview for one of the cricket magazines or simply bustling about.

On the first day of a match Bill Frindall's arrival is stongly reminiscent of those Victorian explorers who nipped about the place in Africa discovering the Congo with a platoon of locals behind them carrying water and food and ammunition, usually on their heads. Bill heads his own procession, and trailing behind him come the helpers with briefcases and reference books and binoculars and pencil sharpeners and stop watches and all other accoutrements of his trade including, presumably, half a bottle of decent Australian white wine, not forgetting the glass, although they seldom carry his paraphernalia on their heads. Bill then arranges himself in the scorer's position with a precision which puts one in mind of Allan Donald positioning his fine leg. Interrupt him or ask a stupid question while this is going on and his expression is not unlike that of a rather severe and irascible Old Testament prophet.

Close observers will have noticed that I have not yet mentioned Christopher Martin-Jenkins. They would be right, and the reason I have not done so is that he has not yet turned up. It is six minutes to eleven, we go on air at three minutes to eleven and CMJ is starting off the commentary. Peter Baxter is quickening his step in the back of the box and looking fiercely at his watch when the door burst open and a slightly dishevelled and mildly puzzled CMJ burst into the box muttering something about traffic and then, in that amiable way of his, he says to our harassed producer, 'Remind me when I am first on.' Backers looks quickly at his watch and says, 'In two and a half minutes,' pretending to talk through clenched teeth. CMJ is not known as the late CMJ for nothing. When I revealed this on air during the one-day internationals against South Africa, I received a letter soon afterwards registering surprise that I was able to have a conversation with CMJ if he really was the late CMJ. I am delighted to be able to tell you he is not that late.

While all this has been going on, the same keen observer will have noticed a good deal of squeaking, and this emanates from our moral guardian and adviser Shilpa Patel. If I did not know it would upset her in extremis, I would be tempted to describe her as Peter Baxter's Girl Friday, but I can see her pursing her lips. Shilpa is officially described within the BBC as a Broadcast Assistant which, in the broadcasting hierarchy puts her somewhere between a producer and, well, a producer and you can't get much closer than that. Shilpa is superbly efficient and she can turn her hand to anything. She books the TMS hotels and, which is much more important, pays the bills; she deals out car park tickets like a skilled croupier at the Blackjack table, she rings me up and asks me if I would like to go to Arundel and cover Sussex's game against the South Africans, she organises the ISDN self-operating commentary equipment I keep in the boot of my car during the summer and she does her level best to make sure we do not suffer from starvation or, more critically, dehydration, during a day's commentary. She keeps us all up to scratch and, most reassuringly for those who feared it was going out of fashion, she thrives upon the gentle art of gossip and, with consummate skill, has taken it to new frontiers. A commentary box, with the same participants for match after match, inevitably becomes a very gossipy place and while you cannot blame Shilpa for that, she was an impressively quick learner. All the beauty in the box comes from her, she is full of fun and has become a essential ingredient of TMS. She caused rather a stir at the Oval in 1995 during the Sixth Test against the West Indies. One morning while I was commentating with Vic Marks, Shilpa gave us both a cup of coffee. When Vic eventually stopped talking, I told listeners we had both been given a cup of coffee. From the back of the box, the rumbling tones of Everton Weekes, who was summarising for us, told me it was remiss of me not to have told listeners that we had been given a cup of coffee by such a beautiful lady. When Vic next relinquished the mike, I told listeners this and as I looked round at Everton, Shilpa was handing him a cup of coffee. 'Oh,' I said, 'I can tell you that she's giving Everton one, too.' And Bill Frindall gave a snort which he really ought to have saved for the millennium.

I knew there was someone I was going to leave out. Each summer we incorporate into the home team the visiting commentator who is supplying listeners in his own country. Dr No comes from Australia – his real name is Neville Oliver and because we are known by our initials on Backers's daily rota of commentators, he has always appeared as NO. It took Brian Johnston about a second and a quarter to call him the Doctor and it has stuck. Gerald de Kok whom I have tried, without success, to christen Absolute, comes from South Africa, Tony Cozier joins us from the West Indies and Brian Waddell from New Zealand. In 1998, it was Gerald's turn again and what fun it was to have him with us. He is the most modest of men and is always dressed soberly and elegantly, reminding me of the clean-cut Boy's Own hero who has just made a hundred in his first Test Match and modestly dismisses it with a wave of the hand saying, 'It was nothing.' He is a decent cricketer himself. I am only sorry that when we were both involved in the long sports programme on Radio Five Live one Saturday afternoon, I failed in an attempt at a leg pull. I was at the Oval and Gerald was at Bristol. In the studio, Nick Mullins, who was presenting the programme, and one or two others, had been singing some of the World Cup football songs and when he next came to me on air, I told him that Gerald had one of the great baritone voices in South Africa. I think Nick realised I was trying to start something, and I had hoped that he would ask Gerald to sing a couple of lines from South Africa's World Cup song. However, he didn't rise to the bait.

The TMS box has always been a natural home for the leg

puller and of course no one was more supreme in this department than Brian Johnston. We have all of us come back into the box when rain has held up play and listened to Johnners talking into the microphone, only to hear him say, to our horror, 'And now here's Henry Blofeld (or whoever) and who better to give you the individual batting and bowling figures of all the Indians on tour'. He would then back away from the mike and panic would set in as I tried desperately to think of some way of getting out of it without making a complete idiot of myself. Much stuttering ensued. After about three minutes which would have been completely incomprehensible for anyone listening and which seemed to go on for about an hour, Johnners, or someone else, would put me out of my agony. 'It's all right, Blowers, we are not on air,' which would be followed by hysterical laughter. It can be extremely dangerous not to treat a microphone with respect and there have been times when the odd swear word has crept through because the commentator 'knew' he was not on air. However much you fear you are being set up, you cannot take the risk. Johnners's irrepressible humour made him see the funny side of almost everything. The only time I ever saw him angry was when the then head of Outside Broadcasts was being ambivalent about the likely future of TMS. It provided a memorable evening during a particularly unmemorable Old Trafford Test Match.

A certain amount of leg pulling still goes on, although it is now mostly confined to Jonathan Agnew's efforts to persuade me to read out faxes he has himself typed out on his computer in the back of the box and which always contain some concealed sootiness. I usually fall into the trap of reading out the most unsuitable phrases and often I don't even spot the naughtiness I have just read out, although the rest of the box is heaving with laughter. This high intellectual pursuit began in 1996 when I read out everything that was put in front of me in perfect innocence. Then, I was told what had happened and the following year I scrumpled up every fax I was given and threw it over my shoulder. By the time 1998 had arrived, I decided that my qualities of detection would allow me to determine which were true and which were false. The first two I read out were signed by Emma Royds and Hugh Jarce and so I have gone back to scrumpling them up. I thought I was being smart when I decided to use Bill Frindall as a sort of litmus test. I gave them to him to read first as he has a considerable sixth sense, but I fear he is in league with Aggers as he okayed a couple of disasters.

Chocolate cakes and champagne are both highly welcome TMS phenomena, not necessarily in that order, or together if it comes to that. Trevor Bailey refers to champagne as 'the medicine' in the sort of tones that usually flutter down to the congregation from those adjacent to the high alter. Wine undoubtedly arrived in the commentary box with John Arlott and I am thankful to relate that it did not leave with him when he retired in 1980. Champagne gives Peter Baxter two major worries. The first is that noisy champagne corks make a delicious and resounding popping noise in the box and he fears our listeners may think an orgy is going on. Then, he is concerned that the name of the champagne house, and per-haps also, the name of the wine merchant who has given it to us, will be divulged to listeners, for that apparently comes under the heading of advertising. He usually responds by thumping a yellow sticker down in front of you on which he has written the simple legend, 'You're fired.' I think it's most uncivilised not to thank your supplier for if you don't he might, just conceivably, forget to send a bottle round next time. There was the occasion when John Arlott put on his most dirge-like voice and told listeners that there was not a single bottle of champagne to be seen in the box and he won-dered how life could have come to such a pass. One of our splendid listeners immediately rang up Fortnum and Mason in Piccadilly and a deliveryman was round within the hour with impressive reinforcements. While champagne and wine were Arlott, chocolate cakes were Johnston. At home, our considerable female audience quite clearly rolled up the collective sleeve and chocolate cakes of all shaped and sizes, and varying degrees of stickiness, chased us round the country from one box to the other. Since Johnners put his cue in the rack, chocolate cakes have been vigorously challenged by those gloriously dark and soggy fruit cakes, encouraged, perhaps, with a dash of brandy. Then, there is the huge basket of shining strawberries which is always sent to us at Lord's in addition to the constant supply of sweets and shortbread and so many other goodies. You can see that there is usually a drop or a bite for any visitor who likes to pop his head round the door.

Visitors to the box are another essential ingredient of TMS. Famous cricketers of yore look in and moan about the present state of the game in England. When things are going better than they are at the moment, players will come up and see us and David Lloyd, who many times worked for us until his elevation to the present exalted position, used to stick his cheerful head round the door. Now that one or two of us have been more than a little critical of the regime he runs, he no longer comes up with quite the same regularity. John Major was a frequent visitor and I think appeared in the box in quick succession as Home Secretary, Chancellor of the Exchequer and Prime Minister, which was quite a hat-trick. He now sits on the Surrey committee with Kate Hoey, to whom I chatted on 'A View from the Boundary' during the Old Trafford Test against South Africa. 'A View from the Boundary' began as a vehicle for Johnners to talk to his many distinguished friends from just about every walk of life, but most particularly from show business. One of the joys of 'rain stopped play' is that we

still get the chance to hear the recordings of his best programmes. After his death, the powers-that-were seemed less
than keen that it should continue during the Saturday lunch
interval but Peter Baxter's tenacity won the day and on the
Saturday of each home Test Match, we take it in turn to interview a carefully chosen victim.

We are the proud possessors of a visitors' book which, over
the years, has claimed some pretty distinguished names. One
or two repeat regularly and love to pop in for a mention whenever they can. One of the downsides of the otherwise sensible
intention to keep all the media together under one roof is that
modern media centres are being built at the opposite end of
the ground to the pavilion. On many grounds, the broad-
casters had been given boxes at the top of the pavilion which
made us highly accessible for the rich and famous who frequent the committee rooms. It remains to be seen whether
these same celebrities will fancy a route march to the other
side of the ground. At Lord's, we have been expelled from the
top left hand turret of the pavilion which has been our base
since 1973 and we are taking our place in the interesting new
Media Centre at the Nursery end which looks like a cross
between a spaceship and a throat pastille with a problem. We
are behind the bowler's arm, which we were not in the pavilion. This is more important for those of us on the radio who
have to describe what happens as it happens, rather than for
the television chaps who comment on what has happened
from the monitor. As long as the cameras are behind the arm,
it does not matter that TV commentators are not. Even so, it
will not be the same.

Another sadness about our move at Lord's is that we will no
longer be able to visit the kitchen just underneath us, which
caters for the players and the committee, and sample the produce. For long years it was presided over with a rod of iron by
that most benevolent of despots, Nancy Doyle who, before her

215

retirement, was awarded the BEM for her efforts. The transition to Linda and her French husband, Alain, a couple of years age has been smooth and seamless. They are a delight and have followed the course set by Nancy; TMS are still supplied with coffee and tea and sandwiches and when occasionally one nips down from the box in the hope of a sharpener, the request seldom falls on deaf ears. For twenty-five years, TMS has been very much a part of the fabric and the family that goes to make up the Lord's pavilion and now it has all come to an end. I wonder if the people who make these decisions ever take considerations like these into account. Originally, we heard that our boxes at Lord's would be taken down and the space used for more seating for members. Westminster Council were not convinced that that was the best idea so the box will stay as it is, and provide a home for the official scorers. What a pity we have not been allowed to stay there, with a perch being found for the scorers on top of the other turret. A lot of raw work is pulled in the name of progress.

For the Fourth Test against South Africa in 1998, at Trent Bridge, we operated for the first time from the splendid new Media Centre at the Ratcliffe Road end, which meant leaving our tiny but old and trusted quarters at the top of the pavilion. Most of the boxes we have become used to, are cramped, but they are jolly places and were a huge improvement on the Dickensian constructions which housed us when cricket commentary began. David Copperfield would have felt at home in the old wooden hutch tacked on to the side of the Old Trafford scoreboard at the Stretford end. We are still at the pavilion end at Edgbaston in a small room alongside the stall that now houses the third umpire and the match referee, and was once the home of the television commentators. It is small and not very comfortable but it's been home for a long time and I hope they don't move us. At Headingley we are perched in the top of the rugby stand in a two-tiered box. The commentators sit at the lower level and peer out under the roof of the stand. It's not brilliant, but like all of them, it has become an old friend.

When people come into the box and listen to our commentary, they almost invariably comment on the informality and friendliness of it all. As you have discovered, to move around is difficult and in some small boxes the art of making way for the next commentator is not easy to acquire unless you are a contortionist, and it's all rather higgledy-piggledy. No one gets angry, and in between the cricket we like to keep listeners informed about our house-keeping problems. We also have to keep an eye on Peter Baxter, who flits about the place with sticky yellow labels which are often presented to us attached to a stop-watch. They say things like: 'At two minutes past, hand to shipping forecast,' or 'Trail the Big Match during the lunch interval – England v Australia Headingley 1981. (Botham's 149 not out). For TMS listeners only.' Another may say, rather testily, 'Stop advertising.' During the Lord's Test, I opened a big envelope to find Nico Craven's picturesque annual account of his previous summer's cricket watching. As I looked at it and started to open my mouth, I got a feverish yellow sticker, yelling, 'Don't mention it. We are reviewing it on Sunday.' This was followed by another, 'England substitute is Bill Bloggs from Middlesex groundstaff.' Then it was, 'Hand TMS listeners back to so-and-so in the studio for a gale warning and continue for SA listeners.' Then, 'Welcome back, Radio Four listeners.' Peter has to keep his eye on the ball every bit as much as we do in order to keep listeners informed and to meet all the junction points. Its no problem as long as you concentrate, which is not perhaps my strongest suit.

Every now and then, I get it wrong and in the First Test at Edgbaston I got it wrong twice in the twenty minutes before lunch. Poor old Peter's hair gets greyer and greyer and his step quickens perceptibly. Mistakes usually produce laughter and snorts in the box and how better to get away from a mistake than to make a joke of it. We may have become an institution but we are far from being institutionalised. I am often asked if I get nervous. I think, if I did, I would be in the wrong job. The strange thing is that although millions of people may be listening, I never feel that we are doing much more than commentating for each other in the box. If I get a chuckle out of Aggers or Vic Marks or the Bearded Wonder, or whoever, I feel I have won. If I was actively aware, on a minute to minute basis, that we were being listened to all round the country and, just possibly, round a fair amount of the world too, I should probably be scared to death and become tongue-tied. Of course, I am delighted that lots of people are listening in but, you see, they are only eavesdropping, and that's different.

Now for the reason we are all there in the first place: the cricket. Every commentary team needs a blend of different styles and different voices and this has always worked well on TMS. The commentators and the summarisers all do it in their own way. CMJ is the cricketers' commentator. His descriptions of play are superb and if you are listening to him describing a stroke, you know exactly what has happened, just as you do when you read his admirable description of a day's play in the *Daily Telegraph*. The only other commentator I have worked with who was as reliable as CMJ was Alan McGillivray, the famous Australian who sadly died in 1996. CMJ likes to keep his bat and pad close together and is always keen to get involved in technical discussions with his summariser which are always interesting and informative. He talks with authority.

Aggers is wonderfully friendly, informal and relaxed. He is very much the modern commentator and he has, inadvertently maybe, changed the style of commentary which CMJ and I learned from John Arlott and Brian Johnston. They talked through the over bringing the summariser in at the end of it and only very occasionally in the middle when they wanted something to be explained or something sensational had happened like a wicket falling. Aggers's commentary almost forms part of an ongoing conversation he is having with his summariser, whom he brings in after nearly every ball. It is all extremely friendly and is delightful to listen to. He has a good sense of the ridiculous, he is informative and amusing, apart, that is, from all those dreadful bogus faxes. He and CMJ kindly tolerate my excesses with the buses, the pigeons, the seagulls, the butterflies and the helicopters, but they have a great piece of luck: they do not have to commentate with me. It is the wretched lot of the summarisers who have to do that. Fred Trueman, in between mouthfuls of his pipe, does not often seem to know what's going off out there. Fred is wonderful when you take him back to a Test Match in which he took part in the fifties or to a famous cricketer he played with. He may be a little less sound when it comes to present-day cricket politics, particularly inside his native Yorkshire, and it is wise to keep away from the subject of Geoffrey Boycott, whom he struck off his Christmas card list a long while ago. Fred is an institution on his own and he also happened to be perhaps the best bowler of fast, late outswingers there has ever been. Then, there is Trevor Bailey, or the Boil, as he has been known since he was once described over the tannoy, while playing in a football match in Switzerland, as Boily. His comments are dry and pithy. He finds much modern cricket incomprehensible and is responsible for those pungent one-liners. 'Can't bat.' 'Can't bowl.' 'Can't play.' In a word, Trevor how would you describe that innings? 'Ghastly.' And so on. He would have got on well with Moses.

Mike Selvey, Vic Marks, Foxy Fowler and Chris Cowdrey are all great to work with and bring their own style and expertise to the programme. Mike is a great realist, Vic a diehard optimist who hates to be too critical, Foxy brings a solid down-to-earth, interpretive touch to it all. Life did not come easy in the Lancashire dressing room and he knows a bit about the survival of the fittest. Like the others, he also has a delightful sense of humour. Chris has a lovely light touch, but there is still a lot of heavy-duty sense in all that he says. They all understand the modern game.

I have to own up to enjoying the theatre of cricket more than anything when it comes to commentating. I love good cricket but when it is not up to scratch, I am easily distracted by all the comings and goings round the ground. If I have a philosophy it is that while the centre of the picture gets most of the attention, it is not a picture without the outsides, the mounting and the frame. I rest my case.

CHAPTER NINE

Plus ça Change . . .

A week after I got back from the West Indies, my right knee
blew up. I had to go in a hurry to the Norfolk and Norwich
Hospital at just about the time when Oxford and Cambridge
were having their first matches against the counties rained or
frozen off. My knee had about half a pint of poison in it and
my surgeon, Mr A.D. Patel, was a self-confessed leg-spinner,
although I thought there was more of the Prasanna about him
than the Chandrasekhar. He wielded a meaningful knife and
septicaemia was narrowly averted. It was from the Alpington
Ward that I perused the early season scores, such as they were,
and I felt rather left out of it. But, more than that, it was from
the Alpington Ward that I went to work on behalf of the
Hoveton St John church roof.

Readers will already know, from the story of my verbal
adventures with Everton Weekes during the Barbados Test,
that I had agreed to speak at the Petersfield Hotel in neighbouring Horning so that the only water to be sprayed around
the church should still come from the font at which, much too

long ago, I had acquired my Christian names. The first date arranged had been in early October but we had had to postpone it because of my subsequent selection as a television commentator for South Africa's tour of Pakistan. Friday, 17 April was then selected as a substitute but I fear that there were a number who were deeply suspicious of my reliability. I alerted a couple of those concerned when I departed to the Norfolk and Norwich as there was now a real chance that I might not be able to turn up, although I insisted that I would. Concern spread rapidly around the Norfolk Broads that night. In the Fracture Clinic on Thursday, 16 April, I told Mr Patel as he pored over the offending knee that, come hell or high water, I was going to be talking to about a hundred punters the following evening. At first, I was afraid the news had not cheered him up, but he recovered nobly and agreed that I should not let them down if it could be helped. He thought about carving me up on Saturday morning before deciding upon that very evening after another close inspection, the thoroughness of which Dickie Bird would have much admired. It was about eight o'clock when, feeling a bit like an Eastern potentate on only a *fairly* good day, I was wheeled in near-record time from the Alpington Ward to the operating theatre, after making a brief stop in a side room where I had an encounter I knew I couldn't win with the charming lady anaesthetist. She put enough anaesthetic in the back of my hand to put a battalion of Grenadiers out of action for a month and, I rather suspect, she cut me off in midsentence, too.

The next day, at six o'clock in the evening, my old friend Rex Neame, whose wife, Kate, was one of those organising the dinner, picked me up at the hospital after first lending me a voluminous pair of bright blue shorts. My knee was bandaged, the bandage was in a splint and I could not get into a pair of trousers. In 1955, Rex had claimed my wicket as the third victim of his hat-trick in the Eton and Harrow match at

Lord's. He has been paying me back ever since. I hasten to add that Eton won the match and I caught him behind the wicket in both innings, though he still claims he didn't hit the ball either time. Trust an Harrovian. Anyway, I did my stuff at the Petersfield, rather moderately, I'm afraid, and tip-toed back into the Alpington Ward well after lights-out.

I was released three days later, and it was another three weeks after that before I took an active interest in the cricket season. I read the scores avidly each morning and I was rather surprised to discover what interested me the most. Unlike Peter Edwardes, the Essex Secretary, I do not consider that the preliminary matches in the Benson & Hedges Cup or, indeed, the later rounds, have performed more than a fairly great service for the game in England, where we need fewer not more one-day competitions. After a number of declarations to try and make up for delays caused by rain, Sussex beat Lancashire and it was great to see that Robin Martin-Jenkins, son of CMJ, took four wickets in the Lancashire innings and made 63 which played an important part in taking Sussex to victory. I was also pleased for Robin Marlar, who had taken over as Chairman of Sussex when the club was about to fall apart eighteen months before and was now beginning to see the good effects of all that he had done. Sussex may never win very much, but they are a club of great character, they have produced great cricketers and are as much a part of the game's fabric in England as Surrey or Yorkshire. Ed Giddins, back with Warwickshire after serving an eighteen-month sentence for failing a random drug test, was among the wickets, and good wickets at that – how Sussex must have wished they still had him. Mike Gatting and Phil Tufnell could not get a game for Middlesex whose new Australian tutor, John Buchanan from Queensland, was clearly a hard taskmaster. Then there were all the unknown names which crop up each season, and I found myself scurrying through the papers to see which of the cricket writers would tell me how they bowled or where they played their strokes and answer the questions that any cricket scoreboard will automatically raise.

The 1998 season was played out with the increasingly noisy debate between those wanting to see dramatic and immediate change to the system of county cricket and the Championship in particular, and those determined that the present setup should continue, rumbling in the background. It was an argument which produced strong feelings on both sides. In 1997, as we have seen, Lord MacLaurin's plans to resuscitate county cricket and therefore the Test side, had foundered when the counties refused to agree to his suggestions. The Benson & Hedges competition was to be abolished and the one-day plans in general were tinkered with and a new competition introduced, but none of this was in the least relevant to producing a stronger England side which should have been the main objective. With too much one-day cricket being played, it was inconceivable that we should scrap the Benson & Hedges with one hand and introduce a new one-day competition with the other.

The overall situation had grown worse by the time that 1998 season was underway. England had lost a series they should have won in the West Indies, ending with a batting collapse in Antigua as horrendous as anything they had managed for a long time. With sickening rapidity, this was repeated in the Second Test against South Africa at Lord's when, in the second innings, the last six wickets disappeared for eleven runs. With events spiralling out of control like this, the seriousness of the situation became ever more apparent and the likelihood had to be that a few of the counties who had voted against MacLaurin's plans in 1997 would now change their minds. In the first half of July, an article appeared in the *Mail on Sunday* which said that nine counties would now definitely vote for change and that two of those who were as yet officially undecided were almost certain to join the nine, which would give MacLaurin his majority.

The debate opened early in the season with a powerful statement from the Professional Cricketers' Association. The players now voted by an even bigger majority than they had the year before in favour of change and a league system with promotion and relegation. The PCA were deeply concerned about the fragile state of the England side and realised how important it was to do everything possible to make it more competitive. Seventy per cent of players had been in favour of change at the previous vote; now it was eighty-four per cent. The wishes of the players were swiftly shot down by Peter Edwardes, the Secretary of Essex who, by accident or design, had become the spokesman for the old farts. He went so far as to say that the players did not understand the full consequences of what they were voting for, which they will have found mildly insulting, to say the least. If those who are actually playing the game say how important it is that it should be changed, one would have thought that their views would be carefully considered. I cannot help but wonder if those who are digging in their toes, and refusing to move away from the past, are only concerned with their own bailiwicks and are unable, if not unwilling, to take the broader view. They appear to skirt round the most important issue of all, which is the appalling consequences for the domestic game if England continue to lose. It then becomes a vicious circle because as sponsors and benefactors pull out, England's performances will get worse and worse. Enough sponsors are leaving as it is and although the ECB is not publicly worried, they must, in truth, be highly alarmed at the way things are going. This was reflected by the reaction of the impressively styled Director of Corporate Affairs who, after yet another hideous England collapse, had the temerity to come to the Old Trafford Press Box and read out some waffle saying that

English cricket had never been in better health and was firing on all cylinders. The clinching argument was that one and a half million children are playing cricket. They are; they are playing Kwick cricket which has just about as much influence on what is happening in a Test Match as King Canute had on the advancing waves. The ECB has developed into a child of Brussels, a bureaucratic nightmare, and those in charge do not help themselves if they set themselves up like so many Aunt Sallys. Who do they think they are dealing with? Coping with the backwoodsmen is hard enough without the principal advocates for change shooting themselves in the foot like this. It is laughable.

For cricket to have held its own in the multi-sports filled summer of 1998, it required the England side to do well enough to justify the faith of its supporters. As it was, football won the day much more handsomely than it should have been allowed to. If anyone had been in doubt as to which sport to support, the performance of England's cricketers, which led to one funeral oration after another over the airwaves and in the media, will have rubbed out that doubt. Alec Stewart and Mike Atherton apart, and they are old hat, the only heroes cricket threw up held South African, and then Sri Lankan, passports. The cricketing children of England had no one to deify, let alone imitate, and small wonder if some of them were attracted away from cricket by Michael Owen, Tim Henman and Justin Rose. England's cricket had become a laughing stock although, of course, the weather had been no help for the season seemed to be permanently stuck in the first half of May.

Those who are not prepared to tolerate change at any price would do well to remember that every county's finances are greatly helped and, in most instances, made viable by the annual handout from the ECB of around £1 million for each county. Television contracts have helped to keep the figure reasonably healthy but more money is always needed. In mid-summer, Chris Smith, the Minister for Culture, took the advice of the Committee he appointed and told the House of Commons that he had decided to take Test Matches off the list of protected events which must be shown live on terrestrial television. If they want it Sky, and any other satellite channel, is free to bid for the television rights for Test Matches in England. The bean counters will be hoping they will come in with a whacking great sum which will solve the game's immediate problems. The reality is that the BBC and Sky will probably divide the Test Matches between themselves, and the hope is that the annual revenue from these sources will be considerably above the eighteen million pounds at present. This would have the advantage of making sure that some Test cricket was still available to the huge BBC audience. If Tests were available exclusively to the much smaller Sky audience, it would be enormously damaging to the game just as it has been to rugby football; since they sold out to Sky they have lost something like three million viewers. Cricket, like rugby, needs to be kept in front of the public. Sky's entry into the bidding will surely push the BBC much higher than the ten million pounds they have been reported as paying this year.

There must be the chance, though, that Sky and the BBC will gang up and say to the ECB, 'Now, wait a moment. You can't seriously expect us to pay such huge sums for a failing product. Our viewers will not be interested in a losing side.' If the conversation goes along these lines, the game has a problem. Another possibility is that Sky might say to the ECB that they are not prepared to buy unless the authorities make drastic changes to county cricket to try and bring about an improvement in the overall state of the game in England. Come to think of it, that might be the best way to bring about change, rather than try to convince eighteen county chairmen, many of whom will be playing to different agendas. If the economic screw is tightened enough, the eighteen will have no option but to follow. I should have said seventeen because I cannot see anything making Peter Edwardes desert his sinking ship. These are interesting times.

In the First Test against South Africa, England failed to capitalise on a wonderful first day after they had been put in by South Africa in excellent bowling conditions. Mike Atherton and Mark Butcher put on 179 for the first wicket and England were 249 for 1 at the end of the first day. England went too slowly to their final total of 462 all out, although rain on the last day would probably have prevented them from winning anyway. South Africa were 46 for 4 on the first morning of the Second Test at Lord's before Hansie Cronje and Jonty Rhodes took them to 350. The failure to press home the early advantage was indelibly underlined by that dramatic batting collapse on the Sunday afternoon which saw those six wickets fall for eleven runs. The Third was then played in front of worryingly empty stands at Old Trafford, which both the ECB and the Lancashire authorities tried to play down, but the truth surely was that the public were getting browned off. It was made worse when South Africa won the toss and scored 552 for 5 declared and England were then bowled out for 183. On the last day and a half, Stewart and Atherton fought splendidly, adding 226 for the third wicket, with Stewart making 164 and Atherton 89 before both were out to badly played hooks and after a mini-collapse, a superb rearguard action was fought out by Robert Croft, who batted for 188 minutes and by Darren Gough who survived for twenty overs. In the end, England were saved by the batting of Angus Fraser who, with heroic bravery, kept out Allan Donald for two overs and one ball. Donald, although feeling an old ankle injury, had bowled superbly, taking, in all, 6 for 88. Test cricket seldom has much more to offer than it did on that last day.

The next day I had been invited by Sir Paul Getty to his cricket ground at Wormsley, where his Eleven was playing the Flamingos from Holland. Lord MacLaurin was among those present and we talked for a while about England's cricket. Far from improving, it was getting worse and he knew that something had to be done. Only the day before he had written to all the county chairmen and chief executives asking them to a two-day meeting in the autumn to discuss openly all the options that are available to county cricket. He wanted them to mull over the idea of a two-tier system with promotion and relegation. There was also the plan to have a Super League of six sides backed by two feeder leagues of six sides each with promotion for three counties each year. Then, there was the idea which is growing in favour, of playing regional cricket as a link between county and Test cricket and, of course, there was the chance to discuss the merits of keeping the existing system in place. Lord MacLaurin felt that the worst possible answer was to do nothing which would be, in effect, to let the game drift on downwards. There is no perfect alternative. The players themselves want change and if they do not get it, it will hardly provide them with the impetus to try and put things right within the framework of the existing game. Then, there are those for whom Peter Edwardes is the spokesman and who are supported most notably by Jim Swanton, in admiration of whom I am second to none in almost everything, who seem to feel that the players should not be involved in this discussion although it is affecting their lives, not to say their livelihoods. Bring back the 1950s. In those days, when there were amateurs and professionals, gentlemen and players, the players were told what to do and did it, or else. Those days are long gone. In the late 1990s, like it or not, those who work at the coalface are also involved in the decision-making processes, and so they should be. The point of view which says they are not the people who should decide is insulting their intelligence, for it is effectively saying that although they are in the best position, they are not capable of making a rational judgement. Modern cricketers are an intelligent and articulate lot and it is hardly surprising that they do not take kindly to this approach. They should not be treated like schoolboys. The PCA are as keen as anyone to see the standard of English cricket lifted so that the national side becomes competitive. They play the game and when they say they know what should be done, their views should surely be listened to and respected. It is no use the old farts behaving as if they were all Lord Kitchener: it just will not wash. Peter Edwardes's riposte to the announcement of the proposed meeting in the autumn was to go on record about his views on the way cricket is going. This is what he said: 'I'm bullish about the whole thing. What is happening at the grass roots level is very exciting. Most of the Under-19 team who did so well in the World Cup are finding places in county sides which is tremendous. Schools cricket is beginning to take off again with the money we get from the ECB's foundation and the appointment across thirty-eight counties of development officers. That is having an effect, there is no doubt about that. We're moving in the right direction.'

Those of us who have been watching England play most of their recent Test cricket would beg leave to differ.

The plain and indisputable fact is that after all the words and plans and hopes and expectations and fiddling around of the last few years, absolutely nothing has happened to halt the decline in the standard and the performances of the England side. The stage has been reached where something dramatic has to be done in order, first, to keep faith with the public and to show them that the game's authorities are deeply concerned with the problems and are doing their best to put them right. Secondly we must show the television companies, the sponsors and the advertisers that everyone is doing their best to try and produce a winning England side and to make them feel that their money is not being wasted, and that their support is important. The players themselves need the adrenalin that a new plot will give them as they try to fulfil their part of the bargain. Cricket needs a lift. The stage has been reached where shock tactics are essential if the decline is to be checked. Much mediocre county cricket will continue to be played by too many mediocre cricketers. H.H. Munro (Saki) wrote a short story called 'The Unrest Cure'. It is an unrest cure that England's domestic cricket so badly needs. If drastic measures are not taken, there may be a great many like me, not yet in the final stages of decay, who will never again see England regain the Ashes – which is a sobering thought.

There are so many arguments. Has the stage been reached whereby a continuation of the County Championship in its present form can only be counterproductive to the production of a successful England side? There are too many teams and therefore too many indifferent cricketers. To raise standards, a concentration of excellence in the top sides is essential. Will this irrevocably change the character of county cricket? Would this mean the establishment of a virtual transfer market, with the best young players in the second division going to the sides in Division One? Would this make it harder still for these sides to get out of Division Two? Would the England selectors not look beyond Division One for their Test players? Would a county providing three or four Test players on a regular basis not be handicapped in a fight for promotion or relegation? Would a two-tier system lessen the chances for young players, because counties would stand by their seasoned staff when it came to the important games, which would be more frequent with relegation and promotion? Would a long period in Division Two have a bad effect on membership and sponsorship and, ultimately, on financial viability? Yes, probably, is the answer to all these questions.

Those involved have to decide if they are more concerned with going along as they are and to hell with the standards and we finally drop all ideas of pretending to be a major power in the cricket world. Or do we all roll up our sleeves and fight for the greater good of the England side in the hope that the compensations which will flow from it will more than offset the potential difficulties? The reward of a successful Test side would soon be reflected in television and sponsorship deals and would be passed on in the annual handout. We must not forget, either, what an Ashes victory over Australia does for the morale of English cricket. If England could somehow manage to beat Australia in 1998/99, it would change everything. Unfortunately they are unlikely to, even in spite of the last two heartwarming Tests against South Africa, and so everything must be done to make sure we do not have to wait too long for that elusive victory. England's cricket still needs a kick-start and needs it quick, as the Test match against Sri Lanka showed.

When we left blowers.co.uk in chapter seven, I was facing my approaching indoctrination on the website with considerable trepidation. We were scheduled to go online at midday, the day before the First Test, and we made it but about five hours late. The trouble was a lead which was about two and three quarters times as difficult to find as the Cullinan Diamond but which would allow me to transmit through my mobile telephone. We tracked one down eventually and I left for Chaddesley Corbett and the Brockencote Hall Hotel with a brand spanking new state-of-the-art lap-top which, at that moment, I thought had about as much potential as a hand grenade. I had been given endless lessons in how to perform the simplest of operations such as writing a story and then dispatching it to goodness knows where, and, lo and behold, it was suddenly there on the screen. Miraculous. I had made

Omar and Tony, our providers, who had tried to teach me, write everything down in the simplest terms. The trouble is that it would all go along swimmingly and then, without knowing it, I would touch something and I'd have a page on the screen in front of me which I had never seen before. Blind panic would set in and I knew I would never see the story I was reading through in my life again. There were other times, too, when I pressed the right button and the wrong thing happened. Now, I didn't consider that to be fair. Thank heavens for Omar and Tony who were on the end of the telephone line, making the Rock of Gibraltar look a mere card house.

Johnny Sachs and Anthony Blackburn, who have the misfortune to be my agents and try and keep me on the straight and narrow as far as business is concerned, did a fantastic job getting publicity for blowers.co.uk and we rather surprised ourselves with the number of hits we managed to get during this First Test. Although I am not normally one for jargon, I was getting the hang of the computerese but I wasn't sure whether I should feel proud or ashamed. As Aggers spends his entire life talking about the Lord's website for which he works, I slipped in the odd mention of blowers.co.uk on TMS and my keen ear did not detect any noticeable quickening of the producer's footsteps behind me. Aggers is, by now, an old hand at it and is always in masterly control of his computer as he whisks e-mails or whatever to his huge and avid band of admirers at all points of the compass. Heath Robinson would have recognised an old friend if he had seen me trying to coax my Compaq into action. Anyway, we were up and running on a 365-day-a-year basis. I bash out a piece about each day's county cricket as well as the Tests, so I am up and running at about half past six in the morning. Lie-ins are a thing of the past as I go all cyberspace for two hours before breakfast each day. What a business it has been. The longer I stuck to it, though, the less abjectly stupid I became, even if that's not saying much. The Lord's and Old Trafford Tests did not produce much more than minor disturbances, although on one occasion it was a pretty close run thing. Anyone who looks at the website will have no idea of the emotional burn-out and the frequent near-suicides the whole process produced.

The weather was impossible. Rains, winds and cold ruled the stage and one was left to dream about those lovely hot days lying in the long grass eating strawberries and, depending on your cholesterol, cream, as well as washing them down with something deliciously fizzy. Ascot and Wimbledon made a sandwich of the Lord's Test Match as usual. A couple of days before Lord's, I drove down late in the afternoon to Eton, where I spent an hour walking around Agar's Plough and Upper Club, which is one of the prettiest of all grounds. I walked thoughtfully across the Datchet Lane which is now called something much more unromantic, and dawdled pensively on the Finch Hatton bridge where, early in June 1957, I had bicycled furiously across talking to Edward Scott over my shoulder and slap bang into a bus which was being propelled at an impressive pace towards the Slough Road. I woke up several weeks later in the King Edward VII Hospital in Windsor and Edward Lane Fox took over the captaincy, although it was the weather rather than the Harrovians which overcame his tactical shrewdness in the all-important contest at Lord's early in July.

I stayed that night at Jourdelays with Peter and Sue Thackeray, who gave a splendid dinner party and then, at something like nine o'clock in the morning, I had to speak to what was left of the School Assembly in the Farrer Theatre. School Certificate and various other activities had taken a considerable toll, although I suppose they may have been sensible enough to boycott the occasion in their hundreds. I told them about the time I was third victim of Rex Neame's hat-trick in the 1955 Eton and Harrow match and they all laughed, at me I suspect, rather than with me. It was all very jolly and after about twelve minutes, they all trooped off to get on with the serious side of education and I was left to drive past the dreaded Finch Hatton Bridge on my way to the M4 and London.

Another special cricketing occasion that week had been the exceptional lunch which I am thrilled to hear is becoming an annual event – as long as I can catch the selectors' eye – given by Bas Kardol in a private room at the charming Stafford Hotel just off St James's. Bas is a Dutchman with South African connections, which is why his aide-de-camp on this occasion is the redoubtable Dick Foxton. Dick lives in Johannesberg and is the most hospitable of men and with him, rather like the Commander, you never know what's going to turn up next. Originally, Bas asked Dick to arrange a lunch at the Stafford in June 1997 just before the Lord's Test to celebrate his, Bas's, recent election to the Marylebone Cricket Club. The lunch had been repeated this year and was great fun and a huge success. Cricketing luminaries such as Godfrey Evans, Barry Richards and Trevor Bailey clocked in, Bill Deedes, the most sprightly octogenarian since Jim Swanton reached ninety, was there in between his non-stop journeys to South Africa, Angola and everywhere else in that region about which he keeps us informed in the *Daily Telegraph*, and so was Michael Mellhuish, a former wicket-keeper and past president of MCC who was disgracefully late and took his seat muttering something inaudible about the traffic. David Hallett, the President of Richmond Rugby Club, was there and so was Dick Foxton himself, in his usual unstoppable form. There were about a dozen others whom I have not mentioned because I have forgotten their names and we all took full advantage of Bas's wonderful hospitality. We

235

drank masses of delicious South African wine, both red and white, and it was late in the afternoon when I left, shooing Godfrey Evans off in the direction of some casino whose profits he was determined to swell.

These diversions help to make an English summer what it is. By now, London had the added advantage of the presence of the Commander, who had left Karachi for his annual visitation, and in order to join Mrs The Commander (Shano) who had been in residence for some while. He was in his best form, and his mobile telephone was busier than ever and his gossip well up to scratch. We all ate together several times between his journeys to Chiswick to help keep TWI's cricketing wheels well oiled. The Commander was to have come up to the Third Test Match at Old Trafford in order to appear at one of Wasim Akram's benefit functions, but there was a last-minute hitch. Soon after that, he flew off to Paris for the semi-finals and final of the World Cup and returned more a boulevardier than a centre forward. No sooner had he arrived than he was off for the night to Dubai and Sharjah in pursuit of television rights – and of course, caviar from the Dubai Duty Free. I have never known anyone who, by his mere presence, is able to give everyone such a lift.

The other piece of news was that Geoffrey Boycott – he and the Commander are very close – was back in harness with BBC television for the Old Trafford Test. Before that he had been conspicuous by his absence, having been dropped by the BBC after his troubles with a girlfriend in France which had ended with him being convicted and sentenced in his absence. Apparently he has asked for a retrial, which is his right, and the French authorities agreed, at which point the previous conviction was dropped. The BBC had, one gathered, not been prepared to use him while that conviction stood and now that Boycott's lawyers revealed that it no longer did, the Greatest Living Yorkshireman was once again in all our ears.

The retrial is said to be planned for the late autumn in 1998 which is outside the parameters of this book. Whatever else happens, it will be one of the media occasions of the decade, if not the century. If it goes wrong, I suppose he could end up in the Bastille but, if he does, I expect he'll sort out the room service there too.

I was as spellbound as anyone when Tim Henman made it to the semi-finals of Wimbledon and then perished at the hand of his great friend, Pete Sampras. I thought, for the first time, this year, that he looked as if he really could win it some day. The World Cup in France was an all-pervading, all-consuming event and we soccerphobes had to put up with wall-to-wall coverage in everything short of the *Tablet* and the *Church Times*. Gazza's dismissal before it all began made me realise that in the full scheme of things, Glenn Hoddle's place was somewhere between the Duke of Wellington and Winston Churchill. However, even I was moved to cheering on the night that England lost to Argentina, on penalties too, forsooth. Michael Owen's goal was only rivalled by the seventeen-year-old Justin Rose, when he holed a chip from forty-five yards at the eighteenth on the last day of the Open at Birkdale, to finish equal fourth as an amateur. Of such stuff are sporting heroes made and maybe when England's selectors, who can so often be a byword in stuffiness, give Ben Hollioake or Andrew Flintoff a real chance, cricket will be able to throw up a young hero of its own. That is what the game is crying out for as much as anything: a role model for the kids. David Beckham's free-kick against Colombia was another such but, in the quarter-final, his petulant kick relegated him to the doghouse and England to an early bath and a trip home. There was Adams, too, who played in such a way in that second half as to suggest that he might have won the First World War, let alone the Falklands, all on his own. It was inspirational. England's footballers, Henman and Rose have one thing in common: they all lost, and magnificent though their defeats may have been, they still lost. So too did England's cricketers at Lord's, but with a total lack of magnificence they showed open dissent as umpiring decisions went against them and later claimed, in unashamed justification, that it was only disappointment. It is so important now that match referees and umpires, in all that they do, must not only be stricter, they must also not be afraid of suspending players. If Stewart and the others – Ramprakash was another who was naughty – knew there was every chance they would not be playing in the next Test Match, it would put a stop to this tiresome dissent at once.

The saddest and most reprehensible sporting story of the summer was, I thought, the report that after Argentina had beaten England in the penalty shootout, they sank to the level where they openly mocked the England players afterwards. It's bad enough to lose such an important match on a penalty shootout without having to suffer the hideous behaviour of appalling winners. I suppose, when you think about it, it may go back to the Falklands. On another note, I enjoyed Jimmy Hill's farewell as a BBC television pundit and I shall miss him. He always has his point of view and sticks to it in the teeth of gale-like opposition. His chair is likely to remain empty long after it has again been filled.

There must be a better way than a penalty shootout, even if it is only a longer period of extra time. Of course it's high drama for television, but when all the years and months of preparation come down to this, it is a pity. The Benson & Hedges final at Lord's got to within reach of the cricket equivalent which is a bowlout whereby five people from each side bowl at an unguarded set of stumps and the winner is the side which hits them the most. That would have been equally preposterous. As it was, after brilliant batting on the Saturday by Paul Prichard and Nasser Hussain, Leicestershire made no sort of a fist of it when play restarted in the middle of Sunday. Essex won by 192 runs, which was the biggest margin ever in this, the final Benson & Hedges competition. To think that after all of this we were only halfway through the summer, it really made one feel that the peace and quiet of the ladies' croquet tournament at Budleigh Salterton couldn't come a moment too soon. There was even a problem at the Henley Regatta. Matthew Pinsent, the Olympic Gold Medallist, had the temerity to punch the air a couple of times as his coxless four passed the finishing line in first place. He was severely reprimanded by the stewards for what they described as 'childish behaviour'. But, generously, they said they would take it no further. Those stewards had a bit of luck that John McEnroe did not go to a rowing school.

I did not see as much county cricket as I usually do in June and July, what with the Test Matches and the rain and a topsy-turvy fixture list that looked as if it may have been compiled by those old chums, Duckworth and Lewis. I was lucky enough to spend three days at Arundel watching the South Africans play Sussex and although one day was lost to rain, it is such a beautiful setting in the South Downs that, provided one's umbrella is to hand, it is still hugely enjoyable. The game itself was of little account and probably the most sig-nificant cricket took place in the lunch intervals on the first and last days, when Allan Donald and Shaun Pollock, who had both got it so wrong in the First Test, had a good work out under close supervision. They did not get it wrong at Lord's.

My own memories of Arundel go back to the late fifties when I played each year for the Eton Ramblers against the late Duke of Norfolk's Eleven. We did not start until midday because the ducal party were doing their stuff in church before that. The Duke himself always liked to play and although he batted at number ten, he was probably overplaced; he also liked to get off the mark, which was not always easy to arrange. His arrival at the crease was rather a moment. He would then have been in his early fifties and, wearing an I Zingari waistcoat, he would take his time to descend the steps down the bank from the pavilion and then advance to the middle in stately manner, in what P.G. Wodehouse, writing of Beech carrying a heavy-laden tea tray across the lawn at Blandings, described as a procession of one. I think we usually lost to His Grace's side, which included a mixture of friends who, like the Duke, were on the rotund side as they galloped through the years. There was Arthur Collins, who kept wicket and may have been the ducal solicitor, whom Brian Johnston had, at an earlier time, nicknamed 'old pick and choose' (spelt whichever way). Then there were a number of goodish young players and, last but not least, the redoubtable Robin Marlar, who was the Duke's librarian. He had just retired as Sussex's captain and all those martlets across his chest, on his sweater, frightened the daylights out of us. George Cox, the old Sussex batsman, is once reputed to have said, when discussing Sussex captains, 'We followed Robin Marlar out of curiosity.'

The weekend of the South African game, the Festival of Speed was being held at Goodwood and there was not an hotel for miles around and so I had to stay at the Chequers in Slaugham, about forty minutes away. The browsing and sluicing was not to be sniffed at and it was a lovely drive to Arundel starting on the back road to Horsham where, on the first day, I only narrowly managed to avoid running over a hedgehog.

My next really enjoyable county occasion was on the delightful ground in North London at Southgate which had a week or two earlier seen the return of first-class cricket after an absence of 139 years, when Middlesex played Essex. Now, in the second round of the NatWest Trophy, they were playing Durham. Durham made 240 for 8 in their sixty overs and, after thirty-seven overs, Middlesex were 129 for 7 when Keith

Dutch and Alistair Fraser, younger brother of Gus, joined forces. In seven and a half overs they put on 49 with increasingly daring strokeplay and after Fraser had been yorked, Richard Johnson, who is no mean batsman, took over and saw Middlesex home by two wickets making 45 from twenty-seven balls. He and Dutch put on 66 in seven overs and Middlesex won with eight balls to spare. This was about as good as it gets and there was a distinct similarity between Durham's performance now and England's when victory eluded them in that first Test in Trinidad back in February – and in a few subsequent ones since. Durham thought they had it won and let up and when runs suddenly began to come, they found they could not get it back and the bowlers folded completely under the pressure. It was remarkable to be in North London, scarcely a mile from the North Circular, and yet to be on a tree-lined ground from which the church was the only visible building. The lunch given to the press is unlikely to be bettered at a county match all season. Smoked salmon and large prawns started us off and was followed by delicious red roast beef and a glass of red, appropriately enough, to go with it. I hope Middlesex play there more often.

As I mentioned earlier, the day before I travelled to Southgate, I spent a spectacular day at Wormsley watching Sir Paul Getty's Eleven and the Flamingos. From the moment you enter the long drive, which is not much more than a good three iron from the M40, you are in the presence of something quite exceptional. Already, the scenery is formidable, with the drive winding between trees and paddocks further down into the gentle valley and every so often a discreet sign saying, 'To the Cricket Ground', has been placed at a junction to make sure you don't go the wrong way. Away across the field to the right, the rather squat yellow hall nestles into the trees behind it below the line of hills, impressive, solid and charming. After the slight rise away from the bottom of the valley, the road bends round to the left and there, on your left and below you, is the cricket ground delicately carved out of the floor of the valley. It is simply breathtaking. The surplus earth was used to make sweeping banks on which spectators watch and the pavilion and the lunch tents stand. A little further on you turn into the grassy car park. There is so much room, and you can almost feel the view relaxing you as you gaze across the valley. It is a setting which on its own encapsulates the very timelessness of cricket. The ground is mown in those lovely swathes which are such a feature of Lord's and on the far side is a small, perfectly formed scoreboard with a thatched roof. In *Gulliver's Travels*, it could have been a royal palace. Behind the scoreboard, the fields, amply supplied with cattle, sweep away to the hills which start with grassy slopes but give way to trees well before reaching the top.

Sadly, there are ugly gaps where the gales in the late eighties have left their mark. But now the empty spaces have been filled with newly planted saplings. My host said that he probably would not see the benefit of them himself, but at least he has the satisfaction of knowing that they are there and that someone will. Meanwhile, the game was being played, the unobtrusive centre of a memorable landscape.

The Getty Eleven were a hundred and plenty for the loss of Derek Randall's wicket. The pitch at Wormsley matches the surroundings and the day is only hard labour for the bowlers but, in the circumstances, even they can grin and bear it. When I left the Flamingos were 175 for 1 and heading for victory, and Sir Paul's bowlers could have been forgiven for thinking that Dante had prepared the pitch. Alas, it was time to go and nothing could bring me back to earth quicker than the road-widening scheme on the M40. I heard later that the Getty bowlers had collected themselves and managed a draw.

One evening the following week, I drove to Woburn to speak

after dinner to a group of 'high-powered businessmen' for 'a tight twenty minutes'. We all met at the Bedford Arms. The people I was to speak to were from Dresdner Kleinwort Benson, the merchant bank. Dresdner had recently taken over Kleinwort Benson who had themselves begun life as Kleinworts, on the one hand, and Robert Benson Lonsdale, on the other. On a Monday morning in early October 1959, in a three-piece suit, a stiff collar, probably a bowler hat and certainly a rolled umbrella, I had arrived at Aldermanbury House in Aldermanbury Square to start life as a trainee merchant banker with Robert Benson Lonsdale, King's College, Cambridge having decided after two years that I was too hot to hold. My career in the city was not a success and the bank and I became deeply suspicious of one another. I did not enjoy it, apart from the fact that I was simply hopeless at everything I was asked to do. In 1961, Kleinworts and Robert Benson Lonsdale got together and now my duties took me on a daily basis to Fenchurch Street which I fear I found even more disagreeable.

It was in early June 1962 that *The Times* asked me to cover a cricket match between Kent and Somerset on the charming old Bat and Ball Ground at Gravesend. I rang up Kleinworts and said I was ill, and I think the subeditor wasn't looking or must himself have been feeling ill because the paper used just about every word I had written on both days at Gravesend. I was dreadfully nervous and did not sleep a wink before rushing to a paper shop in nearby Rochester where I stayed the night. I asked for *The Times* but they told me they had sold it but the shop across the street was more amply supplied. I don't remember ever feeling so happy as when I saw they had used all that I had dictated. It was much better than the City.

I was so emboldened by my success that the following Sunday I rang up *The Times* and asked them if they had any more cricket for me. They, or rather a gentleman called Laurie

Wayman who was the most brilliant copytaker and how could
I ever forget his name, asked me if I would be able to watch
Hampshire play Warwickshire for two days at Portsmouth. I
jumped at it and the following day, which was Monday, I rang
up the General Manager of Kleinwort Benson, whose name
was Mr Payne, and told him I had left. He asked me what I
meant and I said that it meant that I would not be coming in
again. There was a long pause and he said something about it
being a trifle irregular but he made no effort to persuade me
to change my mind, which I thought significant. It is amazing what the confidence of my first two press passes did for
me.

Back at Woburn, we had a delicious dinner in the Sculpture
Gallery and I told them a few of the old Test Match Special
stories which they were polite enough to pretend they had not
heard before and then I drove back to London. Quite by
chance it had been one of those evenings which had brought
back a little of my past I do not bring up on the screen all that
often.

CHAPTER TEN

Personal Heroes

Not only has Mark Ramprakash been one of the outstanding batsmen in county cricket for a number of years, but he also possesses one of the best techniques in the contemporary game. It was inconceivable that he should not score a great many runs for England. He was first given a chance against Viv Richards's formidable West Indies side in England in 1991 and in nine innings he made 210 runs with a highest score of 29 and a lowest score of 13. In every innings he played, he did the hard work and played himself in. He looked a Test cricketer but could not stay to prove it. He was not a success but he was not a failure either. The following year against Pakistan, he played in three Tests and failed. His next chance came on the tour to the West Indies in 1993/94, where he managed to score seventy-eight runs in seven innings and on it went. All the time he was a heavy run-scorer for Middlesex and every now and then the selectors brought him back into the England side, but it did not work. There was something wrong in his mind for he had all the technical requirements to make a good fist of it. He was a fiery young man with a fierce temper and at the top level he was continually failed by his temperament. After an extraordinary run of centuries for Middlesex at the end of the season, Ramprakash was picked for the tour of South Africa in 1995/96, where he played and failed in the first two Test Matches and was then publicly cast into outer darkness by the Manager and general panjandram, Mr Raymond Illingworth, who muttered things like, 'over my dead body' and 'never again'. He felt he had been let down by Ramprakash, perhaps prematurely, and Illingworth was to young cricketers who did not fulfil his requirements, much as King Herod had been to the business of procreation. Illingworth had been a wonderful captain and a fine player but it did not work for him as a manager, probably for the simple reason that his nature made him want to captain the side rather than to manage it. The result was that Ramprakash, who was little more than a piece of excess baggage for the remainder of the tour of South Africa, returned to county cricket the following summer a much chastened and disillusioned chap.

To his eternal credit, he did what he has always done and stuck at it. The selectors did not take any notice of him in 1996 but the following year he again scored prodigiously in county cricket. After all else had failed and the Ashes had been kept by Australia, the selectors again allowed themselves to be persuaded by his Middlesex form in time for the Sixth Test Match against Australia at the Oval. All selectors will have played with and against Ramprakash and, of course, one of them was Mike Gatting whom he had succeeded as captain of Middlesex only a few weeks before. After being out for 4 in the first innings, he made 48 in the second, putting on 79 with Graham Thorpe for the fifth wicket and it was these runs which made it possible for England to win the match when Australia, who were admittedly a touch carefree, were bowled out for 104 in their second innings. He had batted well, even if he had been out trying to hit Shane Warne into oblivion.

A few days later, Ramprakash was picked for the tour of the West Indies and when he had been decided upon, David Graveney, the Chairman, made it clear that Ramprakash was going to the West Indies as the man in possession. He was met with a meaningful blank look from across the table by the captain. Ramprakash himself must have climbed aboard the aeroplane for Antigua early in January hoping that he would at least be starting off in the Test side on the back of that innings at the Oval – that is, if he did not appreciate the workings of the Lancashire mind. I strongly suspect that the decision had already been taken by those who were known as the Manchester Mafia and will undoubtedly have included the captain and coach, Atherton and Lloyd, that the number three spot in the batting order would be filled, to begin with at any rate, by John Crawley. I have no objection whatever to captain's perks when the last place in a side is causing problems. The captain knows who he can rely on and will know more about his county colleagues than anyone else round the table. Graham Gooch often fell back on a fellow Essex player while Mike Gatting and Mike Brearley between them had almost all the Middlesex players capped at one time or another. But to bring in a batsman like Crawley now, when the place has been indisputably earned by another, such as Ramprakash, was favouritism.

I daresay, Atherton and Lloyd were the only two in the West Indies who could have convinced themselves that it was such a close run thing between Ramprakash and Crawley, so that hometown views should be allowed to win the day. It was a bad decision and one which might just, in the light of subsequent events, have cost England victory in the first of the Port of Spain Tests when the series, as well as the match, was effectively lost. Crawley, for all his talent at county level, is flawed both in terms of technique and temperament at Test level. Ramprakash, hardly surprisingly, was a good deal less than chuffed when he realised what was going on for it meant that he was little more than a passenger for almost the first half of the tour. The ECB had decided, in their infinite wisdom, that two practice matches before the First Test would be anough and Atherton and Lloyd had decided they would be used to bring the Test side into form. Ramprakash, Robert Croft, Chris Silverwood, Ashley Cowan and Mark Butcher were the five unlucky ones. Ramprakash knew that he had to sit on his hands and wait and be ready to take his chance when it came, but with his temperament it was not going to be easy for him. In retrospect, he may have been glad he did not have to sample the delights of the Sabina Park switchback in the First Test. He will have been highly frustrated by his inevitable omission in Port of Spain and will have been sure he would have made a contribution which would have left the West Indies to make more than 282 in the final innings of the first of those two tests.

An extraordinary incident occurred during the first part of the long Trinidad leg of the tour. Early one evening, a group of journalists were having a glass of beer at the bar in the lobby of the Hilton when Ramprakash suddenly came up and tried to buy a round of drinks. This was unusual, not because he is mean, but because he is not a bar person. The journalists had all just got new drinks and thanked him but declined the offer and one could see from the way Ramprakash walked away that he had something on his mind. He went over to an armchair by the Guest Relations Desk and sat down. Something was obviously wrong. Mike Selvey, who was at the bar, spotted this and went over and sat with Ramprakash who he found was seething. After training with the team that day and going through all the exercises and activities planned by the physical fitness expert who was a full-time member of the party – yes, another – Ramprakash embarked upon some exercises of his own. For some reason, this upset the physical fitness expert, who remonstrated strongly with Ramprakash, and they had quite a run-in. Ramprakash was beside himself sitting in the lobby and was full of all the crazy thoughts that go through people's minds on occasions like these and may even have been considering packing it all in and going home. Selvey did his best to calm him and then had a word with his former Middlesex colleague, John Emburey, who was the bowling coach with the party, and told him he had an unhappy bunny on his hands. Emburey talked to Ramprakash and the heat was taken out of what had been another illustration of heavy-handed central control by the management which, like a creeping smog, stifles all forms of individual expression. My sympathies were entirely with Ramprakash and I was not the only one left gasping at the insensitive way in which he had been treated.

As if this was not bad enough, the night before the second of the Port of Spain Test Matches began, Adam Hollioake was ruled out of the game because of a back problem. The selectors decided that Ramprakash was the man to take his place and so he will have gone to bed happy that night. The next morning he woke up with flu and had no alternative but to pull out. Butcher took his place and played two most important innings. Although he did not get out of the twenties on either occasion, in the second he provided invaluable substance to a side whose knees shook collectively as they approached victory. Butcher stayed until the match was won and Ramprakash must have thought that he would never now get a chance.

One can only imagine how he was feeling when the party arrived in Georgetown for the Guyana leg of the tour. It will not have done much for him to discover that he was at least getting a game against Guyana before the Fourth Test Match.

This was played on a pleasant-enough looking ground called Everest, which was just across the road from the sea, and the permanent stiff breeze, and that is being charitable, made bowling both a problem and a lottery. For three days most of it was done by the spinners on a turning pitch, which was less than ideal practice for the forthcoming battle against Curtly Ambrose and Courtney Walsh. Robert Croft, whose fortunes had been scarcely better than Ramprakash's, now spun out Guyana, a side depleted by the absence of their captain. Carl Hooper's decision to remain in Port of Spain where he had set up home, with his Australian girlfriend, had not been communicated to the Guyanese selectors and Shivnarine Chanderpaul had taken over at the last moment. By then, Ramprakash must almost have forgotten what it was like to walk out onto a cricket ground with a bat in his hand, but he now had his chance. He had not made more than half a dozen when the entire Guyanese side appealed for a catch behind the wicket and the general feeling was that he had hit the cover off the ball. The umpire saw it differently, however, and gave Ramprakash the benefit of the doubt. He went on to make a painstaking sixty or seventy and when the time came he found himself taking Crawley's place in the side for the Fourth Test Match and he was going to bat at number six, with Butcher moving up to three.

For two months, Ramprakash had had a struggle to keep his character and inclinations in check. Now, we were to see the other side of this same character and how splendidly it served both the man himself and his country. He came to the wicket with England in deep trouble in their first innings at 65 for 4 in reply to the West Indies' 352 on a pitch which looked a bit like the road in from the airport, although it did no play quite as badly as its appearance suggested it would. For the last twelve overs of the second day, Ramprakash, looking more in control than anyone else, sheltered behind an impeccable defence, picking up thirteen runs as he went. He could only watch while Thorpe and Russell succumbed to Ramnarine's leg-spin. At 87 for 6, the close of play score, England needed 66 more to save the follow-on and Croft, also a great fighter, was Ramprakash's partner. Ramprakash started things off the next morning with a cracking square cut for four off Bishop, a fellow Trinidadian whom Lara indulged for longer than made sense. While keeping Bishop in the attack, the West Indies captain ignored Ambrose for the entire morning session.

On an awkward pitch, Ramprakash looked a class act. He seemed to have more time than any other Englishman to play his strokes, his footwork was sure and swift and there was a certain panache about it all. A rippling leg glance against Bishop went away for four and when he dropped short, Ramprakash slashed him with a flat bat ferociously past mid-off for four more. His concentration never faltered, not even in the hysterical five-minute hold-up for the dog that crapped at long-on. He and Croft had put on 64 when Croft was caught at first slip cutting at Hooper. Croft was furious with himself and you could see him ticking himself off all the way back to the pavilion. Headley went in the same over and Fraser one run later, at 140, which meant the last pair of Ramprakash and Tufnell had to score 13 more to save the follow-on. While Ramprakash went on, unruffled and in control, Tufnell oozed cheeky defiance. Ambrose was still chewing gum rather moodily at mid-on and third man and Lara made no attempt to catch his attention. In the end, Ramprakash had reached 64 by the end of the innings, and when he walked off the ground, he should have been feeling more at ease than ever before when wearing an England cap. It could hardly have happened on a more appropriate ground for him too, for Ramprakash's father comes from Guyana. I hope there were one or two extremely red faces to greet him in the England dressing room. I would be very surprised if he received any sort of apology for the disgraceful treatment meted out to him at the start of the tour. I daresay there would have been plenty of self-justification instead. In the second innings, Ramprakash made 34 which was also the highest score and confirmed all the excellent impressions he had made in the first. As I watched him, I could not help but wonder how this story would have unfolded if the umpire in the match against Guyana had taken the general view of that catch behind the wicket. That was the piece of luck Ramprakash needed.

When he left Guyana, Ramprakash had made sure of his place in the England side for the rest of the series in the West Indies. What he now had to do was to establish himself as an automatic choice for the foreseeable future. When he was batting in the Fourth Test, there was an authority about him which he had never shown before at this level. Scores of 64 not out and 34 were better than anyone else's but they were not enough to ensure that his name would go down at the top of the list whenever an England side was chosen. He had a lot of ground to make up and he had now to play an innings which put him above most of his contemporaries and left no one in any doubt that at last this remarkable talent had found itself at the highest level of the game. He needed to score a big hundred for England. For some, the first three-figure score in Test cricket is an almost insurmountable obstacle; others take it in their stride. Ramprakash may not have received the kindest treatment during his England career so far, but he had been given plenty of opportunities and had not been able to grasp them. His failures had been consistent. He had more to do, therefore, than a newcomer who comes into the Test side and hits a hundred in his third or fourth Test Match almost without realising it. Ramprakash had now played in more than twenty Test Matches and he will have been as aware as anyone of the importance of consolidating his position with a three-figure score.

After such relative success in Guyana, other players in a similar position might have thought that their work was done and taken their eye off the ball, but not Ramprakash. He did not waste time celebrating a job which was only half done. He arrived in Barbados and set his mind to completing the task. He had an hour's batting practice in the match against Barbados before pulling a long-hop down mid-on's throat. Then, he put his mind round the Test Match. This time, Lara put England in although the pitch looked a beauty. Maybe he felt that after his victory in Georgetown, England would be seriously demoralised and nothing that happened in the first two hours of the match will have made him change his mind. In quick succession, Stewart, Atherton, Hussain and Butcher perished to Walsh, Ambrose and McLean. England's score stood at 53 for 4 when Ramprakash joined Thorpe a few minutes before lunch. A firm push on the off side against Ambrose set him on his way. In Ambrose's next over, Ramprakash pushed forward with firm wrists and the ball flew back in the air just above ankle height to Ambrose, who put his left hand down; the ball seemed to hit the heel and bounced to the ground. At the same score, 55 for 4, the players came in to lunch and Thorpe, who had had treatment for back spasms late in the morning, was not able to continue. The West Indies probably felt Ambrose's dropped catch was unimportant. Ramprakash came out after the interval with Jack Russell, who had been having a dreadful tour, as his partner. I remember feeling sure that there was going to be a depressing inevitability about what was to come.

At least we were able to smile when Russell suddenly pulled Walsh for four and there was a lovely look about Ramprakash's drive to the cover boundary off Hooper. Russell entertained us again, twice in one over, when he drove Bishop off the back foot through the covers and then came forward to drive him past mid-off. Soon afterwards, reality returned when Russell pushed forward to Hooper and was caught by Wallace at forward-short-leg. Thorpe's back spasms had relented enough for him to be able to take Russell's place and Ramprakash gave us something to hope for when he unwound a perfect on drive for four against Ambrose, and on it went. Ramprakash danced to a precise step in that he played text-book cricket. He is a small man and you could feel his concentration as you watched, almost to the point you were afraid to cough for fear of distracting him. You never know about Thorpe. He is such a good player and yet one day a square cut bounces back off the boundary and the next day the wicket-keeper throws it aloft as he claims a catch. Thorpe strides out and wastes no time in getting down to work. He goes about his left-handed business hitting the ball into the gaps, lining the bowler up and deciding how best he can deal with him. His style is not especially romantic but it is mighty effective. Ramprakash, on the other hand, does things with a classical rhythm which certainly quickens the pulse. His strokes are wonderfully satisfying to watch. Sometimes, one finds oneself nodding quietly in agreement as a peerless cover drive races away past cover-point's left hand. Like the very best players, he makes you feel that it is so easy. With Thorpe, you admire his strokeplay and sometimes revel in it but you always feel that it is better left to him. These two complemented each other for the rest of that day at Kensington. What started as a mild irritation for Lara became a bore, and then a downright bloody nuisance. The West Indies captain even turned to Chanderpaul's occasional offerings of spin for three overs but nothing deterred, let alone penetrated Ramprakash's or Thorpe's defences and nor were they tempted to do anything silly and get out. To appreciate Thorpe made the enjoyment of Ramprakash all the more complete. At the end of the day, he had faced 215 balls and hit ten excellent fours in his 80 not out.

That evening, no one will have been more aware of the importance of those next twenty runs. There was all the difference in the world between getting out for 98 and 102. In Ramprakash's circumstances those two scores were worlds further apart than a simple matter of four runs. When the Indian prince Duleepsinhji played his first innings for Cambridge University, he was out for 96. His uncle, Ranji, later to become H.H. The Jam Sahib of Nawanager, was sailing across the Atlantic. The next morning in his lodgings, Duleep received a cable from the liner in mid-Atlantic. It read, 'What happened to the other four?' Ramprakash will have been determined that there should be no similar shortfall.

A measured cover drive to the boundary off McLean soon after the start announced that all was well. Ramprakash got into the nineties and even he was unable now to sit on his entire nervous system. His best shots found the fielders, he lost the bowling for a spell and I am not certain that his supporters in the stands were not a good deal more nervous than he was. He reached 94 and then, without any warning, his nerve snapped and his concentration broke. McLean bowled one on a good length but well wide of the off stump and unaccountably Ramprakash unwound and launched himself into a wild, slashing drive and the ball screwed up in the air and, through no plan of his own, fell into untenanted country in the backward point area and rolled on to the boundary. It might have gone anywhere. It could have been the end and Ramprakash knew it. He collected himself, put his head down and this wild stroke behind him. Minutes later, McLean bowled one which was only just short of a length, on or just outside the off stump and, as quick as you could wish, Ramprakash went back on his stumps and drove the ball through the offside field. It bounced back a dozen or more yards after hitting the brick wall at the bottom of the Kensington Stand and Ramprakash had his hundred.

Although Thorpe got out soon afterwards, Ramprakash mentally regrouped and went about putting the second part of his plan into operation. He kept his head down and his bat straight for just over another two and a half hours. He batted carefully as he went about the business of consolidating England's advantage. There was none of the 'I'm all right Jack, I've got my hundred', followed by a couple of crashing fours and then his wicket. He was still in at tea with 153 against his name and he looked drained. He scored only one more afterwards before he drove at McLean without quite getting to the pitch and the bowler held the return catch by his waist. Ramprakash had batted for 530 minutes, he had faced 387 balls and hit twenty fours. The build up and the circumstances of this innings, and its two predecessors in the Georgetown Test, were more than enough to make Mark Ramprakash the hero of my cricketing year.

Although he did not have a successful time of it in the Sixth Test in Antigua, making 14 and 0, he had done more than enough to be sure of a regular place against South Africa in England. In that series, the story did not come quite to the happy ending I had anticipated, but it has not been entirely unhappy, either. His first innings against South Africa, at Edgbaston, was in some ways a confirmation of Barbados. He played some lovely strokes and was keen from the start to hit the ball; in the second he, like all the others, had a slog on the instructions of Alec Stewart, and got out. Somewhere between Edgbaston and the next match at Lord's, it was as if all the old dark doubts had crept up on him in the night. For the remainder of the series he played as if his only thought was the sheer terror of failure. A fine, natural strokemaster suddenly turned into an ongoing commercial for Superglue. Every time he went to the crease, it was in anticipation of the worst rather than in hope of the best, and he seldom outscored the overs he faced. It was not that he failed to perform a worthy service for England, and indeed his 67 not out in the Fourth Test at Trent Bridge played a considerable part in England's victory. We were left to admire the Guyana introvert rather than to enjoy the cautious extrovert in Barbados.

More disappointing than that, he failed lamentably at Lord's to control the rough side of his temperament. After batting almost twenty-two overs for twelve, he was opened up by a lifter from Donald that the South Africans thought had flicked the inside edge on the way through to Boucher. Umpire Darell Hair, from Australia, gave him out and it was an age before Ramprakash began to embark upon the journey to the pavilion. He was at the Nursery end, and had to walk past Hair on his way out. As he passed, he said something to the umpire who later reported him. Apparently his words were something like, 'What a way to help a man's career, Darell', and I daresay they were spoken with emphasis. This incident was no help to Ramprakash and it was the most stupid thing he could have done. No one knows better than the players that umpires don't change their minds and what good could possibly have come from this petulant behaviour? He was unable to control himself and it earned him an unfortunate interview with Javed Burki, the match referee. He was fined £800 and given a suspended ban for one match. News of his sentence was not given to him until just before his second innings when he was promptly yorked for a duck and there was an element of rough justice in that.

In the first innings of the Third Test at Old Trafford, he was given out, caught behind, sweeping at left-arm spinner Paul Adams and the replays showed that the ball had come off his arm. He had batted with composure for two hours while making 30. He played a noble part in helping England to save the game on that agonising last day when he batted for 46.3 overs for 34 before he was lbw to one which Donald cut back sharply into him and which hit him just outside the line of the off stump. Three bad decisions in four innings is tough going, but some players seem to make their own luck. Then came Trent Bridge, and a 67 not out which took 65 overs but allowed England to whittle away at South Africa's lead until it was down to 38. It was a fine innings but if circumstances had demanded, could he have played in any other way? I hoped that this innings might have caused him to rethink his approach as he had done so refreshingly after the Guyana Test. It was not to be and at Headingly he was still trapped in that wretched cage made by the dark suspicions of his own mind.

Twenty-two overs of immaculate defence produced twenty-one runs in the first innings and then he played a furious square cut at Donald without much footwork and was rather off balance as a result. He felt the ball hit the bottom edge of his bat and then heard the triumphant appeal for a catch behind. That was enough for him and, in his fury with himself, he stalked off without waiting for the umpire. If he had waited, it might have been so very different as he will have discovered for himself when he reached the dressing room. The cameras showed that the ball had bounced before it was scooped up by the diving Boucher. But why did the umpire, Peter Willey, not intervene? He was in the best position to see what had happened and could have stopped Ramprakash and signalled for the third umpire to have his say. In the second innings, Ramprakash may have been lucky to survive an appeal for a catch behind down the leg side when he tried to glance his very first ball. He stayed on to accrue twenty-five runs from twenty-seven overs which were pretty important considering that England won by only 23. In nine rather curious innings, Ramprakash had amassed 249 runs in not far short of 249 overs for an average of 31.12. There is nothing too much wrong with that although his God-given talent should have been outraged that it had to settle for anything less than 51.12. The only conclusion is that Ramprakash's complex character is still not being true to his vast reservoir of talent but it should at least have got him on the tour to Australia, another country where he needs to make up lost ground. This story is not yet over and, in the meantime, I can still think happily back to that heroic 154 in Barbados and what his character did for his batting talent on those two days. Maybe he too, should look back on that innings more often than he does.

Pat Symcox did not play Test cricket until he was thirty-three. He was the only off-spinner in South Africa likely to be serviceable at this level and having stuck his foot in the door, he has made certain that it has not been pushed out. At the age of 38, he came to England with Hansie Cronje's side in 1998, although the spinner's berth in the side was filled in four of the five Tests by the unorthodox left-armer, Paul Adams. In the Fifth Test at Headingley, the selectors decided that a spinner was an unaffordable luxury although, with hindsight, Cronje would have given a lot to have had Symcox's unwavering determination with him in the field, not to mention his considerable batting ability, especially when things got really tight at the end. So, it looks as if Symcox will finish his career with the unlikely record of having made a hundred in his last Test Match. At the Wanderers in Johannesburg, he made 108 in the First Test against Pakistan in February 1998 and became only the third number ten in the entire history of Test cricket to have made a hundred. Symcox had started life as a batsman and had retained some of his interest in the art.

My reason for including him in my list of personal heroes for this year's cricket was not so much his hundred, which I did not see, but his exploits with the bat in Pakistan during South Africa's short tour there in October 1997. It was Symcox's batting which won South Africa a remarkable victory in Faisalabad. There is something rather old fashioned about Symcox's appearance which is both comforting and reassuring. When you look him in the face you know what you are going to get for there are no chameleon-like qualities in South Africa's off-spinner. He plays the game hard and is as dedicated as anyone in the side to the pursuit of victory. He is tall and thickset with tidily kept dark hair which may be thinning a fraction. If you are batting against him, he won't smile at you because he wants to get you out so badly. In the First Test in Pakistan at Rawalpindi, he was angry that Mahammad Wasim was not given out, caught off bat and pad at short leg. Soon afterwards, Wasim drove Symcox to Shaun Pollock at mid-wicket and Symcox was unable to resist the temptation to point fiercely in the direction of the pavilion in case Wasim had forgotten where to go. It was a gesture which earned him a meeting with and a rebuke from the match referee Ranjan Madugalle who, quite rightly, disapproved of such behaviour. There was no chatter to accompany the gesture and it had not been that dramatic or extravagant – he was just letting the batsman know what he thought. Symcox was telling Wasim that he had had enough of him and I am sure that he will have agreed with Madugalle that it was an unwise gesture. Symcox would be a good man to have beside you should the enemy get above themselves.

South Africa won the toss at Faisalabad and Hansie Cronje decided to bat. The pitch allowed the seamers some help early on and then Mushtaq Ahmed stepped in with his leg-breaks and googlies, and at lunch South Africa were in all sorts of trouble at 98 for 7. Symcox marched out after lunch with Gary Kirsten, who had held firm during the morning. Symcox brings to the wicket with him a military bearing which suggests that he is not going to put up with any nonsense. He strides out eager for the battle to be joined and on another day his bat could easily become a hunter's rifle. He takes guard as if he means business and looks down the pitch at the bowler as if to say, 'Now, what have we got here?' He had a quiet look at Mushtaq and played a couple of exploratory drives. This was his way of clearing his throat and preparing for action. When Mushtaq ran in again, all twirling arms and legs, Symcox opened his shoulders and the ball disappeared one bounce over mid-off for four. Mushtaq will have felt that this approach gave him an excellent chance of another wicket. Over came his arm again and with a powerful swing of the bat Symcox deposited the ball far over long-on for six. There were no histrionics from Symcox, there never are provided everyone behaves themselves. He saw himself simply as a foot soldier doing his duty and going about his business. When he had reached 38, he launched a drive against fellow off-spinner Saqlain Mushtaq, who dropped a firmly hit return catch. He then reached his second Test fifty and was looking every inch a specialist batsman. There were no frills, just sensible and composed strokes and when the chance came along, those broad, strong shoulders opened and someone ran back to fetch the ball from the boundary and occasionally from out of the crowd.

When he was 56, there was a most extraordinary incident. He was facing Mushtaq, who bowled him a flipper which scuttled through off the pitch going past the inside edge and on between the middle and the off stumps without removing the bail. The game froze. The players could not believe it and the fielders stood there staring at the stumps, willing the bail to come off. But it looked back and mocked them. The top of the off stump had been pushed a little wider as the ball had gone through and after much discussion and endless slow motion replays, the game continued. The players were clearly bemused, with the splendid exception of Symcox himself, who had been anxious for some time for the game to continue. The bails hadn't come off and he wasn't out and there was no more to it.

By now, Symcox had reached his best-ever score in a Test Match and he celebrated his unusual reprieve by advancing with a massive left foot and driving Mushtaq far over mid-off for six. The 200 arrived and in time the scoreboard showed 222 for 7, known by all cricketers as 'Double Nelson'; the superstitious regard it as a most dangerous moment. When the scoreboard shows 111 or any multiplication thereof, the superstitious like to keep their feet off the ground. The much publicised antics of umpire David Shepherd when the score reaches 111, 222, 333 or whatever, has caused great amusement. The figures 111 mean one arm, one eye and one something else and what that may be I have never had satisfactorily explained to me. Anyway, Double Nelson now did the trick for Pakistan. Symcox faced Wasim Akram and he went onto the back foot, played across the line and was bowled off stump. He turned and departed in the same businesslike manner in which he had arrived. He acknowledged the applause modestly; he was cross with himself for getting out and did not dwell on the fact that he had scored 81 runs. He had batted for just over two hours and had made these runs off 94 balls and had hit ten fours and two sixes while putting on 124 with Kirsten. These are remarkable statistics when you remember the score was 98 for 7 when he first came in. He disappeared into the pavilion looking like a First World War colonel, mildly put out because he had mislaid his moustache.

Pakistan gained a first innings lead of 69 and Symcox was allowed nine overs, none of which were especially memorable, but he was soon back in action with his pads on. In poor light, the South Africans lost two wickets before nightfall on the second day and Symcox now strode enthusiastically to the middle with South Africa perilously placed at 21 for 2. He survived until the end of the day and the next morning clearly relished the chance to play a proper innings. Wasim Akram greeted him with a bouncer and Symcox looked back at the bowler and you could feel the bloody-mindedness welling up in him. 'Right, let battle be joined!' was what Symcox seemed to be saying to Wasim, who pranced in again and got the shock of his life when Symcox came on to the front foot and drove him straight back over his head for four. Again, he played with great composure, defended solidly and put the loose ball away without any fuss, and in his own reserved, unsmiling way, he was enjoying himself. There were not so many big shots in this innings and at lunch South Africa were 79 for 3 and Symcox had been playing the wrist spin of Mushtaq better than anyone. Immediately after lunch, he could resist the temptation no more and he advanced that left foot like a horse in a dressage contest and drove Mushtaq back over his head for six and then drove him over mid-off for the four which took him to his second fifty of the match off 107 balls with seven fours and a six. He was 53 when he drove at Wasim Akram and was dropped by Aamir Sohail low down at first slip and he had scored only two more when his innings ended in the most absurd manner. He went on the back foot to Saqlain Mushtaq and tried to play to leg a ball which turned a long way into him. At the moment it hit his pad, it was possible to see the off, the middle and the inside of the leg stump. It would hardly have hit another set of stumps and yet Mr Mian Aslam, the umpire, had his finger up before the appeal had finished. It was an absurd decision. Whatever Symcox may have felt, once he saw the raised finger, he turned and left for the pavilion with the same brisk walk which had brought him to the crease. No one scored as many as Symcox in the second innings, and Pakistan were left to make 146 to win.

The last had not been seen of Symcox, either. He took over from Shaun Pollock at the Press Box end for the eighteenth over of the innings and in 9.3 tight, economical overs he found plenty of turn and picked up three wickets for eight runs. Wasim Akram swung against the spin and Kirsten held the skier at mid-on. Saqlain pushed forward and was caught off bat and pad at forward short leg and, at the end, Moin Khan swung Symcox away to deep square leg where Donald accepted the catch as if it was the happiest event of his whole life. When Symcox stepped forward to receive the Man of the Match award, there was still not one single hair out of place. He thanked everyone politely as if to say, 'It was nothing' and returned to the dressing room. Symcox is a good, efficient cricketer who goes seriously and modestly about his business and I shall remember his performances at Faisalabad long after more eye-catching contributions have vanished for ever. Symcox is my sort of cricketer.

Jonty Rhodes is another I have saved for the end. I have been guilty in this book of taking him for granted. His eternal brilliance in the field, the joy of watching his every move, the buzz that comes from a player who so obviously enjoys every moment of it, the impossible wizardry in the covers that never fails, have become such a part of the fabric when South Africa are playing, that it all seems old hat. Rhodes hasn't been running for as long as *The Mousetrap*, but undoubtedly familiarity has taken off some of the gloss. During the Lord's Test Match in 1994, I spent one over describing only Rhodes, who was fielding at cover to Allan Donald's bowling, and there was never the slightest chance that I would dry up. I watched Rhodes from the same point of view for one over in the Fifth Test at Headingley in 1998. Donald was again the bowler.

Rhodes was a non-stop blur of action, enthusiasm and a desperate desire always to be involved. Having run most of the way to third man at the end of an over to collect Donald's sweater and cap and taken them to the umpire, he ran off to cover, jumping a couple of times as he turned round to face the batsman. He starts off deep but runs in with the bowler and is only about twenty yards from the bat when the ball is bowled. If it is played out on the off side he is off like a sprinter in pursuit. If the ball has been hit on either side of him, his reactions are astonishingly fast and by the time it is level with him he will already have raced four or five strides towards it and either dives or picks it up and swivels before sending a low, accurate throw to the keeper, from a position lying on the ground if need be. When the batsman plays the ball, he will often think, as happened with Mark Butcher, that it is going far enough away from Rhodes for a safe run to be taken. It is this lightning burst of speed which causes the first doubts in the batsman's mind and makes him instinctively hesitate. By the time his partner has also hesitated, the battle is often lost. If both batsmen had continued with the original run, they might have made it without too much trouble but it is Rhodes's initial speed across the ground which starts the fatal hesitation. The effect is such that Rhodes's very presence prevents the batsmen from taking runs which are safe enough. Add those to the ones he actually saves with brilliant fielding and you will get some idea of his immense value to South Africa.

When the ball is allowed to go through to the wicket-keeper, Rhodes continues running in, almost to the stumps, clapping his hands to make sure the keeper throws the ball to him. He then polishes it furiously, as often as not bending double in order to tighten the seat of his trousers, which seems to be of special assistance to the art of polishing a cricket ball. Then, he straightens up before throwing it on to, say, mid-off, after which he gambols back to his chosen spot in the covers and the process starts all over again.

If the next ball is played to leg, he veers away to his left to make sure he is backing up in case mid-wicket beats Mark Boucher with a wayward throw. When it thuds back into the gloves, he again claps his hands at the keeper. He wants the ball and when he gets it, the polishing starts all over again. The next ball may be driven past him but he will be sprinting after it, covering the ground at a bewildering pace and then there is a blur as he throws himself at the ball, flicking it back just before he rolls on over the boundary. He is on his feet almost in mid-roll and the ball thumps back into the keeper's gloves. The crowd roars its approval, his colleagues clap, Rhodes shrugs his shoulders and jog-trots back to cover.

It is brilliant cricket, great entertainment and grand theatre. This is what we have from Jonty Rhodes – all the time – and we grow blasé and, after a while, do not notice it. I once watched the juggler at Bertram Mills Circus with the same spellbound fascination. When I got home, I picked up three balls and tried to do it. It was hopeless, and yet he had made it look so easy. It's the same with Jonty Rhodes. Sometimes I think I am going to be out of breath just from watching him.

In England in 1998, there was something else for us to enjoy. His batting has always been his problem. He is a certainty for the South African one-day side but he had become interchangeable in the Test side for he had not made enough runs. He knew this and he desperately wanted to play. He is an extremely single-minded chap and he picked up his bat, went into the nets and set about turning himself into a reborn batsman to lay alongside his admirable reborn Christian belief. There is no more sincere or dedicated cricketer. He realised he had to learn to play straight, to hit the ball into the V between extra-cover and mid-wicket, to show the bat-maker's name to the bowler, to come onto the front foot and to stop playing hockey strokes with a cricket bat in his hand, when his bottom hand takes control. When England saw him coming out to bat in the South African first innings at Edgbaston, they will have rubbed their hands. South Africa were four down for not many and the arrival of Rhodes has always given the bowlers more of a chance. A couple of rasping drives through the covers made everyone sit up. His bat was straight, his footwork fast and sure and his intentions were bold. Rhodes looks more like a clean-shaven Boys Own hero than the real thing, and now he proceeded to bat like one. Gone were all those squirts and cuts and pushes square on both sides of the pitch, he had cut down on the paddle sweep too. His left elbow was now higher and he was prepared to leave alone those balls which were wide of the wicket and to which in the old days he was irresistibly drawn. When the bowlers, especially Dominic Cork, pitched short he swivelled and hooked and pulled into the gaps out of the meat of the bat. This was high-class batting by a real batsman, no longer the hit or miss efforts of a brilliant fielder who sometimes makes a contribution. His 95 was a top-class innings and his stand with Lance Klusener made the match safe for South Africa.

Two weeks later, at Lord's, he stepped briskly to the wicket, twinkling with enthusiasm, with South Africa 46 for 4 on the first morning after they had been put in to bat. Rhodes's response was immediate. In his first over, he went onto the back foot and forced Angus Fraser, of all people, past cover for four. There was no hidden agenda about that stroke and England then had the tea interval in which to reflect on it. Soon after the restart Rhodes faced Dean Headley, in his first over. He drove at one outside the off stump and it flew at great pace off a thick edge above Atherton's head at third slip. He got both hands to it but knocked it over the bar, goalkeeper fashion, and England knew they had let a big one get away. Rhodes did not need time to convalesce either, and three overs

267

later he on-drove Cork for four before hooking a short one for six. Then, he drove again and this time Atherton held the catch at slip but it had been a no-ball. At the end of the over he drove again and Nasser Hussain picked him up on the half volley at second slip. Still Rhodes was not fazed and he was soon on the front foot driving Ealham to the cover boundary. He was 47 not out overnight and an on-drive for three the next morning against Cork took him to a fifty which had come in 69 balls with seven fours and a six. Not bad for a man who had come in at 46 for 4.

Then it was Robert Croft's turn and he was twice cut for four as Rhodes made room for himself to play the stroke. A final impish pull for three brought him to his second Test hundred and by the time he was caught behind off the inside edge pushing at Fraser, he had made 117 and South Africa were 283 for 7. It had been a wonderful innings, based on inspiration walking hand in hand with a newfound batting faith. As I left the Lord's pavilion that night, Rhodes was standing alone deep in thought at the top of the flight of stairs above the South African dressing room. He had his hand up to his face and it would have been an impertinent intrusion even to have said well done.

He had a barren Old Trafford and at Trent Bridge luck deserted him. In the first innings he played back and was lbw to a ball from Fraser which looked as if it may have been going over the stumps. Whatever his thoughts, Rhodes walked smartly off. In the second innings it was worse. He had made a couple when he tried to flick a short one from Cork down the leg side and it touched his leg on its way through to Alec Stewart who, along with the other close fielders, appealed as if their lives depended upon it. The appeal seemed to go on and on. The echo hung in the air and umpire Mervyn Kitchen's finger pointed almost horizontally at Rhodes to confirm what, in a matter of seconds, we all knew was not true. This was too much even for Rhodes and it was only with a superhuman effort that he dragged himself away from the crease but he had only gone four paces when his jaw began to move and he had a sharpish exchange with one of the close fielders. Rhodes will have hated himself for getting involved but even saints are human.

His first innings at Headingley was intensely human too. When he had made a robust 19 he pulled Darren Gough and the ball flew just above Mark Ramprakash's head at square leg, and although he had just held an infinitely more difficult catch at mid-wicket, Ramprakash got both hands to this one and could not hold on. Rhodes ran a single and in the next over pushed forward to Cork and Graeme Hick dropped a regulation catch at waist height to his left at third slip. You cannot afford to give Rhodes two lives in his 1998 form, but soon afterwards he drove at Gough and Stewart caught the edge. In the second innings the situation was made for Rhodes and he was back to his best. When he came in South Africa were 12 for 4 and with a certain bustle and flick of the bat, he set about restoring order even though Cullinan's dismissal brought South Africa almost to their knees at 27 for 5. Rhodes now found a doughty partner in Brian McMillan and first they inched South Africa to some sort of composure and then they began to take the attack to the Englishmen. In eight overs, Salisbury was ravaged by Rhodes's footwork and McMillan's powerful wrists. Rhodes's fifty came from 73 balls. He was particularly fierce on anything at all short as he pulled both Gough and Cork for fours, and while he and McMillan were there, South Africa were suddenly winning. Eventually, McMillan's hook found the top edge and suddenly Rhodes's concentration broke and he drove Gough off his legs low to short mid-wicket. It had been a grand piece of batting and when you add his fielding onto it, he must surely be everyone's hero.

When Angus Fraser had Hansie Cronje caught behind in South Africa's second innings at Headingley, it was his fiftieth Test wicket in 1998, a prodigious record. Of course he was a hero, and I have written so much about his bowling earlier in the book. What warrants his inclusion in this chapter was the bravest innings of the summer right at the end at Old Trafford when our beloved schoolmaster, dressed for war, strode out of the pavilion as England's last man, knowing that the one ball left in Allan Donald's present over had to be survived and two more overs from Donald after that as well as two from Paul Adams. Stewart and Atherton had led a splendid fight back but the innings had faltered and now only stoic resistance from Gough and Robert Croft had given England this last desperate chance. Fraser's protection made him look as if he was doing an advertisement for Michelin.

There is something greatly reassuring about the presence of Fraser. When he walked to the middle now, although the situation was desperate and South Africa, and more particularly Donald, were closing in for the kill, I would rather have seen Fraser than a few others who might even have been more able with a bat in their hands. He has a steadfast stride that conveys a no-nonsense approach. He strode out at his own pace, which is quicker than some, his jaw seemed to be jutting out in defiance and he won't have given the South Africans the slightest impression that he was a little nervous about the next few minutes. He took his time to take guard, had a look round the field and settled over his bat. The last ball of the over hummed past him on the way through to Mark Boucher, leaving Fraser grateful that he had to make no real response to it.

Croft not only saw out the next over from Adams but an off-drive produced the two runs England needed to make South Africa bat again. There would therefore have to be a ten-minute break between innings. Three more overs now had to be survived as Donald tore in again to bowl to Fraser. Somehow Fraser kept him out, and although he was peppered on the body, he never gave Donald the satisfaction of seeing him rub the spot. He watched the ball like a hawk and got his bat to it when he had to and twice it was just in the nick of time. Short-leg crouched ever closer and Donald, bowling round the wicket, pitched short, trying to force Fraser to play and pop up a catch to the waiting Kirsten. Fraser ducked and swayed out of the line, he got every part of him behind his bat and the line of the ball. He would not be intimidated.

Another over was survived – somehow. Only two to go now. Croft coped with Adams but was unable to get the single which would leave him to face the last six balls from Donald. Fraser had already dealt with seven of Donald's fastest and nastiest. Now, this great fast bowler, who had already taken six wickets in the innings on a lifeless pitch, pawed at the ground with his right boot like a predator from an African game park, before he started in again. It was a bouncer which flew away to safety off Fraser's arm guard. One was mercifully left alone, another was jabbed down into the ground at the very last moment and even then it was only Fraser's giant boot that prevented it rolling back onto the stumps. Fraser appeared to be the calmest man on the ground. The next two balls were coped with and so it all came down to the final one. If ever Donald had flame pouring out of his nostrils it was now, as he ran in to bowl this final delivery. The superb rhythm of the run-up, the final leap, the arching of the back and the explosion of the ball leaving the hand, and Fraser had to cope with the nastiest ball of all for a number eleven, a yorker. It was too much for him and it thudded into his pads. Donald's appeal was more an agonised yell than an appeal. Umpire Doug Cowie from New Zealand looked long as he weighed up what he had seen. The ball was slipping down the leg side – just – and Fraser received the benefit of the doubt.

Three weeks later, at Trent Bridge, Fraser took five wickets in each innings of the Fourth Test. He wrote afterwards in his column that three weeks before his batting had been all the news and now it was his bowling. He went on to say that life as the new Ian Botham was pretty exciting. I suppose we expect him to take wickets, but for surviving those thirteen balls from Allan Donald, Fraser deserved nothing less than a cricketing Victoria Cross.

My final hero of the year hung up his bat and his boots a good many years ago but, thank goodness, he has still not finally screwed the top back on to his pen. Jim Swanton, E.W.S., was 91 on 11 February 1998 and is still as coherently immersed in the game of cricket as ever he has been and contributes occasionally to the *Daily Telegraph* as he has been doing since hostilities ended in 1945. His knowledge of what is going on and what decisions are being taken and who thinks what, is as acute and as accurate as ever. No one is better informed. One of the joys of the year has been to talk to Jim, in the West Indies during the England tour, at Lord's on the big occasions, or at Canterbury on the Kent occasions. Five minutes with him will invariably let you into a cricketing secret you did not know, give you a pithy viewpoint to chew over and a good story to pass on to whomever you next run into. Wearing an I Zingari or a Band of Brothers or a Free Forester tie, Jim gives off an aura of cricket as no one else I have ever met.

His memory would be astonishing in a man a third of his age and for him, still, no detail, however small, is too insignificant to be taken on board if it is relevant. In his occasional columns, evocatively entitled 'Personally Speaking', he writes astutely about the contemporary scene. One is never left with the feeling that he is regurgitating the past, even if some of his views have been born in a bygone age. All his pieces are well researched and he is the stickler for detail he always was.

When I worked for him on the England tour to the West Indies in 1967/68, he would ask me to take notes for him whenever he left the Press Box and on his return he would cross-examine me closely about each one. Which side of cover did it go? Was it a full half-volley or did he hit it on the up? Was gully where he is now or was he finer as he had been before lunch? Are you sure it was not his slower ball? I was never quite sure he accepted my answers either.

I was lucky enough to have been asked by Jim to play for the Arabs, the club he founded in 1936, and I cannot remember playing any cricket that was more fun. Jim had a healthy desire to win and some of the most hilarious moments came when trying to explain to an irascible Founder why we had not quite made it. When he hung up his boots, he was not averse to captaining the side from the boundary and he could become positively vitriolic if he thought his captain for the day did not know how to set a field for a leg-spinner. Was he pompous and was he a snob? Probably, and aren't we all? And he was much more fun because of it. I had the luck, a long time ago, to stay with him at the lovely house, Coralita, that he and his wife, Ann, built at Sandy Lane in Barbados, and at their house in Sandwich, too, and there was no finer host, nor a much better shaker of a dry martini, either.

I have met no one else in cricket who it has been so worthwhile and interesting to listen to and few people have provided so many other cricketers and cricket lovers with so much fun and entertainment over the years. The stories about him are legendary and no one has had his leg pulled more or enjoyed it so much. Jim is now 91 not out and knowing his attention to detail and his determination as a cricketer, I have not the slightest doubt he will pick up the remaining nine in well-placed singles, out of reach of Jonty Rhodes, too. My abiding memory of Jim during this last year was at a dinner on a luxury cruiser, the *Sun Goddess*, in the deep water harbour in Bridgetown, one night during the Fourth Test Match. Jim was asked to present the prizes for the raffle after a dinner at which there must have been about a hundred people. He did it with all the charm and the panache one would have expected and he made the recipients feel that this was the high point of the evening and the rest of us wish that we had won something too. Before I left Barbados, I heard that Jim had been along to the pro at the Sandy Lane Golf Club for a couple of lessons. Not bad for a ninety-one-year-old.

For those of us who write and broadcast about cricket, Jim Swanton was an object lesson. Will there ever be a better describer of today's events at Lord's in tomorrow morning's paper? If anyone is ever in need of a lesson, and there are many, in producing a succinct and penetrative discussion of a day's play, all they have to do is to listen to a recording of one of Jim's close of play summaries on Test Match Special. We all owe him a huge debt. But it's those golf lessons that win him a place here.

Index

275